D1302476

THE DYNAMICS OF INDUSTRIAL DEMOCRACY

THE DYNAMICS OF INDUSTRIAL DEMOCRACY

by

CLINTON S. GOLDEN

Director, Northeastern Region
Steel Workers Organizing Committee

and

HAROLD J. RUTTENBERG

Research Director
Steel Workers Organizing Committee

"bringing changes into a world resenting change."

CARL SANDBURG

HARPER & BROTHERS PUBLISHERS

New York and London

THE DYNAMICS OF INDUSTRIAL DEMOCRACY

Printed in the United States of America

C-Y

ALLIED PRINTING TRADES UNION LABEL COUNCIL 1

To

PHILIP MURRAY

under whose wise, patient, courageous leadership, as Chairman of the Steel Workers Organizing Committee and President of the Congress of Industrial Organizations, we have been privileged to participate in bringing a measure of democracy to industry.

Contents

Foreword

By Russell W. Davenport

For most Americans, whether employers or employees, the experience of reading this book will be like walking through Alice's Looking Glass. Or rather, walking *backward* through the Looking Glass. When Alice walked through the Looking Glass she left a rational world and entered a crazy one. But when you read this book you move from a crazy world into a rational one. You leave behind the world of the last ten years, in which strikes, lock-outs, and riots marked the inability of men to recognize a common interest or a common goal, and you enter a new world in which a common interest binds men together and a common goal is in some measure achieved. You step, in short, from industrial chaos into industrial democracy.

The two authors of this book have been in the thick of the labor struggle of Our Time. Clinton Golden, Director of the Eastern Region of the Steel Workers Organizing Committee (SWOC), is a dean of the American labor movement, with a record that stretches back nearly half a century. Mr. Golden's personality—a rare combination of kindliness, wisdom, and fierce energy—is known far and wide in the steel country, and no man who has heard him address a union meeting is likely to forget the experience. Harold Ruttenberg, on the other hand, is a member of the younger generation, a brilliant student of industrial political economy, and SWOC's Director of Research. If you extend Mr. Ruttenberg into the future as far as Mr. Golden extends into the past you get a big slice of American history-in-the-making.

Anyway, it is an extraordinary team. And together they have written an extraordinary book. Under the calm leadership of Philip Murray, who came to the head of CIO via the

Chairmanship of SWOC, they and their associates have created a new era in the steel country. From Bethlehem to Buffalo, from the yellow Yioughiogheny to the broad Ohio, they can call every leader of steel labor, and most of the leaders of management, by their first names. They have seen employers pound the desk, laugh, capitulate, or go stubborn. They have kidded, cajoled, argued, damned, and praised. And they have reached conclusions. These conclusions the reader will find set forth beginning on page xxiii as *Principles of Union-Management Relations.* There are thirty-seven of them. Most of them are illustrated by specific case histories. And when they are all joined together the result is that rational world already referred to as industrial democracy.

The authors do not even pretend that their book is impartial. They are partisans—direct, hard-hitting, and, in devotion to their cause, even ruthless. They are men who dare to believe, and dare to stand for what they believe in. Yet for that very reason the reader will search their case histories in vain for mere propaganda or boosterism. Each case they cite rings like a good piece of silver. Though the authors write from a point of view, they do so with conscience. They possess that indispensable foundation of great partisanship, a respect for facts. That some of their facts might be interpreted differently, that even the facts themselves might seem different if drawn from an opponent's files, they would be the first to admit. These are the facts in SWOC's files. They do not purport to be anything more than that: but they *are* that.

What the reader gets out of this book depends largely on the reader's capacity to learn. Most of the material will be utterly new to most readers. The key is collective bargaining. Yet this is a concept which is as yet understood by relatively few citizens. Most people think of collective bargaining in terms of an employer arguing with his employees over a wage increase. Collective bargaining *is* that, but it is also much more. What this book makes indisputably clear is that there are a number of collective bargaining phases. The first, or primitive, phase is reached when the boss first sits down to talk with the union. More developed phases evolve, usually, very quickly. From the stark discussion of wages the bargainers are drawn, by relentless pressures within the shop, to discuss vacations and sick leaves, shop rules and working conditions, an efficient grievance system, safety devices, maternity leaves, severance pay, pensions, and arbitration. When arbitration becomes more or less a matter of course, collective bargaining is well advanced.

Yet there is still a higher phase of collective bargaining. This super-charged phase begins when the union takes an "enlightened" view toward the business and the employer takes a *partnership* view toward the union. In the stormy history of American industrial relations this phase has been reached in relatively few enterprises. Which side is more responsible for the failure to reach it as a general rule, instead of as a shining exception, is a hen-and-the-egg problem that will never be satisfactorily solved. My personal view is that the employers have been more responsible for the failure than labor. Yet I know from experience how difficult it is for employers really to understand the workers' problems or really to grasp what is on an employee's mind when he or she insists upon something patently unreasonable.

As a matter of fact the chief problem that the big boss has, in dealing with labor, is usually the man under him. As a general rule (to which there are plenty of exceptions) the president of a company is apt to be more enlightened in his attitude than the vice president, the vice president more enlightened than the superintendent, and so on down the line. Thus management's *first* labor problem is often the lower fringes of management itself. Besides this, the employer is almost always a trustee for other people's money, and this fact causes him to stress the rights and perquisites of employership. That he tends to over-stress them, or even hide behind them, is perhaps only human.

In any event, as this book amply shows, super-charged collective bargaining *does* exist and is possible. What it means is that labor and the employer are brought into a kind of partnership. This partnership does not overlook the hard fact that their interests are different. It does, however, acknowledge that when the interest of one side is well served, the other side gains. The interests are not the same: but they are unmistakably *mutual.* Hence it is of advantage to both parties to confer on problems that are not merely wage and hour problems, or grievance problems, or even strictly labor problems. The authors give several cases, of which those concerning shop efficiency are the most striking. Labor has always resented "speed-up" schemes, even though it is clearly to every working man's advantage to make himself as efficient and productive as possible. But this resentment can be overcome, and indeed converted into eager co-operation, if the problem of increasing production is put squarely up to the workers and a *joint* plan is evolved. In super-charged collective bargaining, management and labor share the problem of production-for-a-living. If the day ever comes when this sharing is no longer a super-charged operation, but is accepted as a matter of course, industrial democracy will have arrived.

Admittedly that day is still some distance away. Relatively few unions are equipped for this kind of bargaining. Management is exactly right in resenting the intrusion into the affairs of industry of unions whose leaders are bent on their own political advancement, at whatever cost to the business, or of unions dominated by factions working for the destruction of the enterprise system. So long as union leadership has ulterior motives of that sort collective bargaining in the advanced phase is impossible and even absurd. Such bargaining requires careful preparation by labor. The first step in such preparation should be, perhaps, a thorough reading of this book.

On the other hand, as these authors point out, the development of union intelligence hangs always on the development of management intelligence. When management combats collective bargaining, however subtly, the demand within the union for soap-box orators and strong men becomes irresistible. It is impossible for the union, for instance, to build a central committee of political economists and production-minded leaders when negotiations are still in the brick and tear-gas stage. It is equally difficult to do so when management gives lip service to a collective bargaining contract, but really regards the whole business as a nuisance or a threat.

I have particularly in mind a company which signed a contract some years ago, but which has ever since fled from the collective bargaining principle. As a result the contract has cost this company a lot of money and gained it almost no credit. Management recently devised an elaborate pension plan that will cost the stockholders' even more. This plan was in line with the company's long-established policy, to give its employees the *best* in wages, in opportunity for advancement, and in working conditions. But it will fail to increase the workers' loyalty to the management *because it was planned and presented without any consultation with the union whatever.*

Such consultation could have served three practical purposes. First, the plan could have been used as a bargaining point against a proposed increase in wages, and might thus have saved the stockholders money. Second, consultation would have increased the workers' confidence in their union and in its ability to cope with the management. Third, this increased confidence might have encouraged the members, and especially their leaders, to enter upon more advanced phases of collective bargaining: assured of the status of the union they could concern themselves with some of the aims and purposes of management. As it is, the pension plan has gone through, the union is demanding a wage increase, and management is "baffled" by the workers' ingratitude.

This situation is not in the least simplified by the fact that the local of the union involved is rather ineffectual. Negotiating and major policy are in the hands of "outside" officials of the union, who happen to be more or less communist dominated. This means that the management of a firm which believes deeply in the enterprise system, and has made it work, is asked to sit down and "share" management with men who may stand for the destruction of that system—a total absurdity. Still and all, it can be said that this management has been stupid. There is in the unit a strong right wing, very management-minded and intensely anti-communistic. But the net result of management tactics has been to weaken the right wing and to strengthen the left.

The apparent cause of the trouble in the above case has been generosity. Many cases could be cited where the apparent cause has been, on the contrary, parsimony. But as the present volume makes clear, neither parsimony nor generosity is really the point. The point is, rather, the emergence of a relationship—a relationship new to political theory, born of an industrial age, and bursting through the shell of the familiar past. The pieces of that shell lie in fragments around us. The absolute dictatorship of management over the affairs of any company is such a fragment. So, on the other hand, is bossism in labor leadership. These and other relics of the days of Mike Tighe can produce nothing but strife, turmoil, and waste. In their place this new relationship of industrial democracy, quasi-political in character, places the responsibility for production, protection, and profit squarely upon the shoulders of all.

Now of course all this raises the fundamental question of just what "industrial democracy" is, and whether we want it anyway. I shall not prejudice the authors' case by arguing this question one way or the other. Industrial democracy is a lot of things, many of them revolutionary. What it means in the present connection is that labor should have a share in management. To the average industrialist this is a heresy to be dismissed briefly. But the present authors, I feel sure, have in mind an industrial order that cannot be summarily dismissed. They do not advocate taking away from industry that centralized authority which is necessary to the operation of any human enterprise. They do say, however, that enterprise in the industrial age has human and social implications and repercussions, and that management cannot proceed blindly without taking these into account. And they say, further, that these matters cannot be realistically accounted for unless labor has a share in the accounting.

It is as the mere author of a Foreword that I stand on my rights and suspend judgment on this question. But I would urge the reader to do likewise. Indeed, I would urge the reader not to pause very long over points in this book with which he may disagree, however violently. It is more important to see the work whole. The authors themselves do not pretend to have solved everything. But they have opened a broad vista for further exploration.

I, myself, for instance, cannot agree with the authors on the subject of a closed, or union, shop. My disagreement is based largely upon principle. I believe that the union shop, if carried to its logical conclusion—that is, if it were made universal—would actually endanger the existence of democracy. It is a violation of the concept of individual liberty; it would lead to the concentration of enormous powers in the hands of the few; and it would to some appreciable extent diminish, rather than increase, the freedom of work. Yet I do not worry much about this *because if I am right the workers themselves will oppose a universal union.* Their stake in democracy is the guaranty.

Indeed the whole question of the union shop bears far more heavily on the workers than on management. It raises the fundamental problem of the union leader. If the closed shop is necessary for the workers, that is one thing. If it is necessary for the union leader, that is quite another. Unhappily the union shop has been obtained by the leaders *for* the leaders on all too many occasions. Leaders who do not deserve to be leaders find this monopolistic device invaluable in maintaining their power, collecting their dues, and in a general way assuring themselves of maximum safety with a minimum of work. From this charge I want specifically to exonerate the present authors and their associates. It is, nevertheless, a problem that they must face.

On the basis of practice, as contrasted with principle, the authors have presented a most powerful case for the union shop. I will let the book speak for itself. I think it is worth pointing out, however, that their argument derives most of its power elsewhere, namely, from the fact that only in union shops has it been possible even to approach this new relationship which they call industrial democracy and which requires the interest of the workers in the company's welfare. The relationship, not the institution of the union shop, is what clinches their case. They clearly show that, in any particular plant, the winning of the union shop opens the way to the more advanced phases of collective bargaining. In my view, the union shop is merely a device, and if advanced collective bargaining were generally accepted it would not be necessary. In theirs, the advanced relationship cannot be achieved without the union shop.

However wrong my view may be, in the more experienced eyes of the authors, I know they will agree that the *relationship* is the important thing. Indeed this book, considered as a whole, is a definition of the relationship, and is by far the most advanced that we have had so far. That is the primary point, and within it all other points are secondary.

There is one final consideration which is all too often overlooked by orators on both sides of the labor controversy. The key to democracy in industry is democracy in the unions. The success of the Steel Workers Organizing Committee in organizing the steel country and of Messrs. Golden and Ruttenberg in formulating their thirty-seven principles is rooted in the fact that the SWOC unions have not been bossridden. And it is essential to the success of their movement that this standard be maintained. A union is a political body, not in the sense of party politics, but in the sense that it exists of, by, and for its members. It must therefore follow elementary political rules. It must adopt parliamentary procedure, frequent elections, and the secret ballot. Its financial status should be far more public than is the custom. And its sense of responsibility, as an organized (and therefore powerful) body of men and women, should be acute.

It is not always easy to maintain a local union on this basis. At first the membership is keen to assert itself, but gradually the excitement of this new experience wears off. Meetings become smaller. They are attended week after week by those members who have some special axe to grind. Little by little the power becomes concentrated, the fine hopes of the founders are lost, and collective bargaining degenerates into a series of deals between an employer boss and an employee boss.

Many unions, including SWOC, have been able to prevent this devolution. Yet, human nature being what it is, there is always some danger of it, and as in the case of so many other problems in industrial relationships, the solution to this one lies on management's doorstep. Management is sure to be the ultimate sufferer from a boss-ridden union, and it is to management's advantage to prevent the condition from arising. The cure is simple enough: give the union plenty to do. The more problems the management is willing to share with its workers, the more interested the workers become and the bigger do the union meetings grow. Annual renewal of a contract, relieved only by reports from the grievance committee, does not insure broad and active participation in union affairs. But a tough problem in shop efficiency, or in technological dislocation, or even in a pension plan, will arouse interest at once. Many union members will want to participate in such problems, who would otherwise let the local slide along in the hands of its officers. And the result will be a healthy, democratic union which no single man, or clique, is able to control.

As an American I want to thank the authors for this book. And I want especially to recommend a thorough reading of it to those many Americans, whether in the ranks of labor or management, who are puzzling about the future of our world. We are now engaged in a great war. Yet I believe it is becoming apparent to many that this is not merely a war of defense, but a revolution. We are revolting, as our forefathers did, against a bloody tyranny whose depredations on the democratic world had become intolerable to us. The immediate manifestations of this tyranny are Hitler and Japanese militarism. These must go. But there are some things right in our own midst that must go along with them. We are not fighting merely to preserve an old world, but to create a new one. And concerning the nature of that new one the reader will find, in this book, a number of important hints.

New York City February, 1942

Preface

During the last five years we have recorded—pretty much as a clinician records his observations—our vital experiences encountered in the negotiation of collective-bargaining contracts, the adjustment of differences between workers and management under them, and the development of practical techniques through which these two traditionally hostile groups in industry might co-operate. At the end of two years, 1937-38, these experiences began to develop into quite definite patterns, and from time to time, in speeches, pamphlets, and magazine articles, we have passed on some of these evolving patterns to labor-union, management, government, university, and general audiences. The response in all such instances has been enthusiastic and surprisingly unanimous. This indicated to us that both our experiences and the patterns into which they fell were fairly typical. Gradually in the next two years, 1939-40, our experiences started to repeat themselves in a rather systematic manner. At first unwittingly—but later consciously—we applied to each case arising for our attention the conclusions we had come to in previous ones of a similar nature. The results were virtually uniform, indicating that these conclusions had begun to crystallize. Finally, at the suggestion of our publisher, early in the fifth year, 1941, we undertook the task of formulating our experiences into what we call "principles of union-management relations" and of illustrating them with actual cases.

The heart of this book, however, is not so much these principles as the cases—spelled out in detail—illustrating them, because one of the barriers between workers and management is the connotation of words. For example, the expression "union-management co-operation" to workers generally means co-operation between management and their union as coequals for the purpose of increasing production and, in turn, earnings. Yet we have had many management officials oppose union-management co-operation because they placed the accent on the first word and not the latter one of the expression and, as a consequence, came to the conclusion that we were talking about "management by the union." The citation of specific cases largely eliminates this source of misunderstanding and helps to bridge the gulf between the hitherto conflicting viewpoints of the two groups.

Of necessity, the cases cited are kept anonymous. Naturally we would prefer to name names in each instance, but the difficulties in doing this—at least at this stage of growth—are obvious. We would probably write ourselves out of the confidence of most management officials with whom we have relations, if not out of the labor movement itself. Furthermore, to name names would not be fair to the firms and unions involved in the several cases, since they were chosen because we felt them to be typical and not because they are unique. In addition, we have felt freer in discussing each case anonymously than we would have under the other arrangement.

This book makes no pretense of being impartial; it is the work of partisans. Yet, in many ways, a frankly partisan work attains an objectivity hardly attainable by persons in the middle of conflicting forces, because a clear picture of one side of a question cannot help but throw the other side into bold relief. We do claim, quite definitely, that this is a fair discussion, since we have tried, so far as it lies within our power, to portray objectively each case discussed. This, we believe, will be clear to the reader.

The outline of the book falls into three parts. The first deals with union-management bargaining. This covers the larger portion of the body of the book, as it is concerned with the day-to-day problems of collective bargaining generally prevailing in industry. Part Two is concerned with union-management co-operation; it attempts, on the basis of rather limited experiences, to look beyond the function of a union as a mere agency to adjust grievances and bargain over the division of the existing proceeds of production. The concluding part discusses union-management planning, both on an industry-wide basis to solve collective-bargaining problems that are beyond the scope of the individual company and union and on a national basis, with the federal government as a formal part of the arrangement, to solve the intricate economic, social, and political problems that overtaxed our free society before the war and promise to be even more taxing in the postwar period.

We believe that American industry is on the threshold of a new era in human relations—the greatest period in union-management relations. The turmoil and strife of the last decade have merely reflected the transitional character of the relations between workers and management. Out of this transitional period is emerging a new capacity on the part of those in industry, regardless of their different positions, in point of view of responsibility and authority, to work together as a unit—literally with a singleness of purpose and of action for the attainment of a common objective. The reader will not find in this book a detailed proposal for the solution of each of the outstanding economic problems confronting workers and management, though many of them are discussed, because it is essentially a discussion of democratic techniques and not of economic matters. This book is about the dynamics, and not the economics, of industrial democracy. It is predicated upon the conviction that a free society is one of constant change, and that the increasing extension of democratic methods into industry will lead toward fuller production and employment and toward increasing the stature, well-being, dignity, and happiness of the individual worker.

CLINTON S. GOLDEN
HAROLD J. RUTTENBERG

Pittsburgh, Pennsylvania
January 12, 1942

Principles of Union-Management Relations

John Stuart Mill said: "A principle ascertained by experience is more than a mere summing up of what has been specifically observed in the individual cases which have been examined; it is a generalization grounded on those cases." The following principles are not immutable rules of union-management relations, because they are the outgrowth of changing conditions and, as a consequence, are themselves constantly subject to change. Any enduring validity that they may prove to have will depend largely on the continued growth of industrial democracy. These principles are based on the authors' experiences in their respective capacities with the Steel Workers Organizing Committee (SWOC).

The period of time covered by them is a five-year one from 1937 through 1941. The union-management relationship upon which they are based is that generally prevailing in the basic iron-, steel-, and tin-producing industries and more than a score of allied metal-fabricating and processing industries. We make no claim that they apply to all types of union-management relations, only to those prevailing in the basic and mass-producing industries—although in varying degrees they may well have validity in all fields of collective bargaining. Nor do we claim that they are necessarily original with us, only that our experiences have demonstrated these principles to be conducive to the establishment and maintenance of industrial peace and fruitful union-management relations. It is in this spirit that they are presented. The text of this book is built around them, and we have carefully chosen what seem to us to be typical experiences to illustrate these principles.

1. Workers organize into labor unions not alone for eco-

nomic motives but also for equally compelling psychological and social ones, so that they can participate in making the decisions that vitally affect them in their work and community life.

2. Collective bargaining marks the end of individual and the beginning of group relations between workers and management.

3. The initial collective-bargaining practices are influenced in varying degrees by the preunion history of the particular industrial concern and by the fact that genuine union-management relations are initiated by the union.

4. Collective bargaining is an instrument for workers and owners, through unions and management, to solve their problems directly without recourse to the government.

5. Collective bargaining is the extension of the basic principles and practices of democracy into industry.

6. The policies and actions of unions are likely to reflect the policies and actions of management.

7. The attitudes and actions of management largely determine the degree of co-operativeness of union leadership.

8. The time lag in the growth of constructive union leadership, after management ceases its opposition, varies with the extent to which labor assumes responsibility for the development of its leaders.

9. Salesmen and purchasing agents usually possess a more natural ability for handling management's relations with unions than do operating officials.

10. The leadership requirements and responsibilities of management increase under union-management relations.

11. Participation of workers, union representatives, and management at all levels is a prerequisite to the successful administration of a collective-bargaining contract.

12. The peaceful administration of a contract requires the confidence of workers that they will get justice through the collective-bargaining machinery in the settlement of their grievances.

13. Grievances should be settled speedily and as near their point of origin as possible.

14. Grievances should be settled on their merits with no logrolling permitted.

15. Management should frankly acknowledge the role of the union in bringing about improvements in working conditions.

16. The successful administration of a contract requires the maintenance of an effective system of communications for both management and the union, in bringing complaints from the bottom up and relaying decisions and policies from the top down.

17. The nature of union-management relations and the administration of a contract are influenced greatly by the pattern of social relationships in any given community.

18. Workers acquire a qualified property interest in their jobs under a collective-bargaining contract.

19. Each group of workers strives for the kind of seniority rules which it thinks will provide the greatest amount of job protection.

20. Seniority is an instrument designed to eliminate favoritism and discrimination.

21. The power to discharge should not be lodged in a single individual.

22. Workers should enjoy full freedom of opportunity for advancement and promotion.

23. There is no basic conflict between seniority and productive efficiency.

24. A prime objective of collective bargaining is the redistribution of the proceeds of production.

25. Unions should participate with management in distributing the proceeds of each firm's production between its owners and workers.

26. The proceeds of technological changes, laborsaving machinery, and other factors contributing to lower unit costs of production should be shared equitably between owners and workers.

27. The adjustment of wage-rate inequalities should be exclusively on the basis of the merits of each case.

28. The greater the participation of workers through their

unions in setting piecework and tonnage rates, in making time and motion studies, in determining work standards and job evaluations, the greater are the earnings and output.

29. Membership in the union should be a condition of employment.

30. The union shop is a necessary prerequisite for constructive union-management relations.

31. The union shop may be an instrument for either constructive or negative union-management relations, depending chiefly upon management's outlook and the caliber of union leadership.

32. Management's assumption of sole responsibility for productive efficiency actually prevents the attainment of maximum output.

33. The participation of organized workers in management provides an outlet for their creative desires, as it is essentially a creative and co-operative undertaking.

34. Union-management co-operation to reduce costs, eliminate wastes, increase productive efficiency, and improve quality represents a practical program that provides workers with effective direct participation in the creative phases of management.

35. Union-management co-operation tends to make management more efficient and unions more cost-conscious, thereby improving the competitive position of a business enterprise and increasing the earnings of both workers and owners.

36. The natural outgrowth of local-plant and individual-company collective bargaining is bargaining between district or industry-wide organizations of management and unions.

37. The future of industrial democracy depends upon the attainment of full production and employment on a sustained basis during and after the war.

Part One

PATHS TO INDUSTRIAL PEACE

Chapter I: Motives for Union Membership

Workers organize into labor unions not alone for economic motives but also for equally compelling psychological and social ones, so that they can participate in making the decisions that vitally affect them in their work and community life.

"Big Mike" worked in the Pennsylvania Railroad yards in Pittsburgh during the first World War. Workers, not jobs, were scarce then. In his twelve years with the road he had never secured a personal pass. One day "Big Mike" decided to get a pass to visit some friends in Philadelphia. Dressed in his working clothes, he went to see his boss at noon. He rushed into the middle of a conference in his office and brusquely demanded a pass. The boss bawled out "Big Mike" vigorously, commanded him to dress in clean clothes and return in an hour to make his request properly. An hour later he quietly entered the outer room of his office, politely waited until the boss was available, and presented himself in gentlemanly fashion.

"I am back," he began in a low voice.

"Now, that's better," the boss interrupted. "You have come to get your pass to ride the road."

"Big Mike" calmly replied, "No, Mr. Roberts, I just come back to tell you to go to hell 'cause I got a job on the B. & O."

Intertwined with the motives for union membership is the almost universal desire of workers to tell the boss "to go to hell." The causes that manifest themselves in this desire are rooted deeply in the personal lives of workers—in their psychology, and in their social situation—which, in turn, are influenced materially by economic factors. An inquiry into these causes goes back to the time when jobs were plentiful. "Big Mike's" rash action was not exceptional. During the first World War and the nineteen twenties job opportunities permitted workers the freedom to quit when the boss insulted or humiliated them, or when the work was not to their liking. The statistics on labor turnover bear this out.[1] This freedom gave the individual worker a feeling of internal strength. It made him independent. He could maintain his pride and dignity. He had the power to tell the boss off instead of having to suffer personal indignities because of fear of going without a job indefinitely. The individualism of workers, so evident in the twenties when union membership reached a new low point, grew out of this relative freedom of action.

Then this changed, and a revolution in industrial relations followed so fast that management and unions are trying still to catch up with it. The individual worker was compelled to "eat crow" when his boss jumped him, rightly or wrongly. He had to swallow his pride when he was "given hell" in front of his fellow workers. His dignity was reduced to low levels. Because of his family responsibilities he dared not do anything that might cost him his job. To speak up to the boss was one of these things, or it was feared to be. A complaint, or hint of dissatisfaction, about wages or working conditions to a boss only brought the rebuff "if you don't like it here, you can quit." Deprived of their one great individual strength —to change employers—workers groped in the depression for another source of power. Gradually, as jobs became fewer, working time was curtailed, and relief was forced on them, they found a new power in group action. What they could no longer achieve as individuals, they found they could do by joining together. The National Industrial Recovery Act in 1933 merely accelerated the process, it having been pregnant in the national economy. The progressive and large-scale organization of labor unions ever since indicates the extent to which workers have begun to lose their individualism and acquire a group consciousness.

The strike, among other things, is a group expression of "Big Mike's" individual action in telling the boss "to go to hell." This is plainly observable in the early enthusiastic days of a strike and in the initial union-organizing meetings. Workers lost the freedom exercised by "Big Mike," but in losing it they gained the group freedom to tell the boss off. They could go to their strike or organizing meeting to hear their local union leaders and organizers denounce "the slave-driving boss and company dictatorship." The more names their leaders called the boss, the more workers booed, cheered, applauded, stamped the floor, and sang—in brief, they loved it. Back in the plant, significantly, most workers kept their tempers and held their tongues. They left the name calling and "the spouting off to the boss" to the few workers who, for a number of reasons, took the union leadership. This factor accounts for the belligerent type of local union officer in the early stages of collective bargaining. Management, in many instances, believes it would not have a union if it were not for a few disgruntled employees, but the way in which all of its employees strike to secure the reinstatement of one when management fires him soon shows the error of this mistaken belief.

This is not a revolt against the authority of management as such, but against its arbitrary use and abuses. These practices of management down through the years in nonunion mines, mills, and factories, that resulted in the industrial-relations changes of the last decade, set in motion an irresistible desire of workers to "get even" and "crack back." Where labor unions in their early days are preoccupied with "squaring accounts" for their members with management, the latter's chickens are only coming home to roost. A vital path to industrial peace is for management to understand this phenomenon, to be patient and co-operative while it works itself out. If not, union-management relations become immersed in management retaliatory acts against unions and keep in motion endless frictions. Within a usually short period of time the desire to tell the boss "to go to hell," which affords only temporary satisfactions, grows into a positive, constructive desire for participation in making the vital decisions from which workers derive lasting satisfactions.

Of the three motives for union membership—psychological, social, and economic—the latter is most commonly recognized. Workers want to improve their economic status, to secure a larger portion of the proceeds of production, and to make their lives more secure. The economic motive does not require either elaboration or illustration because it is so well known. What is necessary is a critical examination of the doctrine that the economic factors are all-dominating, even exclusive, in union-management relations.

The industrial peace of American industry has been disturbed, in large measure, because of the failure of management and, yes, many labor leaders to understand fully the several motives that impel workers to join unions of their own choosing.

For the past one hundred and fifty-six years—since the Philadelphia printers struck for a weekly minimum wage of six dollars in 1786—union-management relations have come to be viewed, quite wrongly, as economic warfare with periods of truce between strikes and lockouts. The sit-down strikes in Akron, Detroit, Flint, and other turbulent industrial centers, the "Memorial Day Massacre" in Chicago, and the bloody war in Harlan County, Kentucky—just to recall a few of the highlights in the "warfare between Capital and Labor" during the last decade—have served to perpetuate the ingrown American attitude that the relations between management and unions constitute an ever-recurring, inevitable battle between the "sons of toil" and the "exploiters of labor." Industrial strife in American industry over the last several decades has been recurrent for two basic reasons. One is the absolute refusal of management to recognize the rights of workers to organize into unions of their own choosing, and the other is the overemphasis on the economic factors in union-management relations. This discussion is not concerned with the first cause of industrial strife, since the paths to industrial peace are predicated upon management's recognition of the rights of workers to organize freely. We are concerned only with the second cause.

To look upon industrial unrest and the formation of labor unions as springing primarily from economic factors is an oversimplification of the problems of human relations. The basic needs of the human beings who make up American industry's working force are threefold:

1. Economic—an adequate plane of living and the necessary amount of job and wage protection.
2. Psychological—the personality needs of freedom of action, self-expression, and creative outlets.
3. Social—the ties and bonds of group relations and community life.

Workers seek these three things in their jobs. When they fail to find satisfaction for all of these needs, or any one of them, in their daily work, they seek the fulfillment of the unsatisfied need or needs outside. This finds expression in many forms of individual and group activity. We are concerned solely with the manner in which workers seek a well-rounded life through union membership, and the extent to which they find satisfaction of their threefold needs through their unions. Union membership is not an escape or a substitute satisfaction, but a means for workers to find direct satisfaction in their daily jobs for economic, psychological, and social needs.

Which is the most important motive is an academic question. The practical consideration is that all three are important; no matter why a man or woman in industry says he or she is doing a certain thing at a given time, that person is moved at the same time by psychological and social factors as well as by economic ones. All three motives are enveloped inside of human beings, are at work in varying degrees and in different ways, and are inseparable from those persons who are moved by them. To take out one motive and examine it, and then another, is often misleading because it leaves the implication that the other motives are less crucial. We discuss the psychological and social motives separately since the economic one is so widely recognized and easily discernible, and not because it is less important. The following cases*

* All persons, companies, unions, and cases discussed throughout the book are from the authors' experience, but the identity of each, except where specifically indicated otherwise, is disguised for reasons noted in the Preface.

have been chosen for illustration because they bring out the noneconomic motives for union membership that give the economic one such a dynamic, irresistible force.

Al Risko was a star footballer in high school. When he graduated in 1929, Al was the town's idol. He got a year's scholarship to a preparatory school for his athletic ability but was unable to move on to college because the family needed his help. An uncle who was a foreman in the steel mill got him a job. This was in July, 1930, when Al finished "prep" school. For a few years Al looked upon his work—he ran a crane for fifty-eight cents an hour—as an interlude between "prep" school and college. His dreams were the college campus, football stardom, and maybe the movies. The depression grew deeper, Al's family was harder hit, and his wages were cut ten per cent in 1931. Al just looked upon the cut as another postponing factor in his college dreams. In 1932 his wages were cut fifteen per cent, to forty-five cents an hour. His father lost out at the glass factory. Meanwhile Al had married a schoolgirl friend. The next year, when Al became a father, he finally realized nothing would come of his dreams and he had better come down to earth.

His uncle tried to interest Al in his work; pointed out how he might someday be an electrician, maybe a gang boss at two hundred dollars a month. He went to night school, studying to be an electrician. In 1934 he was still running a crane, earning, with the restored wage cuts, fifty-eight cents an hour. As a steppingstone to becoming an electrician Al had his eyes on a millwright's job. When the employee-representative election came up in 1935, Al's foreman suggested that he run for representative of his department. Al was elected. Before this he had paid little attention to the representation plan. All the fellows called it a company union, and it never held any meetings except for the few representatives. Inside the company union Al did what he thought would win him a promotion. When the Steel Workers Organizing Committee (SWOC) started its organizing campaign in June, 1936, Al, upon the hint of his foreman, came out against "the racketeers and agitators intent upon disturbing the peace for their own selfish interests." The foreman gave him a five-cent-an-hour raise.

Al was popular in town. A handsome, six-foot youth, Al always had a smile for everyone. The men in the mill had made him one of their own, because of his personal tragedy in not getting a chance to be an "All-American." Gradually the men chilled toward Al. They passed him by, few even nodding to him. Al was bewildered. His wife complained that the ladies were cold toward her when she went shopping. His father told him that he never thought he had raised a "damned scab." The SWOC, or "CIO" as the union was popularly called, was welcomed by most of the men in the mill, but Al had not been around long enough to learn why the older fellows were for it. He soon learned.

Openings developed in the millwright gang as work picked up toward the end of 1936. Al exercised patience awaiting his turn for promotion, but it did not come. College-trained boys were being brought in to fill the vacancies. Al could not understand this and, fed up with it all, he got drunk, was off work a few days, but only found it worse when he went back in the mill. He argued with his foreman, but to no avail. His uncle could only offer him the comfort that in his case he was thirty years becoming a foreman. Al had come to know the general manager of the mill as an employee representative. He went to him.

"I've been for the company," Al complained. "Why ain't it for me?"

"We gave you a five-cent raise," the manager replied.

"Is that all a fellow gets for being a heel with all the men?" Al demanded to know.

The manager reminded Al who was the boss, and that his time was limited.

Back in the mill, Al found life miserable. The older men shunned him, and the young college boys looked down on him. After the company recognized SWOC the older men started to talk to Al again, not friendly but understandingly.

"Hello, Mr. Risko," they would greet Al. "What's become of your company union?" they would taunt him. Al replied with a sheepish look. A little while later the men made a gesture to take Al back into their good graces, and asked him to join SWOC. Al asked for time to think it over. He began to ask questions. "What will I get out of it?" Al asked.

Each man answered Al's question in the light of what he himself expected to get by joining the union.

"You'll be a regular guy again, Al," one man replied.

"We'll see that you get what's comin' to you, Al," another worker added, "and that they stop detouring college kids into better-paying jobs that belong to us."

One of the men assured Al that he would "get more money."

"We'll get something you can't put in words or take home right away in your pay envelope," a gray-haired worker said, "but by the Lord in Heaven we'll know we got it."

This gray-haired worker was in his late forties, somewhat below average height and unassuming except that he looked at you in such a way that you knew his eyes were on you. His name was Bert Edwards. After returning to Wales from four years in the British Army in the first World War, he came to this country and became an American citizen. In his youth Bert had known unions, and while learning his trade as a tin-plate roller he had gone to night classes conducted by the union. In America he naturally followed his trade and had worked at it in several mills before coming to this steel mill near Pittsburgh in 1928.

Though a recent immigrant, Bert's problems were typical of the older immigrant and second-generation American workers with whom he worked. He felt them more keenly, perhaps, than did his fellow workers, because he had known something better in group relations and community life. The town was dominated by the company. The company-owned houses were rented only to those workers who demonstrated their loyalty. After three years of commuting thirty miles a day, Bert finally secured a company house for his family.

Life in Steeltown was different from what Bert had known as a boy in Wales. The company ran everything—the borough council, the school board, and the county government. The men just did not have a thing to say about these matters. Bert's next-door neighbor was a big Irishman, William Francis Collins, whom everyone called Bill. He began working for the company in 1911, just a few years after the mill was built. He grew up with it. He was an electrician and his duties took him from department to department, repairing motors and cranes. Bill took considerable pride in reminding everyone that he had helped to install the machines on which they were working. He was popular in the mill, numbering many foremen and superintendents among his close friends. He had always been a "loyal worker" and had never questioned the company's rule in the mill or community.

When the depression hit the town a feeble effort was made by the company to aid its employees, but the slump was too much for it. Bill thought something could be done to relieve the misery and suffering by voting in a new town administration. Here he committed a cardinal sin. Bill registered as a Democrat in 1932. Still worse, he actually spent some of his spare time winning votes for the Democratic party. His superintendent called him on the carpet. "Don't you know that working for the Democrats is going against the company?" he asked.

Bill counseled with Bert, who advised him to stick to his guns. Before long Bill started to lose turns in the mill. He was laid off for a week because he failed to answer an emergency breakdown call promptly. Everyone knew why Bill was not faring so well, and activity for the Democratic party ceased in Steeltown. But this traditionally Republican Pennsylvania mill town voted solidly for Franklin D. Roosevelt in the fall of 1932.

For several years before this incident things never seemed right to Bert. He did not know just why. He was a good worker and, as far as outward appearances showed, a complacent one. Bert somehow could not understand the men with whom he worked. They seemed to drift for themselves. Bert had no feeling of belonging, of being a part of this "big dirty business of making steel." He had learned, from losing several jobs in this country, not to talk back to a foreman. "A boss in this country," Bert observed, "has more power than the King of England."

Bert had learned never to run a roll against the grain, but his foreman had not. When a roll broke before its "time," because it had been reversed, the foreman laid off Bert for a week. "Could I appeal?" Bert asked. "I once tried to show the dumb ——— why a roll should always run in the same direction, but then he gave me two weeks off. I took it. What else could I do? My wife complained about our moving a dozen times in six years because, she claimed, I was too proud to keep my mouth shut for the sake of my family. My mother-in-law was ill, and moving was extra hard on her.

"My oldest boy—he was just a lad then—would ask me if I lost my job again. His mother would tell him not to question his father. I couldn't stand it around the house during those penalty layoffs, so I'd go down to the beer tavern. Prohibition was still law, but the town was wide open. At the tavern the fellows would say, 'Take it like a sport; you can't do nuthin' about it.' They did not know that they could do something about it or, if they did, they were afraid to talk."

Bert was telling us his story in our hotel room in New York City one evening between conferences with his company in 1939. He was a full-time member of SWOC's staff now, president of his local union, and in the mood to look back.

"So much has happened since 1933," Bert continued, "that it seems like a dream that took place in a night. Time sure goes fast when a fellow's busy doing things he likes doing. Steeltown's changed. Big Bill Collins is council president. Imagine that! Things in the mill have changed. The company comes running to me every time they have a problem involving the men. The men have changed. I can mind when they were afraid of their own shadows. Now it's all I can do to keep them from pulling the switch every time they've got a grievance. I feel like I belong in this man's country now. The men ain't busted up into a dozen different bunches. We're all one now. The foremen ain't the dictators they used to be. The fellows are self-respecting union men. And to think how they used to be herded around like a bunch of sheep! I'm the same Bert Edwards I've always been, but I sure feel different inside."

Al Risko is secretary of Bert's local union. Al joined the union out of a feeling of futility with regard to promotion, a realization that once he got into the mill he was stuck there. Bert joined to overcome a feeling of frustration resulting from the lack of any voice in the things that counted on his job, and the feeling of not being part of a permanent group. Both workers also joined for other psychological and social reasons. Al learned that one had to conform to the prevailing attitudes to be a regular fellow in the mill, and that to defy these attitudes meant breaking the social ties that he and his wife had in the community.

Bert's case went deeper into the social situation. He found much in common with his fellow workers that never existed before the depression, or they found it with him. Slack work and curtailed job opportunities forced them together. Few were better off than the others. They found their individual problems to be the same. This nurtured a bond of friendship among them. Judged by standards in the nineteen twenties, individual workers were failures—for which they could do nothing by themselves. On the street corners and in the beer taverns during the idle days of the depression, the individualism of American workers, as known in the twenties, died—forever. Group action grew out of the helplessness of individual workers to solve their problems. The depression created a new social situation in the coal patches, mill towns, and factory cities that found expression in the kinship of union membership, collective bargaining, and a new status for American workers.

Workers, like other folk, need a means of self-expression and an outlet for their creative drives. In the case of John Rider these other essentially psychological or noneconomic needs went begging for more than three decades. John brought a committee of five into our Pittsburgh office in March, 1937. They were not from a steel mill, but from a cork plant that employed seven hundred men and four hundred women. John's committee worked in the original plant of an internationally known cork-products firm. Its personnel policy and paternalistic practices had been cited by management as an ideal example for years. Wages were high for this type of light work. The forty-hour week and overtime pay had prevailed since 1933. Liberal vacations were granted. The employee-representation plan had been advertised as being the ideal form of labor organization. Social affairs were held regularly for employees and their families. Knowing all this, we were skeptical about John's claims that his fellow workers wanted to form a CIO union. We gave him, however, a batch of petitions addressed to the CIO, authorizing it to bargain for the signatories. We instructed John's committee not to return until a substantial majority signed the petitions. Frankly we did not expect to hear from them for some time, if again.

A week later John returned with his committee enlarged to thirty. It consisted of all the representatives and alternates of the company union who, that morning, had voted to dissolve it. John returned the petitions with over one thousand signatures. The committee demanded that we call a membership meeting—which we did with misgivings, because the previous day management had advanced wages five per cent. John Rider had been with the company continuously for thirty-two years, having started when he was twelve years old. He was a subdued individual, small, quiet, and a little gray at the temples. He was chairman of the company union and commanded the respect of his fellow workers. Why should this seemingly cowed man, we asked ourselves, lead a revolt against the management that admittedly had treated him so well?

The meeting was a surprise. The men seemed to have brought their wives and children, the women their husbands, the girls their boy friends, and the boys their girl friends—at any rate, many more than a thousand persons crowded into the hall. This was a Cork Workers Town Meeting, the first time these cork workers and their kinsfolk had ever been together for serious purposes. Membership meetings were not allowed under the company union. John was unable to act as chairman and turned the gavel over to the scheduled speaker.

A sound moving picture of the meeting would have contained more than enough material for a dozen movies and a score of novels. Organized discussion was impossible. The only business transacted was the election of a small negotiating committee. The only speaking one of the authors did was with a gavel. The time was consumed by more than five score of workers. Some spoke only a sentence, while others took as much as twenty minutes. Once a speaker got the floor it was his. Each worker, with feeling or brilliant humor or both, just recited personal experiences in the plant that he or she did not like. Some of the more humorously told personal incidents virtually threw the audience into hysterics.

"It's about time something like this happened," a comely girl said. "We have got to stand on our own feet. They do everything for you but provide you with a husband, and I even know girls who they got husbands for. And them what ain't got time to get pregnant, they get foster kids for."

"They lay out my work with so many instructions," a middle-aged man complained, "that there's nothing left for me to figure out for myself. The only reason they keep half of us there is 'cause they ain't discovered a machine yet that would take our place."

A member of the committee, who later irritated the plant manager considerably, said, "When the company does you a favor, they think they own you body and soul for the rest of your life." And he cited a few examples to make his point.

In their faces, as they alternately applauded, cheered, booed, and stamped their feet on the floor, one could see the same kind of emotionally satisfying expression visible in the faces of huge audiences at intensely absorbing athletic contests. The chairman, after five and one-half hours, was able to adjourn the meeting only by promising another one three nights later. The next meeting was as well attended and lasted an hour longer. It was a repeat performance, except that one of the authors had half an hour to explain the contract he and the negotiating committee were going to submit to the management. This was the only organized business transacted. Before the final contract was signed, five meetings lasting a total of thirty-odd hours were held in one month.

The key to the meaning of this phenomenon lies not alone in the nature of the meetings but in two incidents involving John Rider. During the conferences the plant manager took issue with John on whether the company could grant further wage concessions. "You do not know whether we make or lose money on natural cork," he said to John, "and you should accept our word for it that it's a losing part of the business."

John rose to his feet. Up to this point he had been listening mostly. In contrast to his naturally quiet manner he rushed to the manager's desk, pounded it to emphasize his words. "You've done my thinking around here long enough; from now on I'll have you understand I've got a mind of my own and, the Lord permittin', I intend usin' it."

Halfway back to his chair, John swirled around and returned to the desk to pound out another sentence. "You're makin' money on natural cork, and if you think I'm too dumb to figure that out you're the biggest lunkhead I ever knew."

The other incident took place several months later. The "Little Steel Strike" was on, but it made little difference to John Rider and his fellow workers. They had won their victory, and were enjoying it. They rented a large river steamer and took their members and their families—this was virtually everyone eligible for union membership—for a day's ride on the Ohio River. John told us about this afterward. "We sure had one swell boat picnic. Everyone had a great time; no one was hurt. We managed it all by ourselves. Not a single bit of help did we get from management and, boy, we didn't want it. And we made expenses."

John Rider joined the union in his forty-fourth year to give a meaning to his personality, to overcome a feeling of personal inadequacy, and to find a means of self-expression—all of these things having been denied him by his rigid industrial life. He was hardly conscious of the motives that moved him into union membership; nevertheless, he was moved deeply. John was confident that he could think for himself and manage things for himself, and he derived extreme personal satisfaction in proving this confidence in himself justified. He was no longer that anonymous person whose only distinction was that he had worked for the same company more than thirty years, but the head of a union to whom his fellow workers looked. After all these years John was somebody, and it made him happy. You could see it in his eyes.

For his fellow workers the compelling motives that made them join the CIO were an urge for self-expression, a desire to have a voice in the things that counted to them in the plant, an outlet for their creative drives, and the freedom of action to work out their own destiny in their own way. Economic motives seemed to be secondary. Wages were raised six cents an hour over and above the five per cent raise granted at the inception of the union, but this ten-dollar-a-month raise was acknowledged in a matter-of-fact way. John Rider and his fellow workers were more concerned with getting things out that had been bottled up inside of them for all these years, and with contemplating the prospect of being able to do things for themselves that would give a meaning to their personalities and a purpose to their lives. The paternalistic policies of management—doing the thinking for its employees, giving them things, and trying zealously to keep everybody happy—made these workers feel subservient when they wanted to be proud, and made them seek that something that was terribly important to them but lacking in their rigid industrial life. A make-or-break factor in the continued success and usefulness of labor unions is the extent to which they provide their members with the things these cork workers sought in becoming union members originally.

Fletcher Brown, a large, likeable Negro steel worker, joined the union for economic motives primarily, but not entirely. He appeared as a witness before the Steel Labor Relations Board created by Congressional action in 1934.

The board was holding a hearing in the old Postoffice Building in Pittsburgh on the motion of a local union to hold an election in its mill. The board's jurisdiction was confined to cases of demonstrated industrial unrest. A corporation attorney was cross-examining Fletcher. He showed conclusively, so he felt, that there was no unrest in the mill or in the town. Then he turned to Fletcher and demanded that he tell the board where all this unrest existed that the union was alleging.

Fletcher looked at the retired admiral who was in charge of the hearing, slowly leaned his huge bulk forward, raised his right hand to his breast, stared in the attorney's face, and said, "That thar' unrest I'se speak of is rawght here in ma he-art!"

Everyone in the room laughed, and the board called a recess. This attorney has admitted since that no other witness ever set him back as did Fletcher Brown with his forthright, simple, honest answer.

Fletcher did not point to his stomach and say he was hungry, though he was—literally his family was ill-housed, ill-fed, and ill-clothed. He instinctively went to the root of his unrest. It was in his heart, yet he had joined the union certainly to better his family. These motives were clear enough, and powerful enough, to explain why Fletcher was a union member. But he had joined also for other motives that, in spite of his economic circumstances, seemed equally as compelling, if not more so. Fletcher is a man of tremendous energy, radiant personality, and unusual abilities. His work in the mill was hard, unpleasant, and routine. He was a chipper, taking the bad seams out of billets with a heavy, deafening, body-shaking, air-hammer chisel. The pay was four dollars and fifty cents a day, the work irregular.

In his job Fletcher found no outlet for his tremendous energies, no opportunity to express himself or to show what he knew. Day after day he went to work; year in and year out dissatisfaction grew inside of him; his creative drives—his vibrant personality—became frustrated by the dictatorial type of management under which he worked. Joining the union gave him the chance to clean out of his system the emotional cancer that had been eating at his heart, that had been causing "all this unrest." For the last eight years his local union has had the benefit of his exceptional leadership and ability, which management either could not or would not give an opportunity. Fletcher's relationships with management have changed, and he finds satisfaction in his work that was never there before. His economic status has improved one hundred per cent in the meantime, and his social position is manifoldly better. He is an integral part of a powerful organization of human beings that makes no distinctions because of race, color, or creed.

Industrial workers, particularly in the larger concerns, have experienced a similar life, in varying degrees and in different ways, ever since the rise of the huge corporate production units. Their work smothered their personalities, denied them any satisfying social security, besides failing to give them either an adequate economic return or an enduring job status. The average worker, like other folk, needs more than higher wages and job-protecting seniority rules to make him happy. He needs opportunities to satisfy his personality; outlets for his creative drives; a sense of belonging, of being important and useful, of being a part of a vital, virile, permanent social group—an integral part of a group that will give him a real sense of social security. This is demonstrated by the workers' lives we have examined.

Al Risko receives ninety-seven cents an hour as a motor inspector in the electrical gang. Bert Edwards, who earned three to four hundred dollars a month as a tin-plate roller, is making three hundred dollars monthly now as a SWOC field director, not as much as he once earned but considerably more than his fellow tin-plate rollers, most of whom have since been displaced technologically, are earning now. John Rider's cork-plant job pays him seven dollars a day compared to the five dollars and fifty cents he got before the union. Fletcher's chipping job has been eliminated by scarfers and a chipping machine; but he is earning nine dollars a day working in the soaking-pit department, which is twice his old chipping daily wage. These workers, and the millions they typify, were motivated to join their unions to win these economic gains so that they might provide better for their families. Their financial gains are indicative of the economic benefits labor unions have brought workers generally in the last decade.

They were motivated, like the millions of other union members, also by a quest for security—protection against petty discrimination; arbitrary discharge; technological, seasonal, and cyclical unemployment; and the other factors that contributed to making their lives insecure.

Wage raises, promotions, and job protection are by-products of the psychological and social motives that impelled these workers to organize into labor unions, as much as they are in themselves original motives for union membership. The steel and auto organizing campaigns of 1936-37 are evidence that workers join unions not alone for more money and security. In June, 1936, the steel industry granted paid vacations to large numbers of its employees to offset SWOC's organizing drive. Instead, these economic concessions gave an impetus to SWOC. Three months later, time and one-half for overtime was conceded; and within another two months wages were raised ten per cent to thwart SWOC's growth. Membership, however, swelled so rapidly that a majority of the industry was under contract with SWOC a half year later.

In the hope of weakening the auto workers' union the General Motors Corporation raised wages five cents an hour in February, 1937, only to see it grow stronger. "Little Steel" granted its employees the economic gains won by SWOC in March, 1937, but these workers were on the picket line that summer and, though set back at the time, recovered to win union recognition four years later. These organizing drives, the largest and most important in organized labor's history, derived their strength and success from the failure of management to satisfy workers' psychological and social needs as well as their economic ones. The economic concessions management granted accelerated instead of impeded union membership, and revealed a lack of appreciation of the several motives that impel workers to join unions.

Indisputably the economic motive has been, and is, powerful. The phenomenal success of labor unions in the last decade in raising wages, securing paid vacations, shortening hours, and protecting workers' jobs was made possible by the inequitable distribution of the proceeds of production and by the practices of management and basic economic factors that contributed to the general insecurity of workers. But this is only part of the story.

The dynamic quality, the militancy, and the crusading spirit of the labor movement, especially of CIO, in the last decade were nurtured by the failure of management to satisfy the noneconomic needs of workers. The rise of industrial unions and the large-scale development of collective bargaining date back not alone to the chaotic economic conditions in the 1932 depression but equally as much to the day in that depression when workers realized they no longer enjoyed the freedom of action to tell their boss off, quit, and pick up a job elsewhere. As we look back upon the scores of union meetings we attended and spoke to in the last decade, the purpose they served becomes clear. Here workers would come—and they came in droves—to cheer a speaker for denouncing the boss, whom they dared not denounce face to face. From these meetings workers derived great personal satisfactions. In them Fletcher Brown, John Rider, and countless other workers ranted and raved, and rightly so, against the things in their industrial experiences that frustrated their creative desires, took their personalities away from them, and denied them any substantial satisfaction in their daily work.

These union meetings served as safety valves for the emotional systems of workers. The things that made these workers explode with such emotional outbursts are deep-rooted in the "system of corporate industrial dictatorship and discipline" under which they worked. Like the blissful days of matrimony, the satisfactions workers secure from their first union meetings soon wear off and they seek lasting ones. The labor union then becomes an instrument through which workers seek to replace the "system of corporate industrial dictatorship" with one along democratic lines. The extent to which the industrial life of workers shall be governed by democratic principles is what most of the shooting is about.

Henry Ford[2] once said, "All men want is to be told what to do and get paid for doing it." That is dictatorship, and American workers do not want it. Mr. Ford has learned since that men want a voice in what they do and that they want to participate in determining how they are to be paid for doing it, and how much.

Industrial peace lies at the end of three converging paths, rather than at the end of any single one. The psychological, social, and economic needs of the human beings who make up America's working force must all be satisfied. Labor unions are indispensable in the fulfillment of these needs because they can be satisfied only through group relations. Unions are peculiarly adapted toward this end since they serve workers as a means of self-expression, as a socially integrating force, as a provider of economic benefits, and as an instrument for participation in the productive process. Management by itself, through individual relations with workers, cannot satisfy all three needs. Nor can unions alone. The joint efforts of both are required to provide workers with a well-rounded environment, a happy, prosperous, and secure life.

Chapter II: Art of Collective Bargaining

Collective bargaining marks the end of individual and the beginning of group relations between workers and management.

In the spring of 1941 SWOC representatives met with the management of a large steel corporation to renew and amend the collective-bargaining contract that, four years earlier, ushered in a new era for the steel industry. Philip Murray headed the SWOC negotiators. Management's spokesman was the president of the corporation, a tall slender man in his mid-fifties. He resembled a university chancellor instead of the popular conception of a steel magnate. Sitting across the table from him, one noticed immediately his silver cuff links, conservative blue tie, white shirt, and business executive's blue suit. Frequently he pulled out of his vest pocket a pair of brown-rimmed glasses and pinched them on his nose. The few strands of silver hair on his head, the worried look that never left his face, and the peculiar way he puckered up his mouth gave the conference a burdensome gravity.

The enormous oblong conference room accentuated this gravity. A huge table, surrounded with low-cut chairs, ran the length of it. The walls were paneled with walnut, the floor was covered with a mattresslike rug that matched the orange drapes, and the windows were shaded with steel Venetian shutters that softened the daylight. Small white sound-insulating squares made up the ceiling. The fluorescent lighting completed the ultramodern room. There were also a number of modernistic cuspidors over which the union representatives always seemed to trip. And behind the door stood an old cast-iron combination hatrack and umbrella stand, a silent reminder of what the conference room must have looked like in the days of the original steel masters.

For three days Phil Murray and the nine other union negotiators argued their case. Only the corporation president spoke for management. Never once did he mention the union. He always referred to "our employees" in discussing wages, vacations, union recognition, adjustment of grievances, and other matters. This constant slighting of SWOC irritated the union negotiators, but they strained themselves to be polite.

Finally, in his soft stern manner, Phil Murray leaned over the table and asked him, "Won't you, sir, be generous enough to condescend and mention the union just once?"

His pinch glasses fell, but he skillfully remounted them to reply, "Mr. Murray, we deal with our employees individually as well as through the union—we've always dealt with our employees as individuals."

Readjusting his glasses, he continued, "Why, when I was general superintendent of Tommy's mill"—pointing to one of the union negotiators—"my door was always open for my employees to come to me with their problems."

"All the men used to call your office the 'Lion's Den,' and when they got called in there it was usually bad news," Tommy snapped. A red-haired small man, pipe fitter by trade, Tommy interrupted the conference to tell about his years in the mill before the union, and since.

"I had twenty-two years bargaining for myself, and I don't want no more of it," Tommy began, " 'cause it never got me nothing except what the company gave me. I'd go to my foreman and complain about my wages. But what did it bring me? 'If ya don't like it here you can go some place else' is what the foreman would tell me; and many's the time I felt like goin' some place else. That's changed now.

"When I go in to Mr. Winters, the general super, I get treated like a man. But it ain't Tommy Morgan he's talkin' to; it's the union president he's talkin' with. And it ain't 'cause he likes me that he takes note of what I say; it's 'cause the men are behind me, 'cause they've chose me to talk for them. What do you call that?" Tommy asked, looking the president in the face. "Dealin' with 'your employees' or dealin' with the union?"

The president reminded Tommy that some of the employees did not belong to his union, and that they had the right to bargain with the management for themselves.

"Don't dignify them free-riders," Tommy rejoined, "by sayin' it's a right for them to bargain as individuals. It's no right. It's a union-bustin' scheme; that's what it is. Bargain with you, or your foremen or superintendents, huh—that's a joke. What's Tommy Morgan in that big mill of yours? Another check number; nothin' more. But the union president—man, he's somebody that can bargain with you. Sure, you deal with them free-riders as individuals; and you give in to them, sure. But why? 'Cause they've got any bargaining power? No. 'Cause most of the men are in the union. Take the union away, and see how much bargaining any of them individual employees of yours do."

At this point Phil Murray re-entered the discussion. "Let us examine that last remark of Tommy's," he began, "for there seems to be some confused thinking on your side of the table about individual rights. Theoretically an individual worker has the personal freedom to bargain for himself with organized management, but, as Tommy has testified and we all know, this freedom is a sham. It avails the individual worker nothing to stand up against the power of management and assert himself. To do so is foolish. For years corporate management has made a pretense of this individual freedom. It is an insult to our intelligence to pretend that there is such a thing. The terms of this contract, when they are finally agreed upon, will apply equally to nonmembers and members. Individual workers, not members of the union, can bargain with management for themselves because of the strength they derive from the union's organized power. Take that out of the picture and they would be as helpless as they were before the union. That is why Tommy calls them 'free-riders,' individuals who enjoy the benefits of the union but refuse to join and assume their share of its hazards and costs."

Phil Murray concluded, "You need to clarify your thinking. There is no such thing as equal bargaining between organized management and individual workers. The only feasible bargaining is between management and unions. Whilst you carry on collective bargaining with our union, you attempt to maintain the fraud of bargaining with individuals. That is impossible, and produces confusion and strife. By encouraging individual workers to bargain directly with management you undermine the union and invite trouble. To achieve peace in your mills you should realize that you are not dealing with your employees directly but with their union acting in their behalf."

Failure of management to recognize this fundamental principle is a common cause of disputes. There is an irreconcilable conflict between union-management bargaining and management bargaining with individual workers. The two cannot exist side by side either peacefully or indefinitely. Actually the vital freedom the individual worker enjoys is to join a union of his own choosing without interference from management. He joins with his fellow workers into a group; they fuse their individual strength into a group power. From among their numbers they select representatives who bargain for them with organized management on an equal footing. The individual worker gives up his impotent freedom to bargain individually for the effective freedom of bargaining through a group.

Industrial relations, properly defined, are union-management relations. "Employee relations," "employee-company relations," "labor relations," and other similar terms are obsolete. The union is not the third party but the fourth one in the picture, and balances the relationships between owners and workers. The former have long since hired a third party, professional management, to represent their interests. Where ownership and management have not yet been divorced, workers still bring their unions into the picture to acquire equal bargaining power. Collective bargaining is therefore a human art practiced in industry by groups and not by individuals.

The initial collective-bargaining practices are influenced in varying degrees by the preunion history of the particular industrial concern and by the fact that genuine union-management relations are initiated by the union.

The president of a structural-iron company employing six hundred and fifty workers came into our office during the rapid unionization period of early 1937. He was excited about the proposed contract the SWOC local union in his plant submitted. It covered twenty-two legal-size, single-spaced, typewritten pages. Apparently the union members had thought of everything objectionable in the memory of the oldest one, and then drafted prohibitions against all of them. After trying to get the union committee to confine the contract to the major issues, the SWOC director in charge of the local union felt it would be better strategy to let the committee submit this proposed contract than to compel it to submit the SWOC four-page standard one.

It was a warm May afternoon. The bulky president had taken off his coat and appeared to be exasperated. His associates, the operating vice-president and plant superintendent, seemed no less uncomfortable. Before he could say anything, one of the authors greeted the president, "I hear that you have run into a little difficulty in negotiating your contract."

"We certainly have," he replied. "The men want me to give them the plant to run, to turn over all the profits, and to keep on paying the taxes and foot the losses—and, by gosh, there'll be plenty of losses if this thing goes through."

He was still waving the voluminous contract in the air when one of the authors asked to look at it.

"Well, sir, it looks like your chickens are coming home to roost."

There was dead silence. An apprehensive look came over the perspiring face of the president as he gazed at us speechless but obviously saying to himself, "So these union fellows are supposed to be fair, huh!"

"Perhaps I had better elaborate on my statement about your chickens coming home to roost"—one of us broke the silence—"because there is more to this massive document than appears on the surface. The one hundred and thirty-seven provisions of this proposed contract did not come out of the sky. Each one represents a grievance, and one or more of your employees want these practices to stop. This is their first experience with collective bargaining, and they think the way to stop all the management practices they do not like is to outlaw them in a contract. Let us pick out an example at random.

"Number twenty on page three states, 'Men sent home because of no work shall get paid for two hours.' Let me ask you in all frankness what your practices are in scheduling employees for work."

The president looked at his vice-president, who looked at the superintendent. The latter replied, "We have to call out more men than we need, since some men don't show up and we never know until the last minute just how many we'll need the next shift."

"Suppose you had to pay two hours at their regular earnings to those workers you send home each shift," we asked him. "Do you think you could find a way to schedule your operations so that you could notify each shift in advance how many workers you'll need?"

The president replied, "I won't argue that point. I've heard the men's argument about having to pay for transportation, for their packed lunch, and about the inconvenience. Frankly I did not know this practice was so widespread. We are willing to consider that proposal, but there won't be many men getting the two hours' pay because we intend notifying them in advance whether we need them or not."

"That is precisely what I am driving at," one of us interrupted. "You should go back and thank the committee for drawing up this detailed contract. What you have here is a list of the outstanding grievances that motivated your employees to organize a union. You should consider each one on the basis of its merits. Obviously the way to correct those matters that need attention is not to spell them all out in the contract but to impress your employees with your change of heart and sincerity by proceeding to adjust them as quickly as possible."

This was not all there was to our conference. It lasted more than two hours, but at the end the company officials, still admittedly dubious about the eventual outcome, agreed to continue negotiations. A few weeks later the brief standard SWOC contract was signed.

During negotiations the local union committee was hard-boiled, driving for complete satisfaction on each point, unyielding even on minor details. Pat McGrogan, its chairman, snorted when we counseled "patience" or "be reasonable."

"Listen," he said, blood coming to his face, "we've been kicked around for fifty years and they ain't had no mercy in their kickin' neither, and now, by gosh, we're goin' to do the kickin'. We want our rights, and we aim to get 'em."

The dead hand of the past, unseen but strongly felt, influences the early course of union-management relations. In the first instance this influence is felt through the pioneering, tough-minded, courageous, belligerent workers who first rise to union leadership. These leaders, the modern successors of the hardy, fearless pioneering founders of America, are products of their environment—a violent industrial one resulting from management's indiscriminate use of the power to discharge, blacklist, compel acceptance of yellow-dog contracts, and evict; and, in resisting unions and collective bargaining, management agents have even murdered striking workers. This shameless resistance of management to wage earners' efforts to organize is spread over the pages of the monumental report of President Woodrow Wilson's Commission on the Causes of Industrial Unrest in 1912; the report on the steel strike of 1919 by the Commission of Inquiry of the Interchurch World Movement; the voluminous records of Senator Robert M. LaFollette's Senate Subcommittee on Civil Liberties, 1936-40; and in other revealing pages of governmental and private investigations.

Workers do not forget their lifelong experiences overnight. At the outset they seek to "square accounts" through their newly found power in union membership. Thus the early days, in most cases years, of collective-bargaining relationships are influenced profoundly by what has come before. We shall not call the roll of all these practices, for they are well known. The major ones make their imprint on every collective-bargaining contract. Protection against indiscriminate discharge and against favoritism in hirings, layoffs, and promotions, as well as personal insurance against avoidable indefinite idleness, find expression in demands for seniority. Contract provisions and union policies on the distribution of earnings and related questions of technological change, wage-rate adjustment, time and motion study, and so forth, reflect workers' experiences in preunion days. The union shop—union membership as a condition of employment—besides being inherent in our free society is the direct outgrowth of the violent history of America's basic mass-producing industries. Hence the overwhelming influence of things that have come before runs through the early grievances of workers and the initial practices of collective bargaining growing out of them.

These practices likewise are influenced, in no small measure, by the fact that they are initiated by the union. The union, not management, demands collective bargaining. The union promotes wage increases, standard work hours, vacations, seniority, adjustment of grievances, and other basic tenets of collective bargaining. Management's role, especially in the initial stages, is one of resistance. The dynamic force of union-management relations comes from the unions, from their membership. Workers, for the first time, take the initiative, and leadership falls into their hands. The first collective-bargaining contract has the same significance to a newly organized group of workers as the Declaration of Independence had to the revolting colonists. In many cases management tries to hold onto the reins of leadership by granting vacations or conceding wage raises while workers are organizing and before they have a chance to present formal demands. These efforts are usually futile. The driving force in union-management relations at the outset is the union, and the significance of this factor is obvious throughout our discussion.

The interval extending from the day workers organize and present their first contract demands until management rebuilds its lost position of leadership is a transitional period. How long and intense the period is depends, first, upon the background and, second, upon the manner in which management makes the transition from individual to union relations with its employees. In cases where collective bargaining is accepted gracefully by management and resistance to union organization has been slight, workers soon get over their desires to "get even" with management. The time lag where management's resistance has been bitter and belligerent, of course, is much greater. Whatever the circumstances be, except in cases of management's unyielding opposition and never-compromising acceptance, workers eventually seek to pursue their common interest with management through the processes of collective bargaining.

The confusing and uncertain policies of management in large sectors of industry at the present time result from the fact that union-management relations, in varying degrees, have been going through a period of transition for the past several years. Only now are they beginning to attain some degree of maturity. The thinking of management is becoming crystallized. Unions are growing more co-operative, and both are beginning to face realities. What the future holds in store for collective bargaining, however, remains to be seen. The purpose of this discussion is to give some indication of the greater area into which union-management relations are moving.

Collective bargaining is an instrument for workers and owners, through unions and management, to solve their problems directly without recourse to the government.

A familiar scene in the summer of 1933: a group of workers with lunch buckets under their arms are standing around an old truck which a union organizer is using for a platform. In the background is the red-brick company office building, the windows jammed with management officials listening to the organizer as intently as the crowd on the street. He shouts through the loud-speaker, "The government wants you to join the union." He bases his conclusion on Section 7 (a) of the National Industrial Recovery Act (NIRA). "This section says the boss can't fire you for union activities," the loud-speaker blares, "and, what's more, President Franklin D. Roosevelt, the greatest man that ever sat in the White House, won't let 'im." The speech is long. Frequently cheers and applause drown out the loud-speaker. The gruesome details of the depression and the nonunion shop are repeated time and again. Gradually the audience dwindles away. The organizer announces that he will return for the next shift, and a meeting will be held at seven o'clock in the Fraternal Hall where anybody can sign up for membership. "The government is behind the union," one worker argues with another on the way home or to work. The plant manager phones the top official.

"Hello, chief. . . . Yes, again. . . . What'll we do? That big-mouthed union stiff is agitating the men. . . . What did you say? . . . Too damned many to be comfortable. Does the law say we can't fire them for joining a union? . . . No, I ain't afraid. . . . Sure, we can fire 'em for something else besides belonging to the union. . . . Don't worry; my shirt's on. . . . See you tonight." . . .

Almost a decade has passed since this scene was enacted in front of the mine, mill, and factory gates of America's industrial towns and valleys. Meanwhile workers have won for themselves a new position in industry with the aid of the government. The Union Renaissance, ushered in by the Blue Eagle on June 16, 1933, has been based upon governmental encouragement of the formation of unions and collective bargaining. The failure of Section 7 (a) of the NIRA, lacking punitive enforcement measures, paved the way for the National Labor Relations Act two years later. By April 12, 1937, when the Supreme Court upheld the act, the full weight of the federal government was behind organized labor in its unionizing efforts. A new labor jurisprudence began to take form through the decisions of the National Labor Relations Board (NLRB), and cries went up to amend the "insidious" law under which it operated. These cries, at first quite loud, gradually became less audible as one by one the violators of the law—Tom Girdler, Henry Ford, Eugene Grace, and others—agreed to abide by it. The legal right of workers to organize into unions of their own choosing has become recognized as a basic part of the law of the land, and simultaneously the functions of government have been extended to other labor and social matters.

Organized labor was forced to bring the federal government into the picture. Since the rise of the big corporations more than a half century ago, workers had tried, repeatedly and in vain, to work out their problems directly with management. Each time, however, management said "No!"—and fought.

The steel industry's history is typical of American industry. The early iron and steel masters dealt with their workmen as a group. Andrew Carnegie recognized the steel and iron workers' union, the largest and strongest union during the eighteen eighties, until 1892. In that year he changed his company's policy to "We oppose organized labor, and will deal with our workmen only as individuals." The result was an outbreak of industrial warfare, beginning with the 1892 Homestead strike. This warfare continued intermittently for a quarter of a century as steel workers tried in vain to change the industry's policy back to that of the pre-1892 days. The formation of the United States Steel Corporation was greeted with the 1901 sheet and tin-plate workers' strike. The few local unions that survived this major labor defeat were annihilated in the 1909 strike. In isolated places steel workers tried to re-establish their former organized status, but without success. They lost in McKees Rocks in 1909, in South Bethlehem the next year, in East Youngstown, Ohio, in 1916, and elsewhere. Then came the general steel strike of 1919, but, like the periodic local strikes, it ended in complete disaster. From then until 1933—a period of unbroken industrial peace—the steel industry enjoyed the fruits of its costly warfare with its employees. The price of that peace for the nation's steel workers was servitude. This was the period of the Union Dark Ages in America's basic and mass-producing industries.

The Union Renaissance began in 1933, but it did not bear fruit for four years because of management's maneuver in creating company unions on a large scale. The "employee-representation plans," as they were officially dubbed, however, sowed the seeds for the Congress of Industrial Organizations (CIO). Their significance was that they symbolized the end of the "we will deal with our employees only as individuals" policy. To a limited degree they established the new policy of dealing with employees as a group. The unionization efforts in steel, in part, were frustrated also by the Steel Labor Relations Board, which lacked enforcement powers. The labor board for the auto industry impeded unionization for the same reason. This paved the way for the National Labor Relations Act, which, though enacted in July, 1935, did not become effective until April 12, 1937, when validated by the Supreme Court. In the meantime SWOC signed a contract with United States Steel, and the United Automobile Workers had won recognition from eighty per cent of the auto industry. Since then the ranks of organized labor have grown to nearly ten million workers, and collective bargaining—with the aid of government—has become established in a large part of American industry.

The failure of industry and business—and the lion's share of the responsibility belongs to industrial management—to view America's social and economic problems realistically is responsibl for bringing the government into this field. Especially is this true in the case of collective bargaining. For more than five decades corporate management had been obstinate, blind, and unyielding. Workers have always had plenty of problems, lots of troubles. Each time they organized for the purpose of doing something about them in direct negotiations with management, they were beaten back. When management was unable to do the beating back alone it did not hesitate to get the help of government by the use of police power and court injunctions. Every setback—and management won most of the battles from 1892 to 1933—taught organized labor that it needed the help of government in the form of legal protection. To seek the government's help ran against the natural grain of organized labor, which, for example, opposed federal unemployment compensation as late as 1932. But management's "we shall not be moved" attitude left no alternative. Slowly and reluctantly organized labor abandoned its policy of relying on its own strength and went to Congress, asking for governmental aid in extending the practices of collective bargaining.

There followed a period, then, during which too many leaders of management and organized labor lost sight of the underlying philosophy of collective bargaining; namely, that workers and owners should, and can, solve many of their problems through joint negotiations. Management worked under the illusion that government "hung collective bargaining around our neck," while organized labor operated on an equally fallacious basis that it was up to the NLRB to get collective bargaining adopted. Thus the former pursued a policy of trying to repeal or emasculate the NLRA, while the latter well-nigh killed the NLRB by overloading it with complaints. Both sought to secure industrial peace from the councils of government. Naturally they did not find it there because, in the last analysis, the solution to the problems of unions and management lay in their common local environment. The hectic first six years of the NLRB, surcharged with emotion, tell this story.

The NLRB grew out of management's failure to accept organized workers into the councils of industry on a basis of equality. Somehow this obvious fact was overlooked. So enraged was management by the NLRB that all it could see was the government aiding and abetting union organization. A simple line of reasoning on management's part resulted. "Since the government is responsible for encouraging unions and making us practice collective bargaining" —the reasoning went—"to rid ourselves of 'this damned union business' all we have to do is eliminate the government." From this apriori reasoning sprung the noisy ill-fated campaign to "amend" the NLRA. Management told Congress, in effect, that the act had caused strikes and riots, and in order to re-establish industrial peace it must be repealed for all practical purposes. Some members of Congress listened, but what Congress as a whole heard was a public confession from management that it did not want to accept collective bargaining as a permanent institution. The campaign failed. The Supreme Court and Congress told management to go back home and work out its problems at the conference table.

Organized labor has learned the same thing, though in a different way. The Supreme Court decision of April 12, 1937, upholding the NLRA, set off a wave of NLRB cases. The NLRB in the following month received more than a thousand cases.[1] After four years of anxious waiting organized labor now had a government agency to which it could go, and it went full-splash with its problems arising from management's opposition to union recognition, its encouragement of company unions, and its discrimination against union members. By June 30, 1938, the board was loaded down with thirty-seven hundred and eighty-one pending cases. In 1939 and 1940 organized labor learned to its dismay that NLRB decisions on cases that had been filed two to three years earlier were so long being rendered that they were ineffectual; the local unions affected, in many cases, had become weak or nonexistent. NLRB decisions finding the Ford Motor Company guilty and outlawing the company unions of the Bethlehem Steel Corporation, for example, were hailed as "great labor victories," only to turn out to be quite empty. Gradually unions learned that they could not find the solution to their problems in Washington, D. C.

By 1941 union leaders had returned home to work out their problems directly with management. When Bethlehem Steel undertook to hold company-union representative elections on company property, its workers did not take their case to NLRB. They had already been there and gotten a decision outlawing these company unions, but were still plagued with them. So they went on strike, in Lackawanna, New York, Bethlehem and Johnstown, Pennsylvania, against the company-union elections. In the year 1942 Bethlehem Steel, for the first time, signed a collective-bargaining contract with SWOC. The same thing happened at River Rouge. Ford workers did not take the cases of eight union brothers who were fired for union activities to the NLRB. They had gone there on several previous occasions. Instead they went on strike, and Henry Ford signed his first contract with a union on June 20, 1941.

Organized labor, after eight years of experience with government aid, began to return to its historic policy of relying upon its own strength to achieve its objectives. In both the Bethlehem and Ford strikes of early 1941, the NLRB's functions were confined to conducting free elections for the purpose of determining by which union the workers desired to be represented in collective bargaining. Increasingly, we feel, the NLRB will be an agency engaged primarily in supervising elections of workers. In May, 1941, for instance, a majority of the board's new cases were election petitions. This transition of the NLRB from a collective-bargaining enforcement agency to a supervisor of elections marks the end of that period during which most leaders of unions and management looked to the government for the solution of their problems. Where unions are still weak they will continue to go to the NLRB for help, but as the field of collective bargaining spreads and unions grow stronger the NLRB will handle fewer and fewer complaint cases arising out of organized labor's failure to secure recognition directly from management. The enforcement powers of the NLRB, however, will be jealously guarded by organized labor. The practices of management over the past several decades have made a permanent imprint on the federal statute books in the National Labor Relations Act; it stands as one of organized labor's life-insurance policies.

Collective bargaining is a two-party affair. Management and unions are relying upon it more and more as a means of ironing out their common problems in direct negotiations.

They are no longer looking to somebody else—the government—to solve their problems for them. In a free society private groups can fail to settle their problems in direct relationships only at the peril of their independent existence, because each unsettled social and economic problem eventually finds its way into the halls of Congress. And when the government assumes final responsibility for the solution of these problems, private groups must forfeit certain freedoms and power. Government action in the field of social and economic matters should be in the form of assisting private groups in our economy toward a final solution. This is the essence of the CIO program, which we discuss in the concluding chapter.

Collective bargaining is the extension of the basic principles and practices of democracy into industry.

"Saxon" is a coined word among several thousand steel workers in a well-known mill. We encountered its full force several years ago in attending a local union meeting of these workers shortly after they had won recognition. The meeting hall was packed. Everyone stood to the sound of a gavel. "My America" was sung. The gavel sounded again, and the audience sat down. With dispatch the previous meeting's minutes were read, correspondence was referred to the executive board, a motion to suspend the regular order of business passed to a resounding "Aye," and the presiding officer introduced the speaker.

"We have with us tonight one of our national officers, Mr. Golden, who is going to talk to us about the troubles we have been having at the mill. Mr. Golden."

The recording secretary summarized the speech in his minutes tersely.

Main order of business. Talk by Regional Director Golden. Said local should get along with company as smoothly as membership meeting opened. Said the bosses were all Saxons and slow to adjusting themselves to union contract. Said you could catch more flies with honey than with vinegar, and that local grievance committee should use orderly procedure of contract instead of conducting strikes. Announced he was staying over for meeting with company officials and local officers tomorrow. Questions. Meeting adjourned, nine-thirty.

The question period brought out the fact that most of the difficulties arose in the hammer shop, where several hundred men were employed. The superintendent's name was Mr. Henry Sackson—"Saxon" for short. He had been in charge of the department as long as anyone could remember. His name had become synonymous with the word "dictator" and was applied by the men with reckless abandon to anyone who showed traits of being tough. One of the authors earned the epithet during one of its strikes by ordering the local union to work pending the settlement of its grievances through the contract procedures. The story of Mr. Sackson is that of the autonomous department foreman and superintendent in preunion days.

In his mid-seventies Mr. Sackson still retained much of his youthful vigor. He was of medium height, a little paunchy, and had oyster-gray hair. He sat slumped in his chair as the other management officials rose to greet us when we entered the conference room. The principal grievance involved a hammerman, who had been given a week off for bad work. This caused a two-day strike in the department. Our conference was the outgrowth of the strike, and we got down to the job of discussing the facts and merits of the case.

"Saxon's been pickin' on me ever since the union started," the hammerman began. "In fact, he's had a grudge agin me since I was a representative under the old representation plan. He got sore back in 1934 when I took a couple cases over his head, and told me, 'You squawked to the higher-ups, huh? I'll give you something to squawk about before this is over.' He got mad at me again during the last trouble we had because I said to Mr. ———"—pointing to the company president—"that Saxon was violating the contract. That's why he laid me off this time. My work wasn't bad. Most of the bad pieces "Saxon" threw into my pile after I went home. I've been discriminated against and should get paid for the week I was off, 'cause it wasn't my fault."

Mr. Sackson called the man a liar; said he did not know about the bad work until it was reported to him by the inspector, that to work for him a man had to do good work or get out, and as long as he was running the shop he was the boss and no one was going to tell him how to manage his business. The argument raged for more than an hour, at the end of which the company president agreed to pay the hammerman a week's back pay. Mr. Sackson protested, said that thereafter he was not going to be responsible for either production or efficiency; in fact, he might quit over it. Timidly the president, more than a generation younger, suggested to Mr. Sackson that maybe it would be a good idea if he did retire. This hit the old man unexpectedly. The blood drained from his face, and he looked pale. We all felt sorry for him until he stood up like a jack-in-the-box, grabbed his battered felt hat, jammed it on the rear of his head, rushed toward the door, turned around, and said, "If you don't want me to bust up this ——— damned union, then you can have 'er."

The fact that management seemed relieved at the prospect of Mr. Sackson leaving inspired confidence in the committee. This incident ended an epidemic of "wildcat strikes," and thereafter, except for a brief strike between contract negotiations in 1940, the committee has adjusted its grievances through the contract without resorting to the use of the strike weapon.

Under the system of corporate dictatorship and discipline prevailing in the basic and mass-producing industries in pre-union times, each department of the large industrial firms was set aside as an entity in itself, a small kingdom. Over this kingdom the foreman or superintendent ruled as prosecutor, judge, jury, and executioner. Several operating officials have told us that, as they look back over the period prior to signing their first union contract, they realize that instead of running one company they actually operated a number of independently functioning business enterprises. The total number of these corresponded roughly with the number of departmental superintendents, each of whom was free to hire and fire and run his department about as he pleased with a minimum of interference from top management—just as long as there was some degree of efficiency. The central employment office is a relatively new feature of industrial management. As late as two decades ago the customary way of getting a job in a steel mill was by bribing a boss.

In this type of setup the individual worker was told what to do, and he did it "or else." He was at the mercy of his boss when he had a grievance. Behind the boss was the corporate power of the company. The individual worker had behind him no power at all. He was merely a subject in the foreman's or superintendent's kingdom, and he remained a subject as long as he was a humble one. When and if he tried to get the power of the other workers behind him by organizing them into a union, he was fired. Then he was blacklisted. And when he did find employment, he was required to sign a yellow-dog contract. Some firms were less ruthless but only in method, not in substance. This was the basis on which Henry Sackson ruled. How closely this system of discipline by dictatorship resembles that of nondemocratic states is described candidly by a European university graduate who worked for a year in an American steel fabricating plant.

> The factory reminded me of a European dictatorial state, where bureaucrats plan and order, and citizens work and obey. The board of the company was the government, and the workers were the people, ruled through a centralized hierarchy of officials and controlled by a mechanized system of registration, bookkeeping, time cards, and punch clocks. Like citizens of authoritarian states, we did our individual assignments without knowing their purpose. . . . The foreman was our supreme visible authority. With his superiors, we did not communicate. And the president, with his board members and directors, sat high above us like an invisible, unapproachable God.

Collective bargaining changes all this. The foreman or superintendent's kingdom is converted into a republic. The individual worker, supported by his fellow workers, becomes a citizen. As such he can meet his boss on an equal basis, since he has the power of his union behind him to match the company's power that is behind the boss. No longer is the judgment of the boss beyond question or his authority final and absolute. Each worker now enjoys the democratic right to seek redress of his grievances that may arise from any act of his boss. His union gives him direct access to the superiors of his immediate boss, as he can appeal his grievances to the highest company official or submit them to an impartial umpire for final settlement. Thus collective bargaining establishes an industrial citizenship for workers, enforced by the union-management contract. This parallels their political citizenship. The functions and authority of the departmental boss change under this democratic system which creates citizens of industry. Henry Sackson was a ruler of subjects, and had no patience to become a leader of citizens. So he quit. Most department heads, however, must stay on, and the success of union-management relations depends more on the ability of the foremen and superintendents to adjust themselves to the democratic principles of collective bargaining than it does on any other one thing.

In its broadest sense collective bargaining is predicated upon democratic principles. Democracy is more than a body of faith, more than a belief in the rights of man and the freedoms of citizens, more than a system to govern human relations. Democracy is a program of action. It is the active participation of the individual in the affairs of the community that most vitally affect him and his neighbors. It is effective participation in the affairs of state and the community on the basis of equal opportunity for individuals, possible only through organizations—political, labor, and civic. It is freedom of action for the common good; freedom for the individual to be creative, both for his personal satisfaction and gain and for the enrichment of the community. Creative participation of the individual in the affairs of his fellow men, in fact, is the lifeblood of democracy. Such participation, in varying degrees, is enjoyed by the average citizen in the political affairs of his town, state, and nation. Prior to the acceptance of collective bargaining in his place of work, such participation is denied and repressed. In government the denial of such participation is political tyranny; in industry it is economic dictatorship. Collective bargaining is the democratic instrument through which all individuals in industry —workers, owners, managers, and consumers—can participate in making the vital decisions that affect the local industrial unit, the town in which its people live, right down to the roots.

The only effective way workers can participate is through their labor unions. The written collective-bargaining contract sets forth the extent and nature of such participation, which is determined at the outset by the bargaining power of the union. The written contract is a general constitution upon which a body of industrial law is built. The rules and regulations first set forth in the contract are elaborated and changed from day to day in the settlement of grievances and the interpretation of the contract. Gradually they evolve into a body of industrial common law, developed in a democratic manner. In this way workers enjoy a voice in the economic affairs that mean so much to them. And the old system of corporate dictatorship and discipline is replaced by an essentially democratic one, both in concept and in practice.

The policies and actions of unions are likely to reflect the policies and actions of management.

The sit-down strike is an American product, invented and perfected by management and later adapted by labor unions to serve their own purposes. Management showed unorganized workers the way to the sit-down strike. The lost outdoor picketing strike, broken by housing strikebreakers inside the plant, is the mother of the sit-down strike. We examine the mother and its child.

Summer, 1933. . . . "STRIKE FLARES AT STEEL MILL," the paper headlines. . . . Stretching for more than a mile on the outskirts of town, the steel mill is quiet. The sky is clear except at the eastern end of the mill—where coal-black smoke is gushing out of three smokestacks, the slight wind directing it in three steady streams to the south. Nothing is coming out of the many other smokestacks. . . .

A small band of men is standing around each entrance. At the main gate a two-roomed trailer serves as strike headquarters. Small wooden and cardboard shacks at the other entrances look puny and weak against the huge mill buildings. As a photographer snaps a picture of the streaming black smoke a picket says to him, "They're burning tar in the furnaces. The punks they've got in there can't even cook soup, let alone make steel. They gotta be fed from the outside." . . . At dusk a big moving van, escorted by six police cars with officers standing on the running boards gripping tear-gas guns and grenades, rolls toward the main mill gate. Cautiously several policemen step down from their cars and walk toward the gate. One unlocks it as the others keep guard. The handful of pickets gather together at the side of their small cardboard shack. Once open, the police and moving van move quickly inside the mill gate. The guarding policemen close it and mount the last car, and the caravan races down the mill road leaving a trail of cinder-road dust behind. By this time a crowd of several hundred strikers has gathered outside the gate. One of them stands on the hood of a parked car, and speaks.

"That's the last truckload of food those Cossacks are goin' to take in to the scabs." He reminds the men that the strikebreakers who are eating and sleeping inside the mill are taking the bread from their families' tables. . . .

"BOY SIXTEEN KILLED; STRIKERS RIOT," the paper reads the following day. Early that morning the police had tried to get the moving van out through another entrance. Halfway through the gate the van blew a tire, two others went flat, and it stalled a few yards out from the mill fence. Tear gas was used by the police, mostly inexperienced deputies or imported gunmen, and a young boy standing more than three hundred feet from the mill fence was shot. . . .

"MAYOR TO CONDUCT BACK-TO-WORK VOTE," the next day's paper read. . . . "TEN TO ONE VOTE, RETURN TO WORK," the mayor announces in the evening paper. . . . From three different directions early the next morning, large bands of armed men lead groups of workers toward the mill. The strikers are pitched for battle at each entrance. Suddenly they are showered with small pieces of steel, rocks, buckshot, and tear gas from men standing on mill roofs or at mill windows. A motorcade of trucks and cars rushes toward the gates, spitting out tear gas, stones, and buckshot. The strikers run for cover. The gates are opened. . . .

"MILL WORKERS RETURN TO JOBS," the paper reads that evening. . . .

A hardy but small group of men gather for a meeting in the union hall. The organizer advises them to return to work and try to get their jobs back. He says the national union is preferring charges against the company with the NRA, and that the rights of the men and their union are going to be protected if the union has to go to the Supreme Court. A tired man with bloodshot eyes announces that he had been to the mill for his job but was told to go ask the union for a job, because he was on the picket line and the company had a picture of him there. . . . Dragging themselves out of the hall into the stillness of the evening, hands in pockets, their chests half bared by open shirt collars, the small band of last-ditch union workers looks up at the blue sky—speechless but telling a mighty story by their silence.

Little did they know that though their strike was lost their cause was not. This was not the first strike that organized labor had failed to win. The old-timers could have told them of many that turned out that way before; of strikes that were more bitter, more violent. But the story was the same each time; the union lost. Why? There were many reasons advanced, but they all added up to defeat. Leaders of organized labor said the men would not stick to the union. The men themselves had other ideas, thought something was wrong with the way the strike was run. They did not know what—only that something was wrong. When they finally learned what it was, workers began to change their strike tactics with lightning speed—to the surprise of organized-labor leaders as much as to the dismay of management officials.

The sit-down was not a strike but a wave of strikes. From

the Akron, Ohio, Goodyear Tire and Rubber Company strike of February-March, 1936, to the Supreme Court decision of February 29, 1939, workers, to a large degree, abandoned the conventional outdoor picketing strike for the more dramatic and effective sit-down. The results were phenomenal.

In the sit-down, workers used the tactics management had employed with so much success in breaking outdoor picketing strikes. They housed and fed themselves. They had no picket lines to maintain, no pickets for management to disperse. There were no strikebreakers eating and sleeping inside the plant to break their morale. They had no fear of "scabs" breaking through their lines, no fear that some production might be shipped by bosses and strikebreakers who were staying inside. The psychological advantages that had been management's in an outdoor picketing strike now belonged to them. The initiative for violence was up to management. Company police would have to attack them to try to drive them out of the plant. They no longer had the responsibility for violence that rested with strikers when they had to resist "scabs" going through their picket lines. "Why leave the plant only to have company police club us and scabs crash the picket line to take our jobs?" workers asked themselves. Why not just stay on the jobs, and let management figure out what to do? This they did, and management could figure out nothing except to bow to the unions' demands for collective bargaining.

That was the sit-down, which helped to put industrial unions over the top. So bold and daring was the sit-down as a tactic that leaders of organized labor shunned it for years, only to have unorganized workers employ it with swift effectiveness. Their leaders did not teach the sit-down to them; workers learned it from management, and the newspapers unwittingly gave it a national impetus. Strikers housed and fed themselves inside the plants with as much success as management, for decades before, had housed and fed strikebreakers.

The popular illusion that the sit-down strike is a foreign import, invented by coal miners in Terbovlyé (Jugoslavia),

Pecs (Hungary), and Patowice (Poland) and popularized by "a million French workers," is unfounded in fact. The consistency with which American workers have refused to be influenced by foreign labor developments makes the foreign-product explanation of the sit-down strike highly dubious. The policies and actions of American workers over the decades have been products of an American environment.

We are not discussing the merits or demerits of the sit-down strike; our purpose is merely to point out its origin. We do this to illustrate that the policies of unions are formulated as a consequence of management's policies. To be sure, union policies, regardless of their original motivation, set in motion an interaction of union and management policies; but the initiative to reverse the action-and-reaction circle can be taken only by management. The policies and actions of management are all-determining to the union in the shaping of its policies. For example, the union cannot adopt co-operative policies while management is pursuing hostile ones. By the same token, management has to adopt co-operative policies and prove them by action before the union can afford to drop its hostile policies and follow suit. In our daily work we are guided by the basic policies of management in each particular situation where we advise or formulate union policy. The degree of effectiveness of a union leader charged with responsibility for several local unions will vary, as a rule, in direct proportion to his ability to ascertain quickly and accurately the policies of management in each particular case. In the following chapter we examine this principle in detail as it relates to the type of local, and even national, union leadership.

Chapter III: Development of Leadership

The attitudes and actions of management largely determine the degree of co-operativeness of union leadership.

This story is about the authors as much as it is about a group of local union leaders who—at times not too graciously—dropped their belligerency as management became co-operative.

It begins in the Sokol Hall, Eastburg, Pennsylvania, on the evening of March 24, 1937. Midnight had been set as the deadline for the River Steel Company to sign a contract. When we arrived the smoke-filled hall was packed with more than a thousand restless men, and one of them shouted, "It better be a signed contract or we strike!" Our purpose was to plead for more time in negotiating, because the president of the company had died a few months earlier and the ranking vice-president disclaimed authority to sign a contract. One of us explained that the board of directors would elect a new president with authority early in April, and asked that the strike vote be postponed until then. The strike-hungry meeting was resigned to granting us this extra time when the speaker was called to the telephone. The men anxiously awaited his return.

"I guess everyone wants to know about the phone call," he resumed.

There was a big laugh.

"Well," he added, "you might as well know—the Westridge mill is on strike."

The cheers made the wooden-frame building literally shake.

After relative order had been restored, the speaker continued. "And there is nothing left for you to do but take a strike vote."

While we were driving back to Pittsburgh the company's

vice-president frantically phoned SWOC's director in Westridge and arranged for him to meet the general manager of both mills, who promptly signed the contract. By three o'clock in the morning the fifteen hundred men in Eastburg and the five thousand in Westridge were back at work.

The morning paper headlined, "STRIKE DEFIES CIO HEADS AT STEEL PLANTS."

Back of the desire of the Eastburg workers to strike and the spontaneous Westridge strike is a long history of anti-unionism. It followed the familiar pattern: spies, strikebreaking, eviction, discharge, blacklist, company unions, ad infinitum, that over the years built up an irresistible desire among the men to "get even." The strike was the only way they knew to secure release for their multitude of pent-up grievances. The lightninglike success of their three-hour strike not only destroyed what little confidence the men had left in management but encouraged them to take similar action on future occasions.

Management's hostility to the union-organizing drive had produced the type of leaders most capable of waging war. The Westridge local union leaders had been officers of the company union. One of SWOC's successful organizing tactics was to elect its members as leaders of the employee-representation plans (company unions) and take them over. Bud Barton was elected head of the company union in its dying days, and later became president of the SWOC local union. The men selected him as their leader because he had no children and his wife worked in the glass plant; a worker had first to be prepared to lose his job before assuming the hazards of leadership. This was evident at the initial union meetings, since few workers volunteered to accept an office or committee post. Those who did became semiheroes. The less courageous men looked up to them. "You've got to hand it to Bud," they said. "He's got the guts to take the company on. He ain't afraid of 'em." The older workers knew from experience, and the younger ones had learned at the dinner table, that a man who assumed leadership in the union automatically put his job on "the chopping block." That it might turn out otherwise this time was too big a gamble for most workers to take.

Bud was a bench operator in the cold-drawn seamless-tube department at forty-six cents an hour. He was twenty-nine years old, tall, personable; he wore rimless glasses and was uncomfortable in a coat and vest. By nature he was adventurous. Bud never knew why he was not promoted during his nine years in the mill, except that he probably was not a member of the "right clique." Bud's closest personal friend was chairman of the grievance committee. John Witherspoon was a small thin man. He had an eyebrow-black mustache, wore an oversized felt hat, and always chewed a cud of tobacco in the left side of his mouth. The fact that he had five children, and two brothers in high management positions, made him suspect among many of his fellow workers. But John soon proved that he was on the square; he burned with a consuming indignation against the company. During the twenties he had left a good job in the chemical laboratory as a steel analyst to operate a hardware store. Early in the depression it failed and the only job John could get when he returned to the mill was in the pickling department at fifty-one cents an hour. As chairman of the grievance committee John was tough, unyielding, and always prepared to back up his arguments with a strike.

The other Westridge leaders were also of the militant type. Joe Kitka, a short, stocky young man, was secretary. He had two accomplishments. He was an effective picket-line leader and could compose strong telegrams to company and SWOC officials. Joe was natively honest. Once entrusted with the union's funds, he lost four hundred-odd dollars. Joe sold his car, borrowed some money, and made up the lost funds promptly. The vice-president of the union, Sam Morton, never ran for office in the company union; he considered it a compromise of his principles. He was also the chief grievance committeeman from the steel-foundry department, and the most belligerent of them all. In 1933-34 Sam had been active in the NRA organizing drive and was handled roughly by the company after the NRA had been invalidated. The other grievance committeemen were workers who also had put a chip on their shoulders in the early organizing days and told their bosses, "Fire us if you dare; we're organizing a union."

Unwittingly, the vice-president of River Steel in his complete about-face on the night of March 24th had taught these leaders that the way to get quick action from management was to strike. But he blamed the union entirely. Now elected president, on July 23, 1937, he told the newspapers that in the four months his company had been under contract with SWOC the Westridge local union had conducted thirteen sit-down strikes. The papers screamed,

STEEL HEADS AIR SIT-DOWNS IN MILLS HERE.

A brief colorful account of each sit-down followed this headline, the report on the July 23rd one being an effective sermon against collective bargaining.

> Fifty men in the polishing department refused to go back to work after lunch and were dismissed after they had been idle two hours following demands for a wage increase.
>
> Summarizing its report on sit-down strikes, River Steel officials concluded that
>
> "A general failure of morale is very noticeable since March 25, with the feeling apparent among employees that the door is open now for the raising of all types of complaints, fancied or otherwise, and that cessation of work for any reason, or no reason, is a privilege. Numerous unexpected stoppages keep production in a constant state of uncertainty and make production schedules very difficult to maintain."

The actual facts, of course, were quite different. From the outset management ignored the grievance-adjustment machinery in the contract and would not settle grievances through negotiations. The only way the men could secure the redress of their grievances was for all of them as a body to take them up with management. Consequently the procedure in vogue was for the men affected to stop work and hold a meeting with their grievance committeemen and management. Under these circumstances management, which ignored the pleas of the committeemen, conceded to the men as a body. All of the alleged sit-downs were of brief duration, and in no instance did the men sleep or eat in the mill. Instead of demanding a wage raise on July 23rd, the men in the polishing department protested a dollar-a-day cut in earnings. But in place of granting the men their demands, as had been done in the other twelve cases, the general manager entered the department a few minutes after they quit work and announced, "You are all fired! Get out of here!" He was followed by company police, armed with guns, who escorted the fifty men to the gate. They offered no resistance.

This effort to smear SWOC boomeranged on River Steel. The fifty men were returned to their jobs without loss of seniority, and the dollar-a-day drop in earnings, resulting from the arbitrary revision of incentive rates by management, was restored. SWOC agreed not to quit work to settle grievances, in return for which management agreed to negotiate their settlement through the contract machinery. But few, if any, grievances seemed to get settled in the mill. A flood of cases came into our office steadily for the rest of the year. Each one was appealed in writing to the company president. He rejected seventy-three out of eighty-one on record in our files. A few years later he told us that his policy in handling grievances was designed to liquidate the unions in his mills. He took advantage of the curtailment of forces, resulting from the drop in steel operations, to weed out workers who were the backbone of the unions. The effects of this policy soon became evident to the local unions in the number of lay-off grievances piled high on our desk that we were unable to adjust.

In self-preservation the Westridge local leaders threw a dues-inspection (picket) line around the mill late in December, 1937. Some workers were kept out, and operations were curtailed until the delinquent members put themselves back in good standing with the union. The company president, who thought he had the union 90 per cent buried, denounced the local leaders in the newspapers as "wild men and no-accounts." Little did he realize that the men's confidence in Bud Barton, John Witherspoon, and their fellow officers rose in direct proportion to management's hostility toward them. Apparently feeling that the men generally would revolt against these local union leaders, the company president launched a Committee of River Steel Workers. This was six weeks before the contract was to expire in March, 1938. Lower management officials brazenly succored the rump union. To the Westridge leaders this was an open declaration of war, which they gladly accepted. They put on another dues-inspection line and kept nonmembers as well as delinquent members from going to work. Their local union was reinvigorated by the artificially stimulated opposition. The Eastburg local also put on a picket line, and when the contract was negotiated both locals were at full strength. The company belatedly signed a new contract on March 10, 1938, and the president posted a notice that all unauthorized union activity was prohibited on company property. Within a fortnight the rump union died.

One of the gains of the new contract was the arrangement to settle grievances locally. John Witherspoon was made a full-time grievance committeeman for the Westridge local, and an Eastburg local leader was made an organizer with responsibility for administering the affairs of his union. The general superintendent of each mill was placed in charge of handling grievances for management. In addition, an industrial-relations director was hired. During the next eighteen months we devoted ourselves to guiding these militant local leaders into a constructive and stable relationship. Our efforts were hampered, however, by the uncanny way management had of provoking them just about each time we had the leaders convinced that more could be gained through a co-operative than a belligerent attitude. This was due in no small measure to the unwillingness of the company president to keep his fingers out of the day-to-day union-management relationship. Though there were no strikes during the year following the contract, Joe Kitka, the Westridge local union secretary, wrote one of the authors, on February 17, 1939, that all was not well. Excerpts from his letter are revealing.

. . . The spirit of two years ago that made our local one of the best of the entire SWOC was almost completely ruined through our inability to secure satisfactory settlement of grievances presented to the River Steel management. It is undeniable that these conditions resulted from the utter lack of active support of your office and the subsequent reactionary attitude of the company when it became apparent that your support was not forthcoming. . . .

If we cannot secure a just settlement of a grievance through the proper channels of the grievance machinery, then the only recourse left to the membership is to accept defeat or to refuse to work under conditions that are in violation of our contract. To ask them to repeatedly accept an adverse decision is certainly not conducive to maintaining a spirit of militancy either intelligent or otherwise. On the other hand, had we advised our membership to rebel and to use their only recourse—that is, to refuse to work—it would doubtless have been considered an outlawed strike, though unjustly so, and have been condemned as such by you.

We had persistently restrained the local union from striking. Our hope was that management would eventually get around to handling grievances realistically. A little progress was made with plant officials, but the company president would not let them settle grievances in a way that would add to the union's prestige. Many grievances were settled favorably to the union, to be sure, but this was due less to our efforts than to the hard-driving, belligerent, local-union grievance committees. Our counsel to them to be reasonable brought the rebuff, "The only thing you can get out of River Steel is what you've got the power to take." Management's record, unfortunately, was a convincing body of evidence in support of this view.

Finally in the fall of 1939 the Westridge local went on strike. It was over an unsettled wage-rate case in the open-hearth and bar-mill departments. As in several other similar cases, management refused arbitration. We pleaded with the company president, but in vain. We explained how we had kept the men at work for almost two years, and that the failure to arbitrate unsettled grievances would prevent us from doing this much longer. He remained adamant. No sooner did the mill go down, however, than he signed an agreement referring the case to an impartial arbitrator whose decision was to be rendered within ten days, with the condition that the men return to work in the meantime. But the strike continued. Bud Barton and John Witherspoon opposed the settlement, and it was voted down by twenty-five to one in a secret ballot. The Eastburg local wired the company that it would join the Westridge strike unless the "wage cuts are restored immediately." Barton argued, "We gave the company a chance for more than six months to arbitrate and it refused. Management made us strike, and damned if we'll go back until they give us back the wage cuts."

Witherspoon explained, "This is only one case. We have almost a dozen just like it. Now that we're down, we might as well sweep the deck clean." Two days later the president begged for a conference. He capitulated completely to the union demands; the wage cuts in the open hearth and bar mill would be restored retroactively, and all other cases of the same nature would be reopened and, if necessary, referred to arbitration. The men, on this basis, went back to work.

This strike brought our relations with the River Steel Company to a climax. We submitted to the president a three-point program with the none too co-operative attitude that, if he rejected it, we would help lead a strike at his mills to force him to accept it. The points were:

1. The company president would cease to have anything to do with day-to-day union-management relations at the mills.
2. The industrial-relations director would be given full power to settle all matters.
3. Management would talk to the few recalcitrant employees who were delinquent in their dues, and encourage the few remaining nonmembers to join the union.

After the company president agreed to these three points,

we called in the Westridge local leaders. We told them that their fighting days were over now, and that they had to get down to earth and handle cases on their merits jointly with management. They examined the three-point agreement carefully. Barton looked puzzled, Witherspoon was frankly skeptical, and one committeeman said, "They will have this agreement with Golden busted a dozen times before we get home from Pittsburgh. River Steel is agin unions and always will be."

The committeeman's prediction, fortunately, was wrong. A few days later the company's industrial-relations director visited us. "My instructions are to settle all cases within the framework of operating costs," he began, "and I'm a little uneasy because I never had such authority before. Personally I'm relieved since I have always found men ready to meet you halfway. Your boys certainly have given my boss a bellyful. He never wants to hear the word 'grievance' again."

We assured him that his troubles were not over. "You have to demonstrate your change of heart," one of us explained, "because Barton, Witherspoon, and the other leaders are not the type to be influenced by words. Some of their fellow committeemen, I am confident, will never believe that you have stopped fighting their union. Meanwhile you'll have to exercise a good deal of patience until your employees generally, and their leaders in particular, realize that your company is sincerely desirous of creating a co-operative relationship."

Eighteen months later, April, 1941, River Steel and SWOC signed their third contract. It recognized SWOC as the sole bargaining agency and union membership as a condition of employment for all employees who were eligible for membership. John Witherspoon, now full-time grievance adjuster for both mills, was in charge of negotiations for SWOC and the industrial-relations director for the River Steel Company. Not only had they become able to adjust their own grievances, but they were able to negotiate a new contract. One of the authors called the company president on the telephone at this time. "Well, I want to congratulate you on how well the local unions and your management are getting along now since you have kept your fingers out of their doings," he said. "All you have to do to preserve the industrial peace is to keep right on as a silent observer."

The reply on the other end of the line was weak. "I guess you're right, Clint. I don't know what we'd do in this emergency if we had all of the trouble at the mills that we used to have."

How this change in management's policy enables the local union leaders to look at cases on their merits, and to consider other factors besides how an adverse decision might weaken the union's membership, is demonstrated in a wage-rate case of the centerless grinders at Westridge. A committee of these grinders in the summer of 1941 secured from SWOC's research department rates paid for grinders in other mills, some of which were higher than River Steel's rates. Bud Barton, now full-time grievance committeeman at Westridge, returned with the committee a few days later. He wanted to know whether one of the authors had told the committee that River Steel's ninety-three-cent-an-hour rate was too low. Bud was assured that the grinders' rates that were given to the committee carried no recommendation. "See, I told you the national office would not make such a statement," Bud told the committee, "because our company can't be expected to pay the highest rate in the industry. We have to meet competition. The present rates for grinding are fair. I negotiated a three-cent-an-hour raise back a few months ago. The only way you can increase your earnings is by working out an incentive system for your job." A few years earlier Bud Barton would have used such information to show "what a big bunch of cheap skates the River Steel officials are," and he would have denounced the idea that tonnage rates supplant flat hourly ones "as a vicious speed-up."

John Witherspoon and Bud Barton, unlike many other belligerent local union leaders, have become able contract administrators. Bud is more comfortable now in a suit coat and vest. John still likes his chew of tobacco, but he now wears hats that fit him and his appearance inspires confidence. The union has made them substantial citizens in their community. Both found it hard to change over from fighting management at every step to co-operating on the basis of equality. They did so slowly and carefully, lest in so doing they lose the confidence of their following. For several months they floundered until they learned how to be constructive leaders of men. They found that acting as the spokesmen for the hates and grievances of a group of workers is easy. All they had to do, then, was to give vocal expression to the popular attitudes of the group. The job of giving the same group constructive guidance, often entailing unpopular acts, they found to be much more trying. It is a mark of distinction that Barton and Witherspoon made this transition, because most militant local union leaders, who rise to the surface in the organizing stage of unions, fall by the side when the union moves into the stage of constructive relations with management.

Few of the original grievance committeemen at Westridge have survived the change in management's attitudes and actions. With the exception of two, all have been replaced by workers capable of providing constructive leadership. One of the pioneer Westridge leaders, Sam Morton, for example, was a perpetual source of trouble after management's change in policy. The idea that management no longer wanted to destroy the union could not penetrate his mind. In mid-1940 SWOC placed him on its organizing staff, and set his valuable talents loose in the unorganized sector of the steel industry. When the "Little Steel" firms that engaged in the 1937 strike recognized SWOC, Sam had to be transferred to the properties of one of the two principal steel firms still outside the union fold. His job tenure is secure, however, because he is a good organizer and organized labor still has a large sector of American industry to embrace.

Management, as a general principle, gets the kind of union leadership it deserves. A tough management begets tough union leaders, while a patient, friendly, co-operative management begets a like type of union leadership. Andrew Carnegie knew this, though his earlier acts belied his later words.[1] In 1904 he said:

> . . . The most cheering feature in the relations of capital and labor is that there seems a law at work which rejects the extreme men of both employers and employees and slowly evolves the reign of the fair-minded element which continually makes for industrial peace. . . . There are two sides to all disputes, and also many kindred virtues and an earnest desire for harmony upon both sides. . . . There are fair employers as there are fair workmen, and . . . it is a bad day for both capital and labor when they fail to settle themselves peacefully any dispute that arises between them.

The way in which the segments of the steel and auto industries that resisted the CIO in 1937, for instance, embraced collective bargaining four years later gives substance to Carnegie's words. One of the mainsprings of American democracy is the essential sportsmanship of its people: humble in victory, gracious in defeat. This characteristic of America's workers and managers explains, in large measure, their ability to get along together after years of bitter fighting.

A substantial majority of America's present top-flight labor leaders was catapulted into labor leadership from the ranks of workers, because they were fired for union activities. For better or for worse—we believe the former—the national labor leaders of the next generation will be different, having started their careers under less bitter circumstances. In both cases labor's leaders were born in an environment not of their own making, but an environment for which management is primarily responsible. Labor leadership reflects the industrial environment in which America's workers live and toil; any change for good or for bad will change the type of labor leadership accordingly.

The time lag in the growth of constructive union leadership, after management ceases its opposition, varies with the extent to which labor assumes responsibility for the development of its leaders.

Inside the organized-labor movement there are two points

of view on the question of training union leaders and, frankly, our viewpoint is in the minority. The majority view, in a word, holds that labor's leaders are developed in the crucible of industrial conflict and trained in the arena of union-management relations. Fundamentally this view is sound. Certainly the development of union leaders is largely determined by the industrial environment in which unions are born. As the environment changes, labor's leadership follows suit as a natural matter. Our difference with this majority view is that, unless guided, the change in leadership does not take place fast enough and, further, that it is the responsibility of the organized-labor movement to aid and accelerate this process.

On Sunday, March 2, 1941, Stanley Orlosky, lifelong union worker, a pipe fitter in a steel mill, was expelled from his union after a trial on charges of "violation of obligation to the Steel Workers Organizing Committee." To add to his disgrace, Stanley was tried by union officers whom he had solicited to join the union a few years earlier. He came to our office to appeal the decision of the trial board of his local union. Stanley was powerfully built, stood six feet tall, and the few strands of gray in his black hair belied his forty-five years. He exhibited a soiled membership card in the United Mine Workers of America, Local 405, Loyalhanna, Pennsylvania, dated March 17, 1911. This was secured in his first strike. He lost out in it. Stanley worked the coal fields until 1928, when he was blacklisted and forced to go into the steel mills. The ABC Steel Company fired him in 1933 for being president of the NRA local union, but hired him back in 1934 when the union died. In 1936 he became vice-president of the SWOC local union in his section of the mill and was chairman of the grievance committee until 1940, when the SWOC director removed him from office for violating the contract.

"Being a good union man is agitating—that's what I always knew as a union man—and I got fired for agitating," Stanley complained to us. "The union was organized to have freedom, and not to be fired for talking. The men that tried me in the local, I had a hard time getting to join the union a few years ago. Now they're big union shots. The company has had it in for me since 1933. I'm a thorn in the flesh to it. Now the union sides with the company, and I'm out. That ain't justice. The national office should give me another hearing, and give me back my membership card," he pleaded.

We investigated his case. The talking for which Stanley was fired consisted of charging the incumbent union officers with "selling the men down the river," since they settled grievances on their merits. His idea of a grievance settlement was to get everything or strike. Stanley's leadership was essential to the establishment of the union against bitter resistance, but after it had been fully accepted by management such leadership was a handicap to the development of co-operative union-management relations. His expulsion was sustained by the SWOC national officers.

In this huge mill of more than ten thousand workers, SWOC has five local unions, instead of one, to facilitate the administration of union affairs. Two of the locals are still led by leaders of Stanley's type. Carl Rossi, young high-school graduate, is president of one of the remaining belligerently led locals. He boasts, "I've never lost a grievance case." At joint meetings of the officers from the five locals Carl charges the co-operative ones with "running company unions." He disposes of arguments that costs do not permit granting a particular request with "They're always crying poor mouth." When told his unrelenting pressure for wage adjustments might cut employment, might even put the company out of business, Carl smiles. "Them birds are always crying wolf, and you guys [SWOC district director and co-operative leaders] fall for that scarefish stuff. Not me—that mill will be there when I got whiskers a mile long." Carl and the countless other local union leaders he typifies view the union's relations with management as being predicated upon a continual fight. In those cases, unfortunately still a majority, where management keeps the union at a respectful distance, such a union approach is unavoidable; but where the union has been taken into management's confidence, greater responsibilities face the union and its leaders.

Carl has only one concern in pressing a case of a union member: get for the member what he wants or as close to it as possible. The problem of finding the means to meet the demand is exclusively management's. In winning a case Carl takes all the glory; in losing one Carl gives management all the blame. But Carl never loses a case. A negative reply merely puts the case on the unfinished-business agenda; Carl keeps pressing it until management yields or the member dies. Management, as we discuss fully in Chapter VII, encourages this kind of approach by insisting that union membership be voluntary, despite the union's majority enrollment. Repeatedly we have been told by management, "It is your job to sell the union to the employees." Local union leaders know no better way to do this than to "get things" for their followers, and let management worry about how to pay for them.

Eventually this honeymoon comes to an end. Carl's company has taken SWOC into its inner councils, abandoned its policy of keeping the union at a distance, and says to SWOC's top leaders, "We are co-operating fully with SWOC, have granted the union shop as evidence of our sincerity; but some of your local union leaders still serve us with ultimatums to grant demands by a certain time or they will strike. What are you doing to have them approach these problems in a co-operative spirit, as matters for which they must assume joint responsibility?"

At this point union members, their national officers, intermediary field staffs, and local union leaders face the acid test. They have to demonstrate that under a union shop unions can assume and discharge their responsibilities to the best interests of both their members and the business enterprises upon which they depend for a livelihood. This is primarily the job of top union leaders, since they must show to their followers, on the union staff and in the mines, mills, and factories, the way toward industrial peace and fruitful union-management relations. Before this, however, they must show newly recognized unions how to make collective bargaining work under the difficult conditions of partial union membership.

There are two stages in the development of labor leadership: one is the contract stage; the other is the union-shop stage. In signing the initial contract with a firm, top union leaders automatically assume the task of showing the local union involved, and the union field staff directing its affairs, how to bargain contractually. Likewise in signing a union-shop contract, the national union leadership automatically assumes the responsibility for directing the union involved toward co-operative relations with management. We find ourselves in the peculiar position of having to do both jobs simultaneously with different groups of workers, because SWOC's relations with the eight hundred and twenty-six firms under contract are in varying stages of maturity.

The job of training SWOC's staff and local union leaders to bargain collectively began with the contract SWOC signed with the United States Steel Corporation in March, 1937. An organizing staff specially trained to arouse workers to their opportunities and freedoms had to be recruited by SWOC from among a large group of men who had demonstrated their loyalty to the organized-labor movement. A large majority, by far, were promoted to union leaders as a result of acts by management. Casey McMullin, for example, was a first helper in the open-hearth department of a large steel firm until June, 1935, a week after the National Industrial Recovery Act had been invalidated by the Supreme Court. Management made him a labor leader by firing him for union activity. In this respect he was typical of SWOC's original organizing staff. Overnight he, like the others, found himself face to face with the company officials whom he had denounced for numerous things. Overnight Casey had to bargain collectively and, like most management officials, he did not know how to go about it.

Fortunately SWOC's organizing staff was under the direction of field directors who had experience in negotiating with management; they were drawn from the older unions, principally the United Mine Workers of America. Upon their shoulders, and the national officers of SWOC, fell the burden of converting an organizing staff into contract administrators. Management made the job more difficult than it otherwise would have been. Some companies recognized SWOC; others fought. Hence SWOC's staff had to be qualified to do two diverse things, and do them simultaneously; namely, fight those companies that chose industrial warfare rather than collective bargaining, and co-operate with companies that chose to recognize the union. The Herculean nature of equipping a staff of human beings with these two techniques is fully appreciated by anyone who has had to lead a group of pickets at five o'clock in the morning against company "guards" armed with clubs, tear gas, and guns and five hours later enter a conference with another company to negotiate a contract. Yet this was the smaller part of SWOC's leadership-training job; its success is attested to by the fact that SWOC signed contracts with four hundred and forty-five firms in the year 1937 and, except in a small number of cases, without strikes.

Training local union leaders—the bigger part of the job—has proved to be a continuous process. The qualifications of a successful district director and staff organizer include the ability to train local union leaders in the processes of collective bargaining. SWOC's success in this connection has been limited, therefore, by the respective abilities of its intermediary or full-time representatives. From 1937 to 1942 there has been a seventy-five per cent turnover in SWOC's full-time staff. During this period the caliber of leadership in the more than one thousand SWOC local unions has improved steadily, and the turnover among SWOC's more than ten thousand local leaders has been almost as high. By the spring of 1938 SWOC found it necessary to supplement the efforts of its staff with planned instruction for local union officers and grievance committeemen.

The first step in our formal-training program was the publication of a handbook, entitled *Handling Grievances*, based on SWOC's experiences at the Aliquippa, Pennsylvania, works of the Jones & Laughlin Steel Corporation. In its introduction the handbook states:

Mr. Local Union Officer:
Mr. Committeeman:

This handbook is . . . your guide. . . . The purpose of this handbook is to help you improve your collective bargaining machinery. The objective of this handbook is to show from practical experiences how management-union relations can be improved.

Union collective bargaining in steel has had to overcome many difficulties. Company officials had to bury their hatred and fear generated by years of anti-union crusading. Union officers and committeemen had to forget their distrust and suspicion of management's representatives. The false practices of the company unions had to be thrown in the waste basket. In brief, confidence had to be established. Often confidence had to be created between union and company officials.

Employers' anti-union policies of previous years prevented the development of any body of collective bargaining experience. Therefore, SWOC has had to develop its own body of experience in co-operation with management.

SWOC has not imposed any rigid procedures of collective bargaining on union officers and committeemen or management. Instead the trial and error method has been used. . . .

We hope these procedures and techniques will serve to acquaint our officers and committees throughout the industry with an intelligent and constructive procedure, and will aid them in improving the collective bargaining machinery in their plants, thereby better serving the interests of the workers who have selected them as their representatives.

This handbook and others were supplemented with personal instruction. The training program was brought to the local union leaders in their home communities. Under the direction of Frank Fernbach, University of Wisconsin graduate experienced in training work, assisted by the more experienced staff members, regional conferences were held in forty-four steel centers in 1938 and 1939. Each conference lasted two or three days and emphasized day-to-day problems of collective bargaining: grievance-adjustment procedures, seniority provisions, incentive systems of wage payment, technological unemployment, apprentice training, and so forth. These and related subjects were discussed more intensively at summer camps.

The formal-training program was limited in scope—slightly more than two thousand local leaders participated—and was abandoned at the end of 1939. Since then the training of local leaders has been entirely in the hands of SWOC's full-time staff. The value of the program was demonstrated by the way it accelerated the development of leadership in those local unions covered by it. Bud Barton, John Witherspoon, Joe Kitka, and the other leaders of the River Steel Company local unions attended both summer camps and held training conferences in Westridge each year. The effects of the formal-training program on them are clearly evident in contrast to the development of leadership in local unions untouched by it. Stanley Orlosky of the ABC Steel Company was unable to adapt himself to a co-operative management policy and had to be replaced by a leader who could. The leaders of three of the five locals of this company have changed, but Carl Rossi and the other leaders he typifies still persist in the ways that have been outmoded by a changed management policy. Stanley might have responded favorably to a training program, and SWOC's district director agrees that such training would have enabled Carl Rossi to adjust his thinking by now.

Our experience indicates that the development of local union leadership, which naturally lags behind a changed management policy, is accelerated where the regular work of the union's full-time staff is supplemented by a formal-training program. On the whole, SWOC's field staff and local union leaders have become quite adept in the art of collective bargaining; but unquestionably the effectiveness of SWOC in parts, as in many of the other newer unions, has been impaired by the failure of top union leaders to communicate their ideas and policies down to the ranks more speedily through an all-out leadership-training program.

Such a program will be inescapable as a majority of union members begins to function under union-shop contracts. Already SWOC has had to augment its regular field work to be able to meet its responsibilities with those firms which have extended the union-shop form of recognition to SWOC local unions. As early as the summer of 1938 some firms had granted SWOC the union shop, and SWOC issued its second handbook, entitled *Production Problems*, which outlines a union-management co-operation program that can be undertaken where the union's position is secure and unquestioned. This program is the subject of Part Two of this book. An officer of one of the local unions that has carried on a successful union-management co-operation program was placed on SWOC's full-time staff late in 1940. He has since devoted himself almost exclusively to developing the type of leadership required to administer a union-shop contract in unions enjoying such recognition.

Thus the second stage in the development of union leadership will not be reached until management, pretty much as a whole, becomes willing to place its union relations on a union-shop foundation. The unions, by and large, have met the challenge during the contract stage through the development of leadership capable of administering contracts on a relatively peaceful basis. But industrial peace does not necessarily come when "for-members-only" contracts are negotiated. In moving into the complete form of recognition—union membership as a condition of employment—labor unions cannot afford, in our opinion, to leave the development of co-operative union leaders entirely to the natural course of events. The responsibility assumed in signing a union-shop contract requires the speedy development of competent union leaders to shoulder it. Organized labor, in seeking fuller participation in the affairs of industry and government, will have to be prepared through an all-out program of leadership training. Events in the near future may prove this to be one of the most crucial problems facing labor unions.

For the present emergency, union training efforts, of necessity, will have to be at the level of day-to-day union activity and collective bargaining in the mines, mills, and factories. From a long-range viewpoint, however, the development of union leadership should be approached on a more fundamental basis. The newer unions need to face this problem realistically lest the passing of time ossify their leadership, as has happened, and is happening, in some of the older unions. Because not everyone shares our conviction that life is a constant process of change and adjustment, we are disturbed at times about the future of the great labor organizations that have meant so much to us and millions of others. We are fearful at times lest they become smug and complacent when they become secure. We want them to be always responsive to the interests of their members and the welfare of our nation. We want them to be democratic—to be agencies for the extension and implementation of the democratic process.

To serve such dynamic ends unions need constructive, intelligent, and unselfish leadership. Management needs the same kind of leadership. Yet both are deficient in it. There are outstanding leaders of organized labor and management, to be sure, that fill these requirements, but there are not enough of them and, further, too many of them are past the age of fifty.

Out of the process of change and adjustment during the last decade has come a rich fund of experience. Little of it finds its way into print. Most of it remains locked in the minds of the comparatively few people who participated in the process. We feel that this vast body of experience and knowledge should be passed on to the next generation. We ask the leaders of management and organized labor three questions, simply and directly:

1. Is there not a way in which the experience of people who have participated in these profound changes in forms of relationships between organized wage earners and management can be channeled into an institution of learning dedicated to the training and de-

velopment of intelligent and constructive leadership?

2. Is there any good reason why there should not be an American University of Labor and Management—not just one or the other, but both?
3. Do not those corporations and great unions which have made the necessary adjustments enabling them to live and work together, for their mutual welfare, have a social responsibility to establish such a university?

Speculate for a moment on the effect of unions sending a certain number of their officers and staff members to a resident university for a school year, say, of eight months. Think of the effect of corporations sending their industrial-relations and operating officials to the same place. Here both could exchange experiences and ideas in an environment of inquiry; they could listen to talks by theoreticians and practical men in industry and labor. The union leaders and management officials would be reinvigorated by the change in environment and inspired by the new associations. The younger generation would learn from association with the older. The people who have a vast store of knowledge and experience stored in their heads could come here and unfold it. Such an undertaking, which admittedly is urgently needed, might play an important role in opening an entirely new era of American prosperity and democracy.

And it is eminently practical. There are enough practical men in unions and among management to provide a visiting faculty staff of lecturers and discussion leaders. There are enough trained educators whose interests in such an educational project could be easily aroused to provide the necessary technique for the planning of courses, the analysis of data, and the dissemination of useful information. There are enough unused or partially used university facilities to house the undertaking. A larger part, if not all, of the students' costs could be borne by the union or company sponsoring each student. Eligibility could be determined by the talents of the respective individuals, and not by the conventional university methods. And the other practical problems involved in the establishment of an American University of Labor and Management would not be insurmountable. The big barrier to creating such an institution of learning is the thinking of management and labor leaders along their own particular group lines. But this barrier is not insurmountable. We believe the dynamics of industrial democracy are breaking it down, because the future of organized labor and management is being welded closer together by the force of events. In its broadest sense the purpose of this discussion is to illustrate the nature and force of these events.

A word of warning. Our caustic comments on labor's responsibility for the development of its leadership do not constitute evidence to support those who point an accusing finger at unions for not being "properly led." Because, fundamentally, management sets the pattern of union-management relations. River Steel found its local unions "properly led" only after it put into effect a co-operative policy, and sooner or later all companies that accept the union fully find it led by leaders adequately informed about the firm's problems and the industry's conditions and thoroughly prepared to assume joint responsibility for their solution. Admittedly a goodly portion of the union movement is "properly led," and that all unions are not so guided is due largely to management's failure to concede the union-shop form of recognition on a large scale. When this is done unions as a whole will be "properly led."

The handling of management's side of union-management relations is an all-determining factor: industrial-relations heads, departmental superintendents and foremen, symbolize the company to workers and their union representatives. What they do, and how they do it, is the only way the union becomes acquainted with management's policies, since a changed policy does not become effective until adopted by the operating personnel. Management has the biggest responsibility in the development of leadership: its personnel must first administer a co-operative policy before the union leaders can follow suit, aided or unaided by a union training program. We have been in a unique position to gain an insight into management's handling of union relations. Some officials have been quite adept; many, however, have not. In the concluding part of this chapter we endeavor to pass on, in a generous spirit, some of the principles underlying the development of management leaders that seem to be fairly conclusive.

Salesmen and purchasing agents usually possess a more natural ability for handling management's relations with unions than do operating officials.

The phone rang.

"Mr. Ellis calling," the operator announced.

"Hello, Clint, I'm in a devil of a hurry. I have to go over to Princeton University tonight. I'll have to call off our conference. Can't those cases wait until I get back? I'm going to school for the rest of the week. Imagine an old duffer like me going back to school, and a university at that. I'm supposed to learn how to handle you fellows over there."

The author laughed to himself, and asked, "Do you know who is going to be your professor over there?"

"I don't know," Ellis answered. "Who?"

"Why, A. M. [Mr. Ellis' initials], I am. How do you like that for democracy—an ex-drill tender in an iron-ore mine lecturing an important vice-president of a large steel corporation?"

"Quit your kidding, Clint. It's bad enough I've got to go, let alone you making a joke of it."

It was the fall of 1939. Two days later the author spoke at Princeton University. A. M. Ellis was in his audience.

A. M. had been a member of the old iron workers' union before the turn of the century. He worked in a sheet mill as a lower-paid member of a hot-mill crew until the 1901 strike. The union was destroyed. Many of the men never went back into the struck mills. This gave A. M. his break, and he became a highly paid roller while still in his twenties. By 1935 he was vice-president in charge of operations for his company. The next year he was without portfolio because his

of A. M. Ellis. A slender, red-faced man in his fifties, just getting a little portly, Robert Burt has been in the "selling game" for more than twenty-five years. He has been trained to get people to do things voluntarily. While A. M. could order a subordinate to do something, Burt had to accomplish the same thing by convincing a customer why he should buy his product. This essential difference in training enabled Burt to make a success of his union relations. He became president of his firm while its largest plant was on strike. Just three weeks after SWOC's birth in June, 1936, the thousand workers in this plant came to it for a charter. Piecework wages had been cut and two union leaders fired. Burt was not president of the firm then. His predecessor signed a truce at the end of two weeks, and the men returned to work; a month later he repudiated the truce. The union, in self-defense, struck again, this time for ten weeks. When the directors learned their president signed "something" with the union, they demoted the apostate and put their chief salesman, Bob Burt, in as president. The strike was in its second week and Burt was instructed, "Sign nothing, and operate the plant at any cost." It took him nine weeks, but Burt broke the strike.

The press made much of it, and SWOC's defeat was heralded as its immediate doom. As the organizing campaign progressed, however, the matter soon gave way to bigger SWOC stories in the press. Burt gradually discovered that his troubles did not cease with his "victory." Four months later, March, 1937, he visited SWOC Chairman Philip Murray, who called one of the authors into his office. "Harold, our friend Burt wants to recognize our local union at his plant," Murray said. "I want you to arrange a conference, and see if he means it." The conference was held a few days later. Meanwhile Burt asked the author to lunch with him.

"My plant is in a helluva [he talks this way] shape," Burt began. "I raised wages over thirty per cent fighting you fellows. My costs are out of line competitively and the efficiency in the plant is bad. I lost five good accounts during the strike, and cannot get them back because they are afraid I won't be able to make scheduled deliveries. Everybody is suspicious of everyone else; that is, they are spy-crazy, thinking the next fellow is a stool pigeon. My foremen are nervous wrecks. I am at my wit's end personally. A nasty situation exists in Number One Shop, where half of the men call the others 'scabs.' Most of the best workers are active SWOC members; and since U. S. Steel signed up, a majority of the boys are back in the union. That's why I visited Phil Murray. I want peace in the plant, so we can work together. I wish we had never had the strike; and if we had known U. S. Steel was going to sign up so soon, our story would have been different. Hell, I'm used to getting along with people and, anyway, life is too short to spend most of it fighting."

Little progress was made at the first conference. The local union committee pooh-poohed any idea that their boss was sincere. "He's just recognizing us now because he has to fill a lot of orders," the committee reasoned suspiciously, "and when he has no more orders to fill he will try to break the union again." The contract was signed after a month of heated discussions. Burt's costs remained out of line competitively, but some of the other major problems were solved. He could guarantee uninterrupted deliveries, which helped him regain two of his lost customers, and production increased to prestrike levels as soon as the tension eased. But several incidents prolonged the tension.

The foremen, trained for years to fight unions, reasoned that Burt was forced to recognize the union because of the "law," but that he really wanted them to undermine it. To the worker, his foreman is the company; and every time a foreman jumped the traces the union leaders cried, "The company is trying to break the union. Let's strike." Many times in the first year the plant was on the verge of a strike. The local union leaders, like the foremen, could not take the chip off their shoulders. One got into a fight with a nonunion worker. The foreman fired the union man, but only suspended the nonunion man for a week. This almost precipitated a strike. The author talked on the telephone to the local union president, who was then in the plant, and got the men to stay at work until all the provisions for the peaceful settlement of the dispute were exhausted. Burt fired the foreman, and changed the penalty for fighting on company property to a week's suspension for both men.

Had Burt supported his erring foreman, a strike would have been inevitable. In many similar cases in SWOC's experiences the typical operating official, reared in the "do as you are told, or else" school, supported his erring subordinate, became infuriated at the suggestion that perhaps management was wrong, and charged the union with interfering with plant discipline and management's prerogatives when, in self-defense, it went on strike in support of the discharged union leader. But Burt, reared in the salesmen's give-and-take atmosphere, yielded wisely and graciously. At our advice Burt called his foremen and superintendents together, and told them he would have to let any one of them go who could not get along with the union. This action inspired the union's confidence in Burt's sincerity, and when the second year's contract was signed most of the tension had passed. Except for a half-day strike the plant has operated continuously since. Today Burt's management enjoys a competitive advantage where once it suffered a disadvantage, although average hourly earnings rose from sixty-five cents in 1936 to one dollar and twelve cents in 1941. Union-management cooperation to reduce costs under a union shop, as we discuss in later chapters, has paid big dividends to workers and owners alike in this firm.

Robert Burt never met a union leader until he was past his fiftieth birthday, and knew even less about collective bargaining with unions than did A. M. Ellis. But, unlike the latter, Burt knew from long years of experience how to get people to do things voluntarily. His training was in the conference rooms of purchasing agents, where he had to reason out for his prospective customer why he should buy from him. Then he had to "sell" him. This took patience and a lot of other human qualities. A. M. Ellis was never subjected to such mental exercises. He, of course, had been eminently successful in getting other people to do things, but his method was the iron fist and not persuasive reasoning. The temperaments of these two men were direct contrasts. In four years A. M. proved completely unfit for the job of reasoning things out with union leaders. In less time Bob Burt converted the nasty aftermath of a strike into a harmonious situation, and earned the envied reputation of being the head of one of the few substantial steel-fabricating firms in the Pittsburgh district that showed a profit in the profitless year of 1938.

We do not mean to imply that only salesmen or purchasing agents (their training is similar) make good executives to handle union relations for a company. We merely conclude, from our experiences with many types of management officials, that their temperament is better suited to bargain collectively with union leaders than is that of the typical operating man who has had to rely merely upon his authority to get others to execute his orders. Many of the difficulties encountered in the early days of union-management relations can be ascribed to either the inability or the slowness of management officials with operating backgrounds to adapt themselves to collective bargaining.

The development of competent leadership is as difficult for management as for unions. In the case of the railroads during the early part of the century, many management officials were recruited from the union personnel. No sooner would an able union leader emerge than the railroads would snatch him up as their representative in collective bargaining. This questionable procedure created as many problems as it solved. The president of a large steel firm, when he signed a contract with SWOC in 1937, asked SWOC to release one of its most experienced field directors to head the company's industrial-relations department. One of the authors immediately replied that the SWOC director in question would not consider it, but the company president insisted that the proposition be submitted to him. Although his salary would have been trebled, the field director said, "Clint, it's awful nice of you to offer me this opportunity; but frankly I wouldn't know how to act on the other side of the fence, and I talked it over with my wife and we're just not interested.

Tell the company to get a man with an open mind and give him some authority, and we'll get along with him all right." The head of the company's safety department was given the job, but in the initial years he failed to rise above being a messenger boy between the hostile and often jealous operating officials and the belligerent union leaders. Fortunately the mill superintendent in one of the company's large works rose to the occasion. With him SWOC's director who had refused to join management's ranks worked out effective union-management relations that have been widely publicized.

Here was an operating official who made a success of collective bargaining, but he was as unlike A. M. Ellis as was Bob Burt. Like the latter he was a natural leader of people, a patient man with deep feelings and understanding. His achievements brought him many visitors, all asking, "How do you do it?" He had no ready answer, for there is none. Each group of workers and managers has to work out its own problems in its own way. The techniques and procedures of union-management relations are not the answer, merely the mechanisms. The important thing is the sincerity of purpose behind the actions of management and union leaders; this alone determines the course of collective bargaining, for gain or for loss, for turmoil or for peace. Unions initiate collective bargaining but are unable to make it work constructively by themselves. They need the aid and co-operation of management. At this point something more is required from management than the direction of human beings by dictatorial and arbitrary means.

The leadership requirements and responsibilities of management increase under union-management relations.

A cycle in the evolution of management ended with the large-scale advent of collective bargaining. Up to the middle of the last decade the management of America's mines, mills, and factories was divided into component cells. Each cell resembled a department and was ruled by a foreman or superintendent—we shall call him the "boss." Each boss was chosen to run his department by certain well-defined prerogatives. They were dictatorial in concept and administration, and were expounded in high-sounding words as the "true principles of sound industrial management." Stripped of their verbiage, the meaning of these principles, expressed in the vocabulary of workers and bosses, was respectively, "The boss is the big cheese" and "I'm hired to run this place, and as long as I'm here I'll run it."

The boss was the undisputed ruler of his department; by tradition he made it a kingdom, its employees his subjects, and himself its king. Mr. Henry Sackson, the foreman we discussed in the preceding chapter, ruled so ruthlessly that his name became a community synonym for the word "dictator." Frequently the kingdom encompassed an entire plant, ruled over by a top boss (plant manager or works superintendent). He operated through subsidiary bosses—the latter mere lords over their departments, accountable only to the dictates of their king. Under this type of management workers were vassals. The boss hired whomever he chose. A brave but rare vassal who complained that he had to do two jobs because a newly hired buddy was incompetent was told, "It's none of your business whom I bring into this plant." A discharged vassal was out. He could seek a job elsewhere, but could not appeal for his old job. "Why was I fired?" he would ask. The reply, "It's none of your business." When a new job opened, the boss promoted whom he pleased. A case where an obviously undeserving man got the promotion occasionally brought forth the question, "How come he got the break?" The monotonous reply resounded through the plant, "It's none of your business." Every act of the boss was final, subject neither to review nor to appeal. He need not expound any rationale for his acts or decisions; his job required only that he bark aloud his orders, and enforce them with the power, absolute and unquestioned, to discharge and penalize.

To be sure, there were outstanding persons, department foremen and works managers, who, being natural leaders of men, commanded the universal respect of their employees and enjoyed their voluntary co-operation. They got things done by leading their employees, not by pushing them around with an iron fist. But they were the exceptions. The typical boss was a "hard guy" who earned the universal nickname "pusher boss." His abilities were limited; not much was required of him, since he had the power to say, "It's none of your business."

Organized workers change this. They approach each problem of vital concern to them with the fundamental tenet that "This is our business." Hence the "pusher boss" becomes obsolete under collective bargaining. In his place is required a leader with the ability to win and keep the respect of his employees, capable of managing his department or plant under a system of union-management relations where his every act is subject to the scrutiny of both his superiors and his employees. A penalized worker can appeal his case to his boss and, if unsatisfied with his answer, over his head. Setting a wage rate, raising an occupational wage rate, promoting an employee—these and other daily routine tasks of the boss are subject to the review of his employees through their union-contract machinery. To Henry Sackson this kind of setup was intolerable, and he quit. This kind of setup reveals many pusher-type bosses as incompetent, and they have to be replaced. The type required under collective bargaining has to possess more gray matter than the outmoded "pusher boss." He is not the ruler of a kingdom but the head of a republic. His employees are not vassals but citizens of industry; they enjoy the right to question any of his acts, the freedom to seek redress of their grievances through a system of industrial democracy. An old-time open-hearth superintendent who gave SWOC much trouble in its early days made the transition, and philosophizes, "You must have a lot more English on the ball to boss a bunch of men in these modern days. You can't push 'em aside when they ask questions. Now you have to answer 'em."

Collective bargaining multiplies the requirements of management. The old-time open-hearth superintendent, who got his job, and has held it for years, because he knew how to make steel, now must also know how to handle the human problems incident to the making of steel. Union-management relations compel management to acquire an adeptness in handling both the technical and the human problems in the managing of a productive enterprise. Thus a new cycle in the evolution of management enfolds. Foremen, superintendents, and other operating officials have to devote time and energy today to the human problems in industry that they previously ignored. The requirements of their jobs have become more stringent. Under collective bargaining they have the responsibility of setting the example for union leaders and members to follow in fairness of attitude, promptness of action, sincerity of purpose, courage of conviction, and the other primary principles of human behavior that inspire confidence and trust. The development of leadership on management's side capable of handling human as well as technical problems is, therefore, one of the most important paths to industrial peace.

Management can no more afford to leave the development of this type of leadership to the natural course of events than can organized labor. But the responsibility for training adequate leaders on its side is even greater for management, because this is a prerequisite before organized labor can follow suit. Union members can ill afford to elect a co-operative committeeman to represent them with a belligerent foreman, and national unions likewise cannot afford to assign co-operative staff members to administer the affairs of a local union whose management persists in pursuing policies that are essentially hostile to collective bargaining. Many organs of public opinion, wittingly or otherwise, place the responsibility for industrial peace primarily upon organized labor, but management's responsibility in this connection is clear.

Chapter IV: Administration of Contract

*Participation of workers, union representatives, and management at all levels is a prerequisite to the successful administration of a collective-bargaining contract.**

We spend half of our time settling grievances, or work stoppages resulting from them, that arise, in whole or in part, because management has failed to consult either the union or the workers involved. Sometimes, though less frequently, union officials commit the same error. One of the primary motives for union membership is the desire of workers to have a voice in making the decisions that vitally affect their everyday lives. The written collective-bargaining contract is the means through which workers secure such a voice. This is one path to industrial peace that cannot be by-passed, either by management or by union officials.

In a free society the desire of individuals to participate in the things that are important to them is an inviolate principle of human relations. A wife will object when her husband announces out of the clear sky that he has bought a new car. She may favor such a move, but oppose it in the particular case because she feels strongly that she has a right to be heard in making a decision so important to the family. The vice-president of a company will be huffed for weeks if the president does something for which he is responsible without consulting him. Within our own union, field directors will administer a policy with little enthusiasm, may even oppose it as impractical, not because they are necessarily

* We have weighed our experiences with small firms as against big ones to see if there are any basic differences. Our conclusion is that there are not. The principles of union-management relations in a small firm of one hundred and a big one of one hundred and twenty thousand workers are the same. There is some difference in the speed with which things can be done, and in the speed with which collective bargaining reaches maturity, in a small as against a big firm. But this is a difference of degree, not of fact, practice, or principle.

against it, but because they were not consulted in its formulation. An individual worker or group of workers are no different; they will complain and file grievances against decisions of management closely affecting them that have been formulated without consulting them. In such instances where management has consulted top union officials who, in turn, have failed to take the matter up with those involved, a sharp protest usually arises in the union ranks. Let us look at a few typical examples.

During 1938 and 1939 a SWOC local union in a large engineering plant requested adjustments in wage inequalities affecting more than seventy per cent of the men. The management rejected virtually all of the requests on the grounds that it was not earning profits. In the spring of 1940 business picked up, and the plant manager was authorized to grant wage equalizations not to exceed five thousand dollars a month. He reviewed the grievances filed by the union over the previous two years, distributed the five thousand dollars to take care of most of them, and posted a notice on the bulletin boards listing the adjustments. Two days earlier the union had voted at a membership meeting to open the contract for the purpose of negotiating the wage adjustments "because the company is making money now." Before the mechanics of reopening the contract had been completed, the notices were posted. The union leaders interpreted this as a hostile act intended to weaken the union by denying it credit for securing the adjustments. Whether or not this was the intention of the plant manager is academic; the reaction of the union leaders was natural and predictable.

The men became incensed and decided upon a twofold counterattack. They picked faults with the announced adjustments and demanded a paid vacation, which they had no intention of doing originally. The plant manager agreed to the wage increases, amounting to an additional twenty-five hundred dollars a month, but refused the paid-vacation demand. At the end of the negotiation period the contract automatically terminated. In the absence of a new one the men went on strike. Three weeks later they won the vacation demand, which they took in the form of a week's pay for the last week of their strike.

The plant manager told us at the settlement of the strike, "Unions are unsound when they have their members lose more money striking than they gain in wages or vacations." Like so many other management officials, he could see only the economic side of the picture. He knew the men wanted more money, and reasoned that all he had to do to satisfy them was to grant it. When he did this voluntarily and the men revolted, he was stunned; and when the men lost fifteen days' pay to gain a five-day paid vacation, he was convinced that they were sadly misled by their union leaders. What he failed to appreciate was that the men felt they could afford a few days' pay for the pleasure of "putting the boss in his place." Having been denied direct participation in the final adjustment of wages, the men decided to have a voice in the question of vacations and went on strike until their voice was heard. In making a regular report to the United States Department of Labor one of the authors listed as the cause of the strike "refusal of management to grant vacations." The statistics on strikes lists this one as having been due to economics, when actually it was due to the persistent desire of the men involved to see that the plant manager recognizes their right to participate in making decisions on questions that mean a great deal to them. In dollars and cents this mistake cost the company twenty-five hundred dollars a month, plus twenty thousand dollars a year in vacations for five hundred of the eight hundred workers, plus the immeasurable costs of the strike. The union paid heavily in the form of publicity blaming it for "impeding national defense." Management, as usual, was blameless for the strike in the eyes of the newspapers.

The desire of workers to have a say-so in things of much concern to them works the same way when violated by union officials. The grievance committee in a large mill of one of the big steel firms objected to a revision of tonnage wage rates based on technological improvements in the operation. Failing to agree upon how much, if any, wage revision was in order, the committee proposed that the matter be referred to an impartial umpire for final disposition, as provided for in the contract. Management refused, argued that the grievance was not arbitrable, and instituted the revisions without the committee's agreement. The case was appealed to one of us, who, also failing to secure an agreement with management, likewise proposed arbitration. Management continued its refusal. Shortly thereafter the men quit work and, being in a key department (blooming mill), closed the entire mill within forty-eight hours.

"What are you going to do, Golden?" the company president demanded to know. "You have violated the contract and we will not negotiate until the men return to work." The author, impatient with this unrealistic refusal to agree to arbitration, replied that he had violated the contract in the first place by rejecting arbitration. This was in the fall of 1939, and outside pressure to settle the strike was absent. After the strike was several days old, the company president called in the author and signed an agreement to refer this grievance, and any similar future ones, to arbitration, provided the men resumed work. The author gladly signed the agreement along with him, reasoning that the men were on strike to establish the principle and practice of arbitration and that all he had to do, having secured this concession, was to transmit the agreement to the local union leaders for their acceptance. To his red-faced embarrassment they rejected it, continued the strike, and called for a secret vote among the membership as to whether "the agreement entered into by Mr. Golden should be accepted or rejected." By twenty-five to one the men voted rejection. This happened while the author was out of town, as he had left thinking it would be a mere routine matter to end the strike on the basis of his agreement.

The union leaders and members rejected the agreement on the ground that the company forced them out on strike and they would not end it until their grievance was won. Actually they were against the arbitration agreement because the author had failed to bring them into the conference at which it was reached. This was the Labor Day, 1939, strike at the Westridge mill of the River Steel Company briefly discussed in the preceding chapter. The company president in direct conference with the other author and the Westridge local union leaders settled the strike on the basis of conceding the grievance without arbitration. Originally caused by management's arbitrary refusal to give the men full participation in setting the wage rates in question, the strike was prolonged by the failure of the union's top official to give the men full participation in the strike negotiations. The key to the peaceful administration of collective-bargaining contracts is participation, through regularly established channels, of all persons vitally concerned. This fundamental principle runs throughout the entire fabric of union-management relations.

The peaceful administration of a contract requires the confidence of workers that they will get justice through the collective-bargaining machinery in the settlement of their grievances.

A. M. Ellis, whom we discussed in the previous chapter, had a record for industrial peace that, on the surface, looked perfect. In the twenty-odd mills of his firm there were less than six recorded work stoppages—all of short duration—from March, 1937, to his retirement at the end of 1940. Beginning early in 1941 a rash of strikes broke out in these mills, which A. M. promptly attributed to the co-operative policies of his successors. From his Florida retreat A. M. Ellis proudly boasted that his ironhanded policies in handling the union were responsible for the peace prevailing in the mills during his reign. Actually his unrealistic handling of grievances built up the storm that, luckily for him, did not break until after he left the scene.

Behind the nine strikes, lasting from one hour to three days, that greeted A. M.'s successors in the first half year of their reign was an attitude among the men in these mills that efforts to secure justice through the grievance procedure of the contract were hopeless. The persistent refusal of A. M. Ellis to settle grievances had created this attitude. Economic and political factors were on A. M.'s side. Shortly after the first contract was signed in the spring of 1937, the "Little Steel Strike" broke out. SWOC thus had little spare time to devote to building an effective grievance-adjustment machinery inside the mills and plants already under contract. When SWOC got around to this job late that summer, steel operations took a nose dive and kept declining to below twenty-five per cent of capacity by the end of 1937. By this time more than two hundred grievances piled up in our offices, and they kept coming in during 1938 at the rate of twenty-two a month. Ellis rejected them at the same rate; in fact, our records show only three cases favorably disposed of by January, 1939.

Economics—the mills were working only two or three days a week—proved a strong ally of A. M. He flagrantly disregarded both the letter and the spirit of the contract. Throughout his reign he never permitted a grievance to go to arbitration despite the clearly worded provision of the contract that this action was mandatory on both parties in the absence of a mutually satisfactory agreement. We argued, pleaded, even begged, that cases go to arbitration, but A. M. would just say, "No!" The merits be damned was his attitude. "We ain't bringing no outsiders in to tell us what to do," A. M. repeated to our boredom. We had no happy set of alternatives. We could acquiesce to A. M.'s "No, no, a thousand times no." We could reopen the contract to strengthen its provisions. Or we could wink at work stoppages in the mills to achieve what we had failed to achieve in conference with A. M. The depressed economic situation ruled out the last two alternatives; so SWOC had to tolerate, for the time being, the continued refusal of management to adjust grievances.

Meanwhile the men in the mills complained bitterly about their inability to "get justice" in the appeal of their grievances through the contract procedure. These grievances fell into several fundamental categories: the consecutive-five-day-work-week schedule for continuous operations, time and one-half for overtime, elimination of wage inequalities, a complexity of seniority matters, wage adjustments resulting from technological improvements, and so forth. In writing, in conference, and on the telephone we repeatedly told A. M. that his obvious hostility in rejecting union claims would drive the men to use the strike weapon to adjust matters that he refused to adjust according to contractual provisions. A. M. knew, as well as SWOC did, that the mills were working too infrequently for the men to take such drastic action. He kept repeating "A strike is in violation of the contract" every time we warned him that his policies would lead to a breakdown of peaceful relations. Our only acceptable explanation to the men was, "Your grievances have merits, but management refuses to consider them; so we'll just have to wait until economic conditions improve, because it would be suicidal to engage in strikes prohibited by the contract." The men replied in most instances, "The company broke the contract in cutting wages (or laying men off, or evading time-and-one-half payments—as the case might be) and also in refusing to go to arbitration. Why can't we disregard the 'no-strike' provision of the contract?"

In 1939 and 1940 steel operations picked up, though sporadically until the latter months of 1940. The likelihood of mill strikes faced Ellis in most grievances appealed to him, and during his last two years he conceded, on the average, one out of three SWOC complaints—just enough to keep the mills operating. Like the economics of his first two years, the politics of his last two proved a strong ally of A. M. The campaign to "amend" the National Labor Relations Act was in full swing and, like other unions, SWOC cautioned its members—at times going to extreme lengths—not to strike in violation of a contract because of the obvious aid and comfort this would give the enemies of labor, who were trying to emasculate the NLRA. A. M. conceded one-third of SWOC's complaints begrudgingly, not primarily on their merits but according to how "hot" the local union made things in the particular mill. But he thwarted the normal operation of grievance procedure; he would not, regardless of the circumstances, yield on the question of arbitration. When we became stalemated on a grievance case, we could only urge patience on the men's part and counsel that their complaints would be worked out in the next contract negotiations. We cautioned against strikes in violation of the contract. When work was slack and the NLRA was under deadly attack, our members heeded SWOC's cautions; but when these two restraining factors no longer existed, they let loose. After four years of warning against "pulling the switch" as a method of settling grievances Ellis' employees got weary, and the unbroken industrial peace his boss had publicly proclaimed three years earlier was no more.

From Thanksgiving, 1940, until a new contract was negotiated with this firm in the spring of 1941, most of its mills experienced a shutdown, lasting from as little as an hour to a period of days. The top officials excitedly called for Phil Murray and asked, "What's the matter? Is SWOC becoming irresponsible? Can't you keep your pledge that we will suffer no strikes under our contract with your union? What good is the contract if it doesn't mean what it says? These strikes are embarrassing us with the trade. Our competitors who have never gone along with SWOC are laughing at us. What are we to do?"

Philip Murray replied, "Settle grievances. Your chickens are coming home to roost. You can thank A. M. Ellis for your sorry mess. He was afraid to settle grievances lest a couple more of your employees might join the union and pay their dues. You have violated the contract since it was first signed in 1937 by refusing to refer disagreements to arbitration, and these strikes have a common root. Workers don't strike because they want to, but because they have to. They could not get justice through the contract procedure, so they decided to take things into their own hands. The trouble with you fellows is that you recognized collective bargaining but you have not begun, as yet, to practice it. You have gone through the motions long enough. It's time you got down to real collective bargaining."

A. M.'s successors worked day and night during the first several months of their reign, mostly at the job of cleaning up the mess they had inherited from him. A new and improved contract was signed between their firm and SWOC in April, 1941, and shortly thereafter the backfire against A. M.'s inability or unwillingness to settle grievances was over. Strikes in violation of the contract ceased for several weeks. The men in the mills of this huge firm started to return to the use of the contract procedure for the settlement of their grievances. The actions and policies of A. M.'s successors inspired confidence among the union members that they could get justice through the contract. But this confidence proved premature. The operating officials opposed the co-operative policies of A. M.'s successors. The top officials still persisted in their refusal to arbitrate. This soon became apparent to the men and, once again, they resorted to strike action to get their grievances settled. The number of "wildcat" strikes became so numerous by the end of September, 1941, that the firm's president again called for SWOC top officials. "What's wrong? Doesn't our contract with your union mean anything?" he asked.

One of the authors replied, "Have you ever heard of the word 'arbitration'? Have you ever read that section of our contract providing for arbitration? It simply says that if we cannot agree on a dispute it should be referred to an impartial person for final disposition. Let us look at one of these strikes. Take the coke-works strike in July. It was over relief men in hot weather. Do you know that that grievance was originally presented to A. M. Ellis in July of 1937? That's four years ago. He rejected it. We asked for arbitration. He rejected that. And so far as he was concerned that closed the case. Well, the men who have to suffer the heat from those ovens had another idea about it. They went on strike to get men to relieve them. Then you granted their request. Is there any wonder why other groups of men follow this example! The papers blame us for the strikes, but you know where the major portion of the responsibility lies. We have a big job in rebuilding the confidence of your employees in the contract as an instrument to settle their grievances. The immediate selection of an arbitrator is the first step in this job."

Soon after this conference SWOC arbitrated its first case with this firm—almost five years after its first contract. It is too early to measure the results of arbitration in this case, but as it contributes to the settlement of grievances "wildcat" strikes will diminish in number and gradually cease. Workers do not strike because they want to, but because they have been thwarted in securing justice through the peaceful machinery of their contract. The administration of a collective-bargaining contract is essentially a human problem, since it deals with the ways and habits of human beings, their relations to one another in responsibilities and authorities, and their common welfare. A strike or lockout is less a violation of a legal document than it is the breakdown of union-management relations. Industrial peace, in large measure, is based upon the confidence of union members that they can get justice through the regular machinery for adjusting grievances; and the more this confidence proves justified by the performance of management, the firmer and surer becomes the industrial peace.

Grievances should be settled speedily and as near their point of origin as possible.

"The Unsettled Grievance" is the nemesis of union and management officials alike. Invariably it is found among the several causes of a strike that occurs during the life of a contract, or between contracts, because, like an open wound, a grievance with merit becomes progressively worse until treated. Breeder of distrust, impatience, and strife, the unsettled grievance has been delayed somewhere along the grievance-adjustment route by management or union officials who either lacked the necessary authority to solve it or "passed the buck" to the next fellow up the line. So much for generalities; now let's look at a typical case.

Harry Carman was tired after a tense session with a joint union-management committee, created as a condition of strike settlement. The forty-three-day "wildcat" strike focused upon wages; the men claimed that they were underpaid in comparison with competing steel mills. To determine factually whether this claim was justified was the duty of the committee. Carman, superintendent of the electric-furnace department, spent the May afternoon (1941) explaining to one of the authors and a vice-president of the company, who made up the joint committee, the complicated wage structure in his department. Unwittingly he revealed during the conversation following the formal part of the meeting that there was something else at the bottom of the turmoil in his department. He tells his own story.

"I don't think we would have had this recent trouble in the department if it were not for the ladle cranemen. These fellows had a gripe, and they've kept the rest of the furnacemen stirred up. Long before the strike the ladle cranemen put in for a wage adjustment. Besides being the lowest-paid tonnage men in the furnace crews, they had more work piled on them in recent years. I agreed that they were entitled to some consideration and took it up with Mr. Wicker [operating vice-president]. He turned me down.

"I told the men nothing doing and that if they were not satisfied with my answer they could take it up with their general committee, as the matter was now out of my hands. The case kicked back and forth for months. Reeder [the personnel director] stalled for several monthly meetings with the committee. He took it up with Mr. Wicker but, I guess, got the same answer I did. The general committee meeting with Reeder just before the strike began demanded a 'Yes or No' answer on the case. So Reeder had to say 'No.' I knew that would touch off an explosion, because everyone in my department was watching the case. I told Reeder after the meeting that he should not have said 'No,' but he felt he had stalled all he could on the case."

At the time the strike started, twenty-one wage-adjustment grievances were pending. To grant them all would have cost the firm a little under ten thousand dollars a year. Reeder, the union committee's sole contact with management, lacked authority to review them and kept delaying until he could get the ear of Mr. Wicker, who invariably said, "Nothing doing." Like Harry Carman, the other department heads were not free to act on these matters. The operating vice-president was the bottleneck on all grievances; and despite favorable recommendations from his department heads, Mr. Wicker had granted less than six wage adjustments since the existing contract had been negotiated ten months earlier. As a consequence the union committeemen were unable to "get anything" for the aggrieved union members, who gradually started to criticize them. The men as a whole became impatient and irritated, while the committeemen became angry and belligerent; they reported to a membership meeting failure on settling grievances. Somebody shouted "strike" and before the men knew it they were on the picket line.

All the men who had been watching these cases filed the grievances that they had been holding back. They figured that the only men who would get anything out of the strike were those with pending grievances, and now that they were on strike they might as well throw everything into the pot. A strike has a way of bringing dormant grievances to the surface; that is one of the chief reasons why strikes starting over simple and few things prove so difficult to settle. The public press shrieked about interference with defense. The loss of specialty steels these fifteen hundred men produced allegedly was holding back airplane output. On the forty-third day this strike, which had its origin in management's refusal to concede ten thousand dollars' worth of wage adjustments, was settled at an annual cost of ninety thousand dollars in wage adjustments, plus a ten-cent-an-hour general raise, plus the creation of a union-management wage fact-finding committee whose report brought about further adjustments amounting to an additional thirty thousand dollars.

This costly experience made management self-analytical. The powerless personnel director was placed in the cost department. Mr. Wicker was relieved of union relations, and the firm hired an industrial-relations director with power to settle grievances. Authority was gradually vested in the department heads to settle grievances, and to settle them quickly. The director pursues a policy of having them get credit or criticism, as the case may be, for the settlement of grievances. At this point top management fears, and rightly so, that department heads, close to their men, out of a desire to keep their good will might give the firm away. Operating management officials, who must face day-to-day realities, in addition to being empowered and encouraged to settle grievances arising in their departments, have to learn how to settle them on their merits.

Many firms have standard measurements for judging the ability of foremen and superintendents. One of these is the frequency of preventable accidents in their departments. Under union-management relations the number of grievances susceptible of adjustment appealed out of the department should be another standard by which to measure the performance of department heads. The perfect foreman should be the one who can avoid preventable accidents in his department and who can promptly settle grievances filed by workers under his supervision, besides turning out material of good quality, in sufficient quantities, and at the lowest possible cost. Grievances, speedily settled at their source, are vital though intangible cost factors. Workers should not be denied the natural satisfaction they get from settling their own grievances because their immediate superiors lack authority to settle them. Likewise, department union committeemen should get as much credit as possible in disposing of grievances. In cases involving basic union-management policies, where possible, the final act of settlement should be made by the local union committeemen, workers, and management officials immediately involved. After all, workers, particularly those active as union committeemen, originally joined the union to have a say-so in things of concern to them, and this desire should not be denied them by cumbersome grievance-adjustment machinery that throws the major responsibility for decision on union and management officials who are several steps removed from the point of origin of grievances. When free to pass the responsibility for final decision to higher union and management officials, both workers and lower supervisors are inclined to handle cases from the viewpoint of "How does this affect me?" But when given the responsibility of decision they are more inclined to handle cases on their merits. In the discussion of the following principle we examine how this works in practice.

Grievances should be settled on their merits with no logrolling permitted.

The case of Oscar B. Cottrell, boiler-shop helper in a mill of one of the large steel firms, plagued us from February 2, 1939, to June 6, 1940, and would have done so indefinitely except that the rearmament boom returned Cottrell to the boiler shop. We never met him personally, although his case was repeatedly before us until its underlying cause was corrected. The facts in the case are simple and illuminating.

In the middle of January, 1939, we met with Mr. Roper, management's representative in the final appeal of grievances, to settle five pressing cases. Two SWOC field directors also attended the conference, because the cases came from mills falling within their respective areas. As a whole we were quite successful: two company-wide cases, involving departmental seniority and the continuous-work-week schedule, were settled on the union's basis; one wage-rate case conceded by management brought raises to more than one hundred men, while another rate case was referred back for local disposition. Only one case—that of Oscar B. Cottrell, involving one man—was won by management. It was a meritorious case, and we could have won it had we argued long enough. It was dropped only when Mr. Roper said, "You've won all the other cases. Aren't you going to leave me at least one settled favorably to management on the record?" To our later sorrow we dropped the boiler-shop helper's case; but he never did, and rightly so.

Cottrell's case involved his seniority standing. The contract provided that after an employee had been laid off for more than six months his continuous-service record was broken, and upon rehiring he would begin as a new employee. Cottrell had been hurt in the mill, and the point in dispute was from what date his absence from work should be calculated. Did his six-month-layoff period begin on the date the doctor discharged him, or on the date that he last received workmen's-compensation payments? This question was complicated by the fact that Cottrell had accepted a lump-sum settlement for his disability instead of drawing it in weekly installments. There was only a few months' difference between the union's interpretation and that of the company, but this was more than a technical question; it involved Cottrell's fifteen years of continuous service.

"There will be hell about dropping Cottrell's case back home," the SWOC director observed after the conference. And there was. The local union protested to us. We replied that, no matter which interpretation of the contract prevailed, operations would not increase soon enough to recall him without a break in seniority. This drew a sharp letter of protest to SWOC Chairman Philip Murray. It was now April 5, 1939, and time had come to our rescue. He replied, "There is no opportunity of getting Cottrell back to work without a break in service, since his six-month period has elapsed even under the union's original contention." But the matter did not end there. Cottrell wrote Philip Murray personally. He received the same reply as the local union. Cottrell then took his case to the CIO State Council, whose secretary wrote us an indignant letter about what a "raw deal Cottrell had received." We explained the case to him. The sore, however, was unhealed. The local union appealed beyond Chairman Murray to the SWOC Executive Board and received a final answer on June 6, 1940, sixteen months after we had "horse-traded" the case. "Regardless of what interpretation had been made of the compensation clause of the contract, Cottrell could not possibly have been returned to work without a break in service. This is indeed regrettable, but beyond SWOC's power to amend," the reply stated; "consequently the case has been closed some time ago." But this also failed to end the matter. The pickup in steel operations in the fall of 1940 put Cottrell back to work. He promptly filed a new grievance, claiming that he should get credit for his past continuous service instead of being rehired as a new employee. In the end Cottrell received justice, as management reinstated his old service record.

Cottrell's case has many parallels in our experiences. A SWOC field director established an excellent collective-bargaining record with a major steel firm. Grievances were handled speedily and a substantial majority was settled in the union's favor. SWOC gave much publicity to the development of this relationship, which, unfortunately, proved premature. Early in the second year of our contractual relations a series of protests was made by the local union to the SWOC national office. Simultaneously the company's industrial-relations director complained that the local union was reopening many cases that had been settled unfavorably to it. The SWOC director lost his composure, because the local union committeemen were getting out of control. Three departmental work stoppages, one right after another, brought the situation to a head. At the bottom of it we discovered that for more than a year SWOC's director and the company's industrial-relations director had been pursuing a policy of horse-trading; both were sincere in their purposes. SWOC's director knew he could not get his people everything, and tried to get them as much as he could. Management's industrial-relations head, less experienced than SWOC's director, was trying to keep the peace and make collective bargaining work. As a whole this was to the union's benefit. Seven hundred men in the strip mill, for example, netted a ten per cent increase in tonnage earnings, while a handful of pipe-mill workers lost their claim for a guaranteed hourly rate during breakdowns. However, the union is not a whole but a composite of integral parts. The gain for the many men in the strip mill in no way alleviated the pipe workers' grievance.

In every instance of our experience, logrolling—"You scratch my back and I'll scratch yours"—in the settlement of grievances results in disaster. The union cannot settle one case by forfeiting another without creating turmoil among its membership. Nor can management get away with such a practice, except at the expense of creating still more difficult problems. Each grievance has behind it actual or alleged personal dissatisfactions, and the solution of those cases involving the greater amount of dissatisfaction does not settle the cases involving lesser degrees of complaint.

The application of this principle of settling grievances on their merits runs to the heart of union-management relations. Should a grievance not be settled on its merits because to do so might embarrass a management official? Or might inflate the union's prestige? A clear path to industrial peace is the settlement of grievances on the basis of their merits, no matter whose fingers are burned, no matter what might happen to the prestige of management or union. This policy, though it may embarrass management periodically, or strengthen the union's position, in the long run raises the stature of management in direct proportion to which it is big enough to admit an error. There are times, we have learned from bitter experience, when someone's face has to be saved at the expense of a legitimate grievance, but unless such settlements are eliminated or kept at a minimum they will play havoc with the particular company's union-management relations.

This, in turn, raises the question of union committeemen pursuing grievances that, in the first instance, have little or no merit. Frequently management is forced by union pressure to concede an unworthy complaint, and in as many cases committeemen privately agree the complaint is unjustified but, as chosen union representatives, insist it be granted.

Under most favorable circumstances it is difficult to settle cases on their merits, and often almost impossible as long as the union's recognition is partial and its membership purely voluntary. "It's up to the union to sell itself to our employees," management argues when approached on the union-shop question. The logical outcome of this line of reasoning is for the union to champion individual grievances, at times, to get members. For local union leaders to discriminate between worthy and unworthy grievances under the most favorable circumstances is difficult enough; and when they have to be governed by considerations of how the union membership may be affected, they are less inclined to tell a member or prospective member frankly that he does not have a worthy case. The union-shop form of recognition is by no means a cure-all formula for union-management problems; but, as we shall discuss later, it is a necessary instrument of industrial peace.

Management should frankly acknowledge the role of the union in bringing about improvement in working conditions.

Robert Burt, the company president discussed in the preceding chapter, has been eminently successful in handling his union relations. One reason is that he likes this phase of his work; another, he knows his way about in the intricacies of collective bargaining. In his company the union is part of the official family and not a stepchild.

When the Selective Service Act of 1940 was passed by Congress, management officials were falling over one another in announcing their patriotism. "Company policies" were issued to the press, printed in large type and posted on the bulletin boards, put into letters or booklets and mailed to each employee, and announced from public platforms. These "company policies" set forth how each drafted employee would be protected upon being honorably discharged from "the citizens' army now being mobilized." This attempt of management, which was widespread, to monopolize patriotism stirred union members almost to a point of revolt, and was no small factor in the turbulent union-management picture during the several months immediately following the passage of the Selective Service Act. Vital daily working conditions were affected by these unilateral announcements—explosive seniority questions, for instance, were disturbed—all executed as if there were no such thing as unions in the picture. The general reaction of union members and workers was hostile; they felt that they were being denied an opportunity to show the deep bonds of patriotism existing between them and their country and its government. This reaction was expressed in criticisms of details of the announcements, and SWOC, like many other unions, had to devote much energy to untangling the mess created in so many plants by these quickly promulgated statements.

Bob Burt knew better. He realized that the question of what would happen to drafted employees closely affected the lives of all his employees and collective bargaining in his company. Bob called in the union president, showed him a proposed set of rules regarding drafted employees, and asked for his opinion. The union president promptly grasped the hint and asked for time to study the rules. He called a special meeting of the local union, read the rules, and offered some of his own changes. They were discussed, and several more changes were made by the members. The next day the union committee submitted their set of rules to Bob Burt, who acted as if he had never seen them before. After some argument the union's proposal was accepted by Burt. Later he complained to us, "I gave our statement to the local president so that the union would participate in formulating and giving it effect, and he took and added a few ideas of his own that will cost us several thousand dollars more."

We observed that the local committee showed proficiency in collective bargaining. He replied, "Honestly, I think the committee made some fine improvements over my original statement, and the company is better off with the benefit of their ideas." At any rate, unlike most other concerns, Burt's suffered no turmoil over it, because this obviously patriotic action was shared with its workers and their union.

One of the disturbing factors in the union-management scene is the failure, even at this late date, of large corporations to recognize the role of the union in matters affecting working conditions. Two aluminum-producing firms, early in the defense program, afforded a striking contrast in management's conception of the role of unions in bringing about changes in working conditions.

In the summer of 1940 the Aluminum Workers' Union sought a wage increase and an improved vacation program with pay from the principal aluminum producer. After prolonged conferences the union won a two-cent-an-hour wage raise but no improvements in the vacation program. Only by the most vigorous appeal to its members' patriotism was the union able to get its meager agreement ratified. One plant rejected it, went on strike, and demanded the original union wage request of ten cents an hour. The union's reward for this heroic effort to persuade its members to make sacrifices in the interest of uninterrupted production was a unilateral announcement by the company a few months later of an improved vacation program. The union was not consulted, nor given any recognition for originally proposing the new vacation setup; in fact, its position was jeopardized by management's ignoring it in making this basic change in working conditions. In the immediate months following this incident the company had strikes in three of its plants, one being branded by the press as a Nazi-Communist plot to sabotage national defense. No evidence was adduced to support this charge, although it was clear that management's shortsighted union-relations policies were largely responsible for the industrial turmoil at its main properties.

In sharp contrast to this firm's policy of ignoring the union's role in bringing about changed working conditions, the next largest aluminum producer gave full credit to its employees' labor organizations in a full-page newspaper advertisement that appeared in the country's leading newspapers. It read:

OUR PLEDGE TO THE UNITED STATES OF AMERICA

No greater trust has ever been the responsibility of any generation than that of defending and preserving for posterity the right to live in the freedom of democracy which is ours today. We pledge the resources and facilities of the ——— Metals Company twenty-four hours a day, seven days a week, to supply strong aluminum alloys vital to the defense program. To the fulfillment of this obligation, every employee and executive of this Company, individually and collectively, pledges his energy and unfaltering loyalty. As Americans we cannot do less; as human beings we cannot do more. "This is our purpose and our pledge."

This was not signed in type by the company. It was signed by the company president in his own handwriting, but not alone. His signature was given no more prominence than that of seventeen A. F. of L. and CIO union officers with their union titles. This advertisement was merely symbolic of the company's conception of the union's role not only in changing working conditions but in the problem of production itself. The results are seen in the state of industrial peace at this company's several plants.

A close relationship exists between the industrial peace and the role the union plays in the formulation and execution of policies vitally affecting working conditions. Such policies should be worked out jointly in union-management negotiations; that is the primary function of a union, and to side-step it, in whole or in part, almost certainly leads to industrial strife. The day when management in granting improved working conditions could beat its chest in philanthropic gusto is past; these things, and partial credit for them, now belong to the unions. This principle was incorporated in an award made to a SWOC local union by an impartial arbiter. A précis of it follows.

DECISION OF THE IMPARTIAL UMPIRE-FINDINGS

The SWOC protested the propriety of the Company's action in failing to notify the Union of its intention to grant vacations in 1940 prior to the general announcement made by the company. The latter in its discussion of the matter with the Union maintained that it was not obligated to make such preliminary notice to the Union.

The Company did not violate any technical provision of the Agreement in announcing the 1940 vacation program.

The Company dignified its relations with the Union by recognizing the latter as the exclusive bargaining agency for union members and by entering into a written agreement with it. The

Company, therefore, is morally bound to avoid any act, inadvertent or deliberate, that might be construed to deny, ignore, or embarrass the Union.

Resumption of vacations in 1940 is not quite the automatic act suggested in the argument of the Company. 1938 vacations had been waived by agreement; 1939 vacations had been the subject of discussion which had finally centered on a substitute Christmas bonus plan as the opportunity for vacations during the calendar year disappeared; and 1940 vacations should have been a proper subject for joint negotiations.

The Company article of January 12th added to the uncertainty with respect to vacations in 1940. The general tone of the article suggests that the decision concerning 1940 vacations was purely a matter of Company action. That the Union should become incensed over Company actions that seemingly excluded it from a voice in effectuating the Agreement is not the least bit surprising.

Decision

The Company is bound technically to consult with the Union with respect to the detailed application of the terms and provisions of the Agreement. It is bound morally to consult with the Union with respect to the resumption of terms previously waived or postponed prior to general announcement of such resumption.

The Company is not accused of having acted deliberately to embarrass the Union or indirectly to discourage membership in its ranks in the present issue. In this respect it is given a clean bill of health. However, since its acts were needless and certainly not in the interest of co-operation, their repetition can be avoided. The Company, therefore, is requested to take the following steps in similar situations in the future:

1. Notify the Union representatives of the specific points or action it contemplates.
2. Negotiate with the Union to secure mutually acceptable practice, if such step is necessary.
3. Consult with the Union to secure a mutually acceptable method and text of general announcement.

The successful administration of a contract requires the maintenance of an effective system of communications for both man-

agement and the union, in bringing complaints from the bottom up and relaying decisions and policies from the top down.

A faulty management system of communications is as much responsible for giving birth to unions as is any other single factor. Workers, stymied for years by their foremen, join unions so that they can get their complaints before top management without endangering their jobs. Prior to the union, to do so usually meant the loss of a worker's job. The heart of every union's contract is its grievance-adjustment machinery. This is essentially a communications system designed to bring complaints from the bottom right up to the top, step by step. The first benefit top management derives from a union contract is this effective system for bringing bad shop practices of lower supervisory officials to its attention. An active union committee sees to it that top management is fully informed of what goes on in the mill. Before the contract's grievance machinery was established, management's own communications system failed to bring such matters to the view of company executives one step or more removed from the source.

One of the first concerns of a newly organized union, after it has secured a contract containing provisions for bringing grievances to the review of top management, is to see that policies agreed to by top management are carried out all the way down the line, and not subject to distortions by minor functionaries. Upon embarking on collective bargaining, management, if it is to avoid unnecessary difficulties, has to see that every supervisory person in its organization, down to the seemingly least important one, clearly understands that the firm's policy is to get along with the union. Frequently this may mean, as discussed previously, that some management personnel, accustomed for years to fighting unions, will have to be replaced with persons capable of co-operating with union shop stewards and committeemen. In this job management receives unsolicited aid from the union. This is called, in labor-union parlance, "policing the contract"—seeing that the terms of the contract and the interpretations placed on them in the routine settlement of grievances are followed by every management official. The union will police its contract to the extent of demanding the removal of foremen and others who repeatedly violate it. To see that agreements reached with the union are executed all down the line, therefore, is management's first task in the administration of a collective-bargaining contract.

We are proud of the fact that virtually all SWOC contracts are flexible; that is, their provisions are confined to the major matters—recognition, wages, hours, seniority, vacations, and so forth—and these are set forth in general language, lending themselves to flexible administration and day-to-day interpretation according to changing conditions. SWOC, of course, has some contracts that are the opposite. Their provisions are rigid, inflexible, and binding—no matter how conditions may change in the meantime—until amended or eliminated in contract negotiations. In the latter case the union lacks confidence in management's oral word; its members are distrustful and demand that all actual or feared acts of management considered hostile to their interests be specifically outlawed in the contract. In the former case the union does not consider it necessary to spell out everything that may happen during the life of its contract. Based on management's past performance, the union members have confidence that they will be able to get an equitable solution of any problem that may arise during the life of the contract. Consequently they are content to confine the contract to the major issues, leaving the lesser problems to the grievance committee and management for solution. To develop such confidence is exclusively management's job.

The confidence of union members in management's sincerity of purpose and oral word is an almost certain result of an effective management system for carrying out policies worked out in union-management conferences. A rigid provision on a secondary matter has crept into SWOC's principal contracts. It provides from two to four hours' pay for workers reporting to work but sent home for lack of it. Prior to the insertion of this work rule into the contracts it had been agreed upon orally under the old ones. A grievance had been made about the injustice suffered by a man who packs a lunch and spends transportation fare to work but does not get any gainful employment that day. Management agreed that such cases should be partially compensated. The settlement of this grievance, for all practical purposes, became a part of the contract with the same force and effect as any of its specific provisions. This is the manner in which work rules should be developed; and they have no place as rigid provisions of the basic collective-bargaining agreement, primarily because as conditions change these rules may have to be altered accordingly. The union-management relationship should be fluid enough to allow for such day-to-day changes. But some of the mill superintendents and department foremen, failing to see such a provision in the contract, continued to be careless in scheduling workers and frequently many were sent home. A separate grievance had to be made out for each worker so aggrieved, and fought through the grievance machinery.

Management, in this instance, had failed to see that its agreement with the union to give partial compensation in such cases was clearly understood and lived up to by its foremen and superintendents. As a result the pressure was so heavy on SWOC's negotiating committee with the major steel producer that it had to insist upon the inclusion of this provision in the 1941 contract. A faulty communications system from the bottom up gave impetus to unionization in the first place, and a faulty method of communicating from the top down will give impetus to union demands for a rigid, inflexible contract dealing with even the smallest matters.

This problem of communication exists in all types of organizations, the labor union being no exception. In our daily work we are constantly aware of difficulties encountered in having policies executed all the way down the line in a manner to preserve their original spirit and accomplish their designed objective. The labor union suffers, particularly among its local union leaders, from the same attitude that management encounters among its lower supervisory officials; namely, "Let 'em find out for themselves. I'm not going out of my way to tell 'em. Why should I stick my neck out! I'm not responsible for it." In the latter case top union leaders receive unsolicited help from management. Many of our daily telephone calls are from management officials bringing to our attention something they think we should know, and which we usually hear from them for the first time. As a rule these messages deal with contemplated local union actions that the reporting management official thinks are in violation of the contract. Frequently the SWOC director in charge of the particular local union learns of the matter for the first time in the same way. This is particularly the case if the local union plans something contrary to either its contract or SWOC rules and regulations.

By and large the union's full-time staff accurately reflects top union policies and communicates local matters from the bottom up; in fact, one of SWOC's major problems is to get its staff to refrain from reporting so many local matters to the top and handle them locally. The point at which the union's communications system is most defective is at the level of the local union. But in the same manner that the union reports acts of minor supervisory officials to top officials that the former do not want known "in the head office," management reports acts or planned acts of local union leaders to top union officials that the former make no effort to report themselves. Thus a collective-bargaining contract, by its nature, takes up the slack in the system of communications of both management and the union.

The effectiveness of the union's system for communicating union policies from the top down to the last local union officer and member is closely tied in with the training of union leadership. SWOC has published handbooks dealing with handling grievances, production problems, technological unemployment, industrial training, union-management co-operation, and other matters. We are not too happy over the fact that these publications are read more carefully and extensively by management personnel than by our own staff, local union leaders, and members. These publications were also written for management on the premise, as expounded in this book, that the more enlightened management's policies and actions become the greater the likelihood of local unions following suit. In many instances local union leaders who had paid little, if any, attention to a SWOC handbook when they had received it in the mail devour its contents overnight after some management official has quoted it or otherwise called it to their attention.

SWOC's communications system follows a set pattern. We have periodic staff conferences of field directors between constitutional conventions. Top SWOC officials with the assistance of their field directors develop policies to be carried out by the latter. When their organizing staff is not at the conference, the directors return home and call meetings of their staff. Here they relay the policies. The organizers, each in charge of a number of local unions, then communicate the matters to local union leaders and members. On crucial matters the directors often call conferences of all their local union leaders, who in turn carry the message back to the membership. This system, at times, is supplemented with letters from SWOC officers to the staff, and to the local unions, dealing either with lesser policies or with matters that cannot wait for one of the periodic staff conferences. This system is most effective in conveying intra-SWOC policies, and least effective in passing on SWOC's collective-bargaining ideas and policies.

In discussing a union-management problem with a company executive we often encounter the following line of argument. "Yes, that's your philosophy of collective bargaining, and I agree with your idea for handling the matter; but that's not the way your boys in my plant look at these things. They have their own ideas and, unhappily for us, they vary too frequently from yours."

This gap between the formulation of basic collective-bargaining policies at the top of SWOC and their comprehension and execution at the level of the local union is being bridged, in part, by SWOC's regular full-time organizing staff. But, as we point out in the preceding chapter, an all-out leadership-training program is essential to bridge it adequately. Each set of local union leaders has to face many difficult problems. A common complaint of management is that the union-management relationship does not permit it to communicate its side of the story directly to its employees. This reflects a lack of confidence in the local union leaders' ability to relay to their members such complicated matters as earnings, freight rates, basing points, and so forth. Measured against their backgrounds, which afforded little opportunity to master such matters, local leaders have made great strides in recent years. Obviously, however, there is still a deficiency in this respect, which makes extensive union-training programs increasingly necessary.

The development of a communications system, effectively working both ways, in many respects is a mechanical problem, but because the conductors of the information and policies are human beings its perfection is a slow process. Management and union leaders have to work at it day in and day out, and the neglect of the contract's administration, for even one day, will show up eventually in confusion and industrial strife. There are other matters also that vitally affect the industrial peace but over which neither union nor management officials have very much, if any, influence. These we discuss in the concluding principle of this chapter.

The nature of union-management relations and the administration of a contract are influenced greatly by the pattern of social relationships in any given community.

Industrial peace in a free society is the product of a healthy, stable, and productive environment. Men and women in industry can influence their environment in many respects, but to a large extent both as individuals and as organized groups they are dominated by its social influences. Throughout this discussion we are concerned with the methods and degrees by which management and union leaders, in practical ways, can create the kind of environment most likely to produce peace and keep strife at an irreducible minimum. The extent to which industrial peace can be nurtured, unfortunately, is limited by the social forces in each community that become the master of management and unions alike. In different mine, mill, and factory towns the dominant social influences have a far greater effect on the state of industrial peace than do policies carefully worked out in collective-bargaining conferences. To a certain point the social environment can be shaped toward peaceful relations by union-management acts; beyond that point social conditions that have been developing for years literally gather up both management and union and throw them at each other in bitter warfare or into peaceful conferences, as the case may be.

The turbulent auto and comparatively peaceful steel "labor situations" during the latter part of the thirties demonstrate how greatly union-management relations are influenced by social conditions. Various explanations of this contrast, in our opinion, fail to penetrate the basic causes for the epidemic of sit-down and other types of strikes in Detroit, Flint, and other auto-manufacturing centers, while at the same time steel workers in Pittsburgh, Homestead, and other steel-producing towns made the transition from individual to collective bargaining with very little, if any, strife. In fact, even in the "Little Steel" towns that were the scene of some of the most violent warfare of the last decade, union-management relations developed peacefully after the fighting subsided. But in the automobile industry, generally speaking, warfare was chronic for many months after the first contracts were signed in 1937. Was this contrast due to the type of union leadership in auto and steel, to the kind of opposition offered by management in the two industries, or to the fact that General Motors fought while United States Steel voluntarily granted union-recognition demands?

These explanations are superficial. To attribute the contrast to union leadership is an injustice to the United Automobile Workers' officers and undeserved flattery for SWOC officials. The difference in management-opposition analysis fails to take into account the high degree of proficiency that steel management achieved over the years in union busting, equaled by few auto-management executives. The different approaches of the biggest auto and steel firms also fail to explain the contrast, because the auto-strike epidemic did not discriminate between auto firms that opposed or acquiesced to union recognition; and, further, instead of experiencing a strike epidemic after the big strike, "Little Steel" firms gradually found themselves bargaining peacefully with their workers' unions, which they had tried in vain to destroy. All these explanations fail to go to the root of the situations in auto and steel—the contrasting social environment in Detroit and Pittsburgh, in Flint and Homestead.

Along the Monongahela River in the Southside and Hazelwood sections of Pittsburgh you can find elderly men, retired from the steel mills, talking about "old times" in the beer taverns that have faced the mills and furnaces since shortly after the Civil War—except for a few years underground during the Prohibition Era. These retired steel workers will tell you about the time they helped build the first open-hearth furnaces, or stood around as boys watching Number Two Blast Furnace being built. There were no fences or stone walls around the mills in those days. They will tell you about the union they had when there was no Wagner Act or President Roosevelt or CIO. The 1892 Homestead Strike is one of their favorite stories—how the Hazelwood men tipped off the strikers that the Pinkertons were coming up the river by barge, and how the Hazelwood men answered the strikers' call for pickets. An old-timer will tell you how his father was killed in the mill back in 1896, about how the men in his day would walk off their jobs for a few minutes to get a drink in a near-by saloon. His oldest son, you will learn, died in action during the first World War and, he will just as proudly tell you, his other two boys work in the mill. Finally he will tell you, almost with tears in his eyes, how he has three grandsons working in the mill and that "little Jimmy's wife had a baby boy here a few days ago, and I just saw him last night and he's big enough to handle a pair of tongs already."

Like the soot-covered houses in the shadow of the mills and hanging from the hillsides, these old-timers symbolize the social environment to which they migrated from Ireland, Britain, or the European continent and which they have influenced while raising two generations of steel workers. Pittsburgh's and Homestead's first large immigrations were in the decades preceding the big-time growth of the auto industry. By the time CIO revived union organization and collective bargaining, these and other steel towns had become stabilized over several decades. Sons and grandsons made up most of the working forces in steel, and community disciplines had been established. One of these disciplines, learned through long, bitter experience and passed on from generation to generation, was not to join unions rashly, as that meant strikes, and hardships, and losing out in the mill. SWOC's organizing campaign was based on the appeal to join a modern union that could establish collective bargaining peacefully. SWOC organizers, before getting members, had first to break down the fear that joining the union meant strikes. Many of SWOC's early members were men who had reconciled themselves to losing their jobs before signing the union-application card, and not until it was abundantly clear that SWOC would win in the end—unlike the disastrous 1919 strike—did its membership swell to overwhelming numbers. The years had made steel workers set in their ways. A strike disrupts their community and personal lives so tremendously that, we have found, only the sharpest provocation will cause the men who make steel to take drastic action.

Following union recognition in the spring of 1937, the community disciplines were reflected in the steel mills. The first union contracts were given a chance to work—"Let the union see what it can do" was the prevailing attitude. Steel workers assisted, or at least did not impede, the orderly establishment of union-management relations at the outset of 1937. They did this not because they were any better led or less bitterly opposed than auto workers, but because they were dominated by a social environment that had cast them into accustomed routines which they did not lightly upset. In

Monessen, Aliquippa, the Southside and Hazelwood parts of Pittsburgh, and a few other steel towns the first SWOC contracts were preceded by twenty-four- to forty-eight-hour strikes in 1937. They were more a form of community rejoicing over a victory already assured, however, than a conventional strike against management. Though it would have been better to have enjoyed such an emotional release, most steel towns did not engage in mass rejoicings. Those which did returned to work and stayed at work; they did not periodically disturb their community life by striking. The work stoppages that have taken place under collective bargaining in the steel industry have been neither frequent nor chronic, but the result of the temporary breakdown of bargaining procedures.

The steel towns that suffered long strikes in 1937 felt that they had been discriminated against. They went out for a brief victorious strike and found themselves engaged in a long disastrous one. The "Little Steel" workers had been waiting to see how "Big Steel" would come out and, when they saw a peaceful victory there, joined SWOC by the thousands in pursuit of the same thing. But they were foiled; their union membership turned out to be neither successful nor peaceful. Eighteen SWOC members were killed, many injured. Stoically the "Little Steel" workers took their defeat in stride and went back to work, except those who were "blackballed." Then, significantly, over a four-year period they rebuilt their decimated union. They won reinstatement with back pay and paid vacations for their "blackballed" brothers. They established collective-bargaining relations without a signed contract. And, finally, they secured such a contract early in 1942—all within the framework of their community disciplines without again disturbing their accustomed routines, once they had been restored after the shattering "Little Steel" strike. Communities composed predominantly of newcomers could hardly have achieved such a feat.

A few auto-union leaders, unaware of the dominating influences of the steel towns' social environment, charged

SWOC with being a company union whose members were not as militant as the auto workers. These leaders, since removed from office in the auto union, likewise did not realize that the militancy of auto workers, about which they boasted, was merely a reflection of the auto town's social environment and not something of their own making. This environment in Detroit and Flint, for instance, was the very opposite of that of Pittsburgh, Homestead, and the other steel towns, since the first working forces in steel had been recruited in the eighteen-eighties and eighteen-nineties, when the flow of immigration to the United States was unrestricted. In these decades Detroit's population, for instance, grew moderately. From 1900 to 1910, the decade that witnessed the birth of the automotive industry, Detroit experienced its first big rapid growth—a population gain of sixty-four per cent, to four hundred and sixty-five thousand. In the next decade it jumped one hundred and eleven per cent, to a million people. The nineteen-twenties added another half million, and only during the last decade has Detroit's growth subsided. The period of greatest expansion in the auto industry, significantly, coincided with the period of restricted immigration to this country. Thus almost half of Detroit's auto workers migrated after the 1921 depression from other parts of the United States. The first generation of auto workers is still dominant, therefore, while the second and third generations overshadow the first in steel.

Consequently, the 1937-38 auto-strike epidemic was not something that either union or management leaders could have avoided; it was thrust upon them by their engulfing environment, which the following basic factors have been shaping for almost three decades.

1. Absence of extensive industrial background and discipline of auto workers.
2. Rapid growth of the auto industry.
3. Acuteness of periodic seasonal shutdowns.
4. Severity of the depression in the early thirties.

These factors created a social situation in which waves

of strikes and lockouts could be expected. During the turmoil in the industry's union-management relations in the late thirties we talked to scores of men and women—union leaders, shop stewards, plain union members, passive auto workers, and those who were hostile to the union. Their attitudes toward pay and time lost in strikes, the frequency and outcome of them, though expressed in different terms and from various viewpoints, had a common theme. An auto worker, not hostile to the union nor enthusiastic about the several strikes in which he had been in 1937 and 1938, expressed this theme characteristically.

"I came to Detroit in 1920 as a boy," he began, "to visit an uncle I hadn't seen since before I went to France in '17. When I got back home from the war in '19 work wasn't so good and I bummed from one little pickup job to another. My home's down near Morgantown, West Virginia, and most of the work's in coal mines, and my mother never wanted me to be a miner; so she gave me money to come to Detroit, hopin' my uncle could get me work. He got me in at Briggs, where I worked until the next year when things got real slack here. I went home but found work just as bad there, so after a few months I came back to Detroit. This time I went to work at Fishers. I've worked for Dodge, Chrysler, Budd Wheel, Murrays; you see, I've always been a body man—that's Detroit, work today and look for work tomorrow. The CIO says it's changing that, but they have to show me. I've been in Detroit, here on East Side, for eighteen years almost, and I don't see how the union's going to stop 'em from layin' you off for a couple-month stretch between models, or for a day or week when your line is down. In 1931 and '32 I was out for months at a time, and these past years work ain't been what it used to be. It took me a long time to learn that you've gotta make your dough stretch, but there's no gettin' away from it. You've just gotta save when you're working so you don't starve the rest of the year. I don't see where the CIO makes any difference. I go to work, and the place's on strike," he emphasizes, throwing his head back forcefully, "so I lose a couple days; but I catch up on that at the end of the model season, 'cause they gotta get out so many cars anyway."

We ask about the union.

"Sure, things are better and the union makes gains; but I spent as much time on strike this last year as you usually lose between models. Don't get me wrong. I ain't complainin'. The union's O. K. by me, but I ain't takin' no lead in it. Just belong and pay my dues. Don't matter much to me. Work today or strike or go home 'cause the line's down. All the same to me. You work or you don't—that's Detroit. When they send me home 'cause the line's down, or they quit producing cars for a couple months, nobody cares about what I think on losin' time. Only when it's 'cause of a strike. Detroit's Detroit—always losin' time. No difference, if the union makes me lose time. I'm used to that. You gotta be to get along in Detroit."

This man—typical of his fellow workers—had reconciled and adjusted himself to the unstable conditions of his adopted city. Like the other towns inspired by the auto industry, the motor capital never had a chance to settle down as Pittsburgh and other older steel communities had done long since. From 1902 to 1910 the infant industry was getting started in a hectic atmosphere. Detroit more than doubled in size in the next decade as the industry grew, seemingly without an end. The 1921 depression halted growth, and the industry was about to enter a period of consolidation when it burst into its most feverish decade. Mass importations of workers from abroad had been stopped by Congress, and "labor scouts" were sent to the overcrowded coal fields and nonindustrialized states to get auto workers. The twenties in Detroit was a time when an individual auto worker secured jobs in Murrays, Fishers, Budd Wheel, Briggs, Chrysler, and Dodge—all in the space of a few years. By the thousands workers, mostly without any of the usual industrial disciplines, invaded Detroit, Flint, Pontiac, Toledo, and other auto centers for six or seven months of work. They then returned to their homes all over southern, midwestern, and eastern United States and southern Canada until the next rush season in auto. The industry was so busy its workers never got a chance really to settle down, to get a feeling of really "belonging" in the auto towns. Steel workers, though they also came mostly from a nonindustrial environment, arrived three to four decades earlier and through the generations acquired the industrial disciplines and a sense of "belonging," if not to their steel towns at least to the parts dominated by their particular nationality group.

Not so in auto. Before the industry could become stabilized the 1930-32 depression seized it, and the men and women dependent on autos for a livelihood were thrown into unemployment. Chronic seasonal unemployment had already made the auto towns unstable, but the mass unemployment of the depression made the instability acute. The years 1931 and 1932 saw relief riots. The years 1933, 1934, and 1935 were lean, hard years for auto workers, completely idle at least three to four months a year and only partially employed the rest of the time except for a few peak months of auto output—certainly not the kind of work opportunities conducive to a stable social environment. In steel the depression also virtually destroyed work opportunities, but steel workers bunched up and stuck close to their homes awaiting an upturn; while the itinerant auto workers of the twenties became stranded in the auto towns or went "home." Gradually, in '35 and '36, they began to return to Detroit, Flint, and other auto centers as the industry picked up. Then came the 1936-37 auto boom, the first since 1929, and along with it unions, collective bargaining, and a strike epidemic, dramatized by the sit-down technique, that frightened a nonunion industrial nation into embracing collective bargaining.

So unstable were social conditions among auto workers that their strike epidemic became almost chronic. This was especially true of the vast majority who had stuck, by choice or otherwise, close to the auto plants that enjoyed only sporadic bursts of activity during the early part of the thirties. News commentators attributed the strikes to the assembly line, to the "reds and radicals," and to the "agitators and irresponsible leaders of labor." These and other superficial explanations built a public opinion that to this day is not fully aware that the 1937-38 strike wave in the auto industry was merely an expression of the social instability prevailing in auto communities. A hindsight reappraisal shows that the auto towns' social environment, through a hectic strike period, forged an instrument—labor unions—to stabilize auto-plant and community life. The extent to which the auto workers' union had done this already in part, and promises to complete it in the current and succeeding decades, is proof of the fact that not the assembly line, or agitators, or "irresponsible leaders," but social conditions were at the root of the epidemic of strikes and lockouts in the auto industry.

Both the union and management administrators of collective-bargaining contracts in the auto industry have been greatly influenced by the factors that go to make up the composition of a community. Though they experienced more work stoppages under their contracts during the 1937-40 period than did the steel industry, in many ways they were more successful—because the seniority rules worked out by the auto-contract administrators, as well as union organization among auto workers, contributed to the development of a stable, peaceful, and productive environment in the hitherto turbulent and unstable auto communities. This development by no means is complete, but it demonstrates how industrial peace is as much the outgrowth of a community's environment as it is the result of sound union-management relationships. The latter is such an important factor in a local environment, however, that the two are inseparable. But, no matter how conducive the social make-up of a community may be to peaceful relations, union and management leaders must actively continue the collective-bargaining process day in and day out.

Perhaps one of the most vital influences collective bargaining brings to bear upon a community's environment is the manner in which it provides job security and, in turn, family security. Seniority, the subject of the next chapter, is the method by which collective bargaining attempts to assure this security that is so essential to the development of peaceful and constructive union-management relationships.

Chapter V: Quest for Security

Workers acquire a qualified property interest in their jobs under a collective-bargaining contract.

In the days of feudalism the vassal could say to his lord, "You can give me land to till, sheep to herd, and other chores to do. You can make me fight your wars, and truly I am yours to do with as you choose; but, alas, you must feed, and clothe, and shelter me!"

The chattel slave, less than a hundred years ago in our own country, could say to his master, "You can whip me, you can make me do your work, you can sell me on the slave mart, and you can acquire me by auction; but, praise the Lord, you must give me food to eat, garments to wear, and a place to rest my weary body between long hard labors!"

For freedom, liberty, the right to stake a claim and say it is his, to go in business for himself, to be independent and on his own, the common man down through the centuries risked, gave up, or had taken from him his security. In return he gained a free heritage, but in gaining it jeopardized a vital essential to his family well-being—security, as the Industrial Revolution created the largest group of insecure individuals in the history of mankind. To his employer the industrial worker, for all his advantages over the vassal of the fourteenth and the slave of the nineteenth century, could not say, "You can pay me what you please, you can work me as long as you decree, and you can make me work in a firetrap and under unhealthy conditions; but, damn your soul, you must employ me so that I can eat, and sleep, and exist!"

Collective bargaining in England and more recently in the United States of America has tried, with some success, to recapture for the industrial worker that security enjoyed by the vassal and the slave—without losing the great advantages of a free society. In other countries these "great advantages" seemed so empty to the common man that he bartered them for some old-fashioned security with tyranny.

That they proved no bargain for him in these countries is not our present concern, except in so far as this holds a warning for us: that the failure of a free society to provide the common man with the necessary requirements of personal security may tempt him to barter his free heritage for these minimum requirements of family happiness. The quest for such security is one of the compelling motives for union membership; literally, the industrial worker joins his union to be able to say to his employer, among other things, "This is my job, and as long as I fulfill it and until I voluntarily choose to give it up, under my union's contract with you, you cannot take it away from me, nor can you compel me to take a lesser one, nor can you deny me a better one to which I am entitled —except, of course, in case of industrial layoffs."

The unions have introduced a new doctrine into American industry (accepted for many years by British industry); namely, once management has hired an employee who makes good, except under agreed-upon circumstances, it must continue to give employment, or preference for employment, to that employee until such time, if ever, as he chooses to quit his job. Thus under union-management relations, governed by collective-bargaining contracts, workers acquire a qualified property interest in their jobs—which they seek to make as inviolate as the most sacred interests of real-estate property.

Property is purchased with labor. For example, John Doe buys an acre of land for one hundred dollars which he spent one year acquiring. Consequently, for one year's service he acquired an acre of land. No other person can take this land from John Doe unless he voluntarily sells it or forfeits it by failure to pay taxes or other encumbrances. The same principle, varying only in detail, entitles the industrial worker to a qualified property interest in his job. John Doe, for instance, works for the ABC Steel Company five years as a craneman, longer than any other qualified worker. This entitles him to the ownership of the craneman's job unless he voluntarily gives it up or forfeits it by the infraction of a rule agreed upon by his union and management. Another worker with only four years of service, say, has second claim to the same job, but he will not own it outright until he has worked on it longer than any other qualified worker. Thus by virtue of years of service workers acquire possession of their jobs, which is implemented by the seniority provisions of collective-bargaining contracts. As each seniority rule is agreed upon by unions and management, and every new interpretation becomes a precedent for similar cases to follow, a body of common law in industry is being built up that guarantees to each worker a property interest in his job. Union membership assures job protection, and only those individuals who claim seniority or property rights in a job as their sole asset—with children, a wife, sickly mother-in-law, doctor bills, etc., ad infinitum, as liabilities—can fully appreciate how precious and valuable—dearer, in many ways, than life itself—is this asset of seniority.

Seniority, of course, is only part of organized labor's program to provide workers with some measure of security.

Today, as a result of organized labor's efforts over the years, the industrial worker can say to his employer:

"If I am hurt while in your employ, you must pay me workman's compensation!

"If I am killed while in your employ, you cannot cast adrift my widow and children without paying workman's compensation!

"When you lay me off because of slack work, I shall receive unemployment-compensation benefits!

"When you lay me off because I'm too old to work any more, I shall receive old-age benefits!

"You may not fire me for union activities!"

To these measures of security, collective bargaining adds seniority or job protection which enables the industrial worker to say to his employer:

"This is my job to have and to hold as long as I do it well and keep within the rules!

"You shall not fire me wantonly, without cause, or on the spur of the moment!

"You shall not make me suffer from discrimination or favoritism!

"You shall not pass me by in promotions indiscriminately!"

Seniority is only a step in organized labor's social-security program, since workers still suffer from technological unemployment, seasonal and cyclical idleness, lack of an adequate health-insurance program, and other causes of insecurity. These causes, in the main, are beyond the scope of union-management relations at the level of the individual productive unit or competitive company, and require the concerted action of management, government, and organized labor on an industry-wide and national basis. Nor does seniority provide any measure of security for the large body of citizens, mostly young and old people, for whom there are insufficient work opportunities; their problem likewise requires national action for solution. Collective bargaining provides some measure of security only for those individuals who have jobs, and our concern in this discussion is with the manner in which seniority assures job protection to workers after they secure, and prove qualified to hold, a job.

Each group of workers strives for the kind of seniority rules which it thinks will provide the greatest amount of job protection.

On May 24, 1938, when the steel industry was operating at thirty per cent of capacity, one of the authors received the following letter from the wife of a steel worker.

I am taking the privilege of writing you concerning the CIO and the ——— steel company.

I suppose you are aware of the fact there is dissension among the men and the union, the cause being the company has taken orders from No. 1 department where they were having trouble over seniority rights into another dept. stating it was an economy measure—a very clever trick to undermine the union, because the men voted for department seniority.

The president [of the union] said these men are just the same as fired. I think the union led these men into a trap. They certainly knew the strip mill would displace men—the covered wagon can't compete with the strip. Why didn't they make some agreement in case one department was discontinued?

The old men have no chance of getting in any place even though things start up again. My husband has been employed up there 26 years, and after all these years he is let out. What chance would he have to get a job anywhere else I ask you? We have five children and need an income now worse than we ever did before.

The only satisfaction the union gives the men is if their department starts they will get work. Everyone is agreed they will never have enough orders to run both depts. I always was under the impression that the union protected the men—in this case it is protecting the company because the men were not intelligent enough to see the handwriting on the wall and vote for plant seniority.

I think that is where they needed a good union to inform them what to do for their own protection—now over two hundred men have withdrawn from the union and it threatens to spread all over the mill—the men are scared to death. Before the company took care of their old men just as things picked up they put them back to work. They feel the union has been a detriment instead of a blessing.

I think myself they have made a horrible mistake by allowing them to centralize their orders in one dept. Mr. Golden I would be very grateful to you if you would find time to drop me a few lines to enlighten me on this matter.

Very truly yours,

[signed] Mrs. Henry M——

If the union had voted for plant seniority and this lady's husband had had only seven years of service in the shipping department, she would have protested that "the men have been trapped into voting for plant seniority, and my husband was bumped out of his job [or had to share thirty-two hours of work per week down to twenty-four or sixteen] because some man from the sheet mill has twenty-six years of service with the company, and this entitles him to take the bread out of my children's mouths. My husband only makes seventy-five cents an hour, and those sheet mill men who earned three and four dollars an hour for so many years should be better able to stand the depression than my husband. I think seniority should be within each department only."

Seniority rules begin from the bottom, and seldom are handed down from the top. Each worker or group of workers asks only one question about a proposed seniority rule, "How will it affect me?" Mrs. Henry M—— knew little, and cared less, about the general principles of either plant or department seniority; her concern, eloquently stated, was, "We have five children and need an income now worse than we ever did before." That her family might have been better off with department seniority in the long run was no consideration to her, because she felt, as a British economist once said, that "in the long run we are all dead." Her needs were immediate. It is the unhappy lot of industrial workers that their needs are always immediate. Thus their prevailing attitude is to take care of things today and worry about tomorrow when it becomes immediate, and in formulating their demands for seniority rules each group of workers is guided by a single idea—what will guarantee the greatest amount of job protection!

The minutes, dated October 15, 1938, of a meeting of all grievance committeemen from the nine plants of the Ohio River Steel Corporation give conclusive testimony on the approach of workers to the problem of seniority.

> . . . The Steelville committeeman stated that inasmuch as they had gained all they could out of plant seniority he thought that now was the time to drop it. This was in regard to the Hot Mill men, who had gained by plant seniority. . . .
>
> King, of Pinewood, talked at length on how they were working seniority in the Pinewood plant; in some instances they are using plant seniority and at other times they are working departmental. . . .
>
> The Irontown committeeman explained that they are working under verbal agreements of departmental seniority. He explained one case where they used plant seniority, but after a meeting with the supervisors they again agreed to work under departmental seniority, and in his opinion departmental seniority

should be used as all had been gained in the Steelville plant that could be under plant seniority. . . .

Ohio River Steel, to the extent it followed seniority at all before the union's inception, practiced departmental seniority rules. The first SWOC contract was signed in the spring of 1937 and, though the seniority provision was of the most general sort, departmental seniority was followed under it. In December of that year the corporation was compelled to abandon, on a permanent basis, an obsolete hand-style sheet works, employing fifteen hundred, that was a department of an integrated steel mill. An obsolete tin-plate works, also employing fifteen hundred, was abandoned likewise at another, but nonintegrated, steel works. In each instance an entire department was eliminated, and under departmental seniority the men involved were out in the cold. The situation created at both works defies description; work was slack, opportunities for transfers almost nonexistent, and the communities were in a social-revolutionary frame of mind. In Lakesmouth the displaced sheet-mill workers got the entire local union to vote for a general strike in all the corporation's mills "for the purpose of seeing that the sheet mill men are taken care of." That the strike almost took place, and would have if operations had not been so low, is indicative of the nature and intensity of the problems the displacements caused both management and the union. Out of all this came a conviction of management that seniority should be on a plant basis. The union demanded and secured plant seniority for the time being, which served to strengthen management's conviction further. In May, 1938, the corporation issued to its managerial forces an interpretation of the contract's seniority clause, which placed the major emphasis on plant-wide seniority; continuous service was defined as "the current unbroken service in the plant or mill." The operating vice-president and his assistant in charge of industrial relations told us, "We have learned from experience that this is the best way to handle seniority."

In the next three years they learned that their experience

had not been complete when they issued their pronunciamento in the spring of 1938, as it violated two principles of group relations, namely:

1. Policies affecting the security or job protection of workers cannot be formulated and handed down from the top by either management or union leaders, or both.
2. Each group of workers has to work out its own destiny in its own way, on seniority or any other matter that vitally affects its welfare.

We tried to get the corporation to make its seniority rules more flexible to meet different conditions in the nine plants, but in vain. Plant-wide rules were carried to such an extreme that while one employee was temporarily laid off because his department was slack another employee from another department on the basis of plant service would be transferred to his job when operations picked up. In such cases the temporarily laid-off employee cried, "They've robbed me of my job!" The objective of such transfers, of course, was to stabilize employment as much as possible by giving a few extra days' work to employees whose departments were working only part time. We agreed with this objective and favored such transfers, but only into departments that did not have any of their employees temporarily laid off. Otherwise the employees, whose property interest in their jobs was based on departmental service, felt, and rightly so, that someone was stealing their jobs. But the corporation could not see it and supported its position by claiming that an employee was an individual on the pay roll, while SWOC contended, and most firms agree, an employee is an individual on the pay roll or temporarily laid off through no fault of his own. In an intraoffice memo one author wrote to the other about Ohio River Steel's seniority pronunciamento:

> The management will never make these proposals on seniority work. The men will continually raise hell, and I guess the only workable course is to let the management learn from experience,

and it will abolish some of the rigidity of these rules case by case and plant by plant.

The controversy between SWOC and Ohio River Steel raged for three years and, though the management still holds to plant-wide seniority in many respects, the June 11, 1941, contract recognized that the best way to formulate seniority rules is from the bottom up, and that each group of workers in the several plants should work out its own seniority setup. After providing for departmental seniority in cases of promotion or demotion and for plant seniority in cases of inter-department transfer, increase or decrease of forces, the contract reads:

> It is understood and agreed that the preceding rules represent a general standard, the application of which is subject to local rules to be jointly agreed upon between the Grievance Committee and Management of each plant or mill.

For all practical purposes in each of the firm's nine plants and mills this amounts to departmental seniority, except in those instances where plant-wide rules provide the men affected with better job protection.

In many situations the union ranks are split on what kind of seniority rules should be in force, as one set of workers will get better job protection through departmental seniority, or even job seniority, than through plant-wide seniority, which another set of men prefers. Here the rule of the majority is the only solution, for all a union can hope to do is serve the best interests of the greatest number of its members. Workers generally are persistent in recognizing that the fellow with the longest years of service should get the "breaks." At any rate, management can feel confident that when the union committee presents seniority demands they have been carefully threshed out in the union meetings and among the members in the plant. But, of necessity, the union's approach to seniority rules is frankly opportunistic; it is job protection the union members want, and they fit seniority rules into this desire and not job protection into seniority rules.

Seniority is an instrument designed to eliminate favoritism and discrimination.

"It's not what you know, but who you know that counts in this plant," a member of the union negotiating committee told the vice-president of a large aircraft firm during the discussion on seniority.

The vice-president retorted, "That's a dastardly statement."

When this sharp interchange of words was repeated by one of the authors at a mass meeting of the local union, it struck a popular chord. Whether or not the committeeman's feeling was justified is secondary; the fact that he and many other workers in the plant felt this way, however, is significant. A group of workers, as a rule, will tolerate almost any kind of reasonable situation, as long as it is felt everyone is getting his share of the "breaks" and all are getting equal treatment. When someone gets a "break" that the group feels is favoritism or discrimination, dissension develops and a grievance is filed in protest; and, if the grievance-adjustment machinery is not working properly, a strike may result to correct the "injustice." The aircraft firm's vice-president, being several steps removed from the plant, did not know that his policy of "rewarding the deserving on the basis of application and ability" had been subverted into a labyrinth of shop politics—"playing favorites"—in making work assignments, granting promotions, and giving individual wage raises. We knew this to be the case, because that is why the thousand men in the plant had so solidly joined the union.

One of the union organizer's standard appeals to an unorganized group of workers is, "Join the union so you can get a square deal. When you get a contract with seniority protection you don't have to worry every morning when you get to work whether you'll have a job when you come home at night; you won't have to worry about the boss firing you because he don't like the color of your hair, or of promoting a younger man to a job you should have because he's a member of the same fraternal order as the boss; and you won't have to shine the foreman's shoes [or some other colloquialism] to get a nickel raise or a better job—it'll be yours if you have the years of service to get it and can do the job. Join the union for the sake of your wife and kids." . . . This is perhaps the organizer's strongest appeal, and consequently seniority is one of the most difficult provisions of a contract to administer in the early stages of collective-bargaining relations.

Seniority—a set of rules designed to give workers prior claim to a job over others with fewer years of continuous service, provided they can fulfill its requirements—is the only equitable method, proved practical of administration, to eliminate favoritism and discrimination among a group of workers. The arbitrary decision of management is replaced with a set of rules. The human element—prejudice, inclination to favor one individual over another for intangible or other reasons—in governing the relations of a group of workers to one another and to management is reduced to a minimum. "Seniority" and not John Smith, or Paul Jones, or some other management official, gets the brunt of denunciation and criticism from a worker who is dissatisfied with a decision that adversely affects him and, being an inanimate set of rules, seniority can absorb these periodic outbursts of emotion graciously. And, unlike an unsatisfactory arbitrary decision of management, an equally unsatisfactory result of a seniority rule is more palatable to the aggrieved individual, because the latter is something of his own creation. He has had a voice in its formulation and, what is more important, he can change it if he can persuade a majority of his fellow workers that it is unfair. If a majority, however, feels the rule is fair, then the aggrieved individual has the assurance that when the shoe is on his foot he, and not the other fellow, will get the "break." But there is no such assurance in an arbitrary decision of management. Further, when an arbitrary decision of management gives the right fellow the "break," other workers have no guarantee that they will get similarly fair treatment when it is their turn, whereas a seniority rule carries this implicit guarantee for every member of a group of workers.

The introduction of seniority rules into the management of a productive enterprise is a radical departure from most previous practices. This is evident from the bitter controversies between union and management officials over the interpretation and application of the seniority provision of their initial contract. Promotions and decreases of forces are the two principal points of controversy.

"When I have a vacancy to fill, must I give it to the oldest employee, and pass up younger employees who I think are better qualified to fill the job?" management asks.

"When I have to cut my forces, do I have to let some really good men go just because there are men with more years of service in my plant?" management asks.

Both questions are typical and self-revealing; management may have felt that it has always taken care of its oldest employees, but, in practice, foremen, superintendents, and other supervisory officials—not bound by seniority rules—have been guided by considerations other than an employee's length of continuous service, in promotions, the cutting of forces, transfers, and the recalling of furloughed workers. The invariable reply of the union to these two questions is, "Yes, lay the youngest off; and the oldest man should always get a crack at any advancement in his department [plant or crew, as the case may be]."

Management's consistent comeback is, "We are responsible for the efficiency of this plant, and we have got to see that the best employees are taken care of. We cannot give up our right to use our working forces to the best interests of the company as a whole. The union isn't going to tell us whom we can place on a job, or whom we must lay off when work is slack."

Essentially this is a reflection of management's desire to maintain its freedom of arbitrary decision in matters of promotions, layoffs, etc., which is diametrically opposed to the fundamental tenets of seniority. The arbitrary power to promote, lay off, etc., is one of the prerogatives management loses under collective bargaining; these matters become the joint concern of management and union officials, to be determined by an agreed-upon set of rules. Most management officials, in our experience, have found it difficult to become accustomed to this basic change in the determination of the relations of a group of workers to one another and to management. Many firms instruct their supervisory officials to select "the best of the oldest employees, and not the oldest of the best employees" in promotions, force reductions, etc. Naturally the union vigorously opposes such an interpretation, because it fails to do away with management's arbitrary powers. It abrogates seniority rights.

"If the boss says I ain't as good as the next fellow, then he can throw my continuous-service record in the wastebasket," the dolomite pitcher or steel roller objects, adding, "Well, I say that ain't seniority."

The union's interpretation of seniority is that the oldest employee capable of performing the job should get the promotion or be retained on the pay roll during a period of force reductions in preference to another employee equally qualified to perform the work but with fewer years of continuous service. Eventually the union's interpretation prevails, because it cannot provide its members job protection as long as management has the arbitrary power to promote, lay off, and so forth. Thus the conflicts over seniority narrow down to the question of an employee's ability to perform the work at hand. All other matters of promotions, demotions, transfers, increases or decreases of forces, are governed by a set of rules, called seniority. The management of a productive enterprise by a set of rules, instead of arbitrary decision, is the only practical method of reducing favoritism and discrimination to a minimum, and seniority, being based on length of continuous service, is an equitable method of guaranteeing fair treatment to a group of workers. As long as a worker can perform the work, his equity in his job is protected against wanton discrimination and petty favoritism of lower supervisory officials.

The power to discharge should not be lodged in a single individual.

Pat McGinnis, a bricklayer earning one dollar and twenty-eight cents an hour in the open-hearth department of a major steel mill, climbed out of the ladle he was relining and walked to the other end of the pit. He scaled a huge ladle and called down to his friend Joe, who was setting a nozzle, "Do you have any spare tea balls?"

"Ya, in my locker. It's open; take a couple, but don't forget to pay me back," Joe shouted up.

For several minutes Pat and Joe kidded each other—until the foreman hollered, "Hey, Pat, what the ——— are you doin' up there? Get back to your ladle and start slappin' them brick together, you big lazy ———" The foreman heaped a lot of abuse on Pat while he was climbing down from the top of the ladle.

"Say, listen, I ain't done nothing wrong," Pat remonstrated. "What are ya always pickin' on me for? And I don't like those names you called me."

The foreman exploded, "Why, you Shanty Irishman, I've a notion . . ."

His speech was temporarily halted by a series of hard blows to the face and body. Pat was on the throwing end of the fists. The foreman tried to fight back, but Pat floored him quickly again.

Lying on his back, the foreman, his nose bleeding profusely, shrieked, "You're fired, you're fired, you're fired, you're . . . huh . . . oh . . ."

Pat had picked him up and knocked him down for the third time.

By now a large group of men had gathered around to see the fight—quite a rarity, not in the town, but certainly in the mill. The superintendent broke through the cordon of men, demanding, "What's goin' on here?" The situation needed no explanation. Turning to Pat, who was calling the foreman too yellow to stand up and fight, the superintendent commanded, "Get out, McGinnis. Go draw your time."

The men did not quietly return to their jobs. One of them shouted, "If Pat goes, we all go." Soon they all picked up the slogan, and before the superintendent could get the foreman on his feet the entire bricklaying crew was on the way out of the mill—it was a strike in violation of the contract.

Forty-eight hours later the SWOC field director got the bricklayers to return to work with the understanding that Pat's case would be taken up promptly and, if necessary, referred to arbitration. Management refused to reinstate Pat and his case went to an arbiter, who rendered his decision several weeks later. It read:

On November 12, 1940, Patrick McGinnis, a brick-mason, was formally discharged for striking his foreman while on the job. Four pertinent facts seem perfectly clear:

1. McGinnis' action in striking his foreman was definitely an act of insubordination.

2. On the morning of Nov. 12th he was not using his time with sufficient effectiveness to have avoided comment from his foreman.

3. His record of employment with the company was evidently not of such a character as to support the conclusion that he was irresponsible, quick-tempered or subject to sudden irrational surges of temper.

4. The foreman definitely contributed to McGinnis' emotional outburst on Nov. 12th. The exact nature of his remarks and actions is of secondary importance. Whether the outburst was disproportionate to the seriousness of his comments is beside the point. Explanation of McGinnis' response lies in the pattern of their relations over a period of time rather than in the incident of Nov. 12th. . . .

My decision is based on these conclusions:

1. Injustice with respect to discharge is an admissable cause for reinstatement. . . .

2. McGinnis' act of insubordination cannot be approved or white washed. There is no justification or excuse for McGinnis' outburst. There may be reasons to explain it, but it still remains an act of insubordination and as such merits disciplinary action. . . . McGinnis had no right to take matters into his own hands

and seek personal settlement with his fists. His insubordinate act therefore must be strongly disciplined. . . .

3. Both the foreman and company management must share in the responsibility for McGinnis' collapse of self-control. The only evidence to support the company's position that the foreman was not "riding" McGinnis consists of his denial of the charge, a normal reaction in self-defense, and of McGinnis' failure to file a formal grievance or to lodge a complaint with higher executives. Undoubtedly McGinnis should have filed some such complaint but his failure to do so doesn't in itself constitute proof that he never was "ridden." The weight of evidence is all in favor of the reality of a long-time damming up of bitterness based upon personal animosity between the two men; and the foreman was a definite party to this process. . . . McGinnis' precipitate act was certainly not without cause. . . . Certainly a less inept foreman and a better informed management would have gone far in preventing the development of the crisis of Nov. 12th. . . .

4. The discharge of McGinnis is an unfair extreme of disciplinary action that is not warranted in view of all pertinent considerations. The seriousness of discharge to the employee needs no elaboration. It represents the extreme of economic punishment. It not only involves a cessation of earning power with all attendant hardships, but mars the man's record thus complicating and extending economic woes. Discharge then should be resorted to only in the most extreme instances where its use is beyond dispute. Disciplinary control can be maintained without wielding the discharge shillalah whenever the need for discipline is provoked. Discharge should follow insubordination only where the insubordinate employee alone is at fault and has shown that he is too much the non-conformist for effective teamwork in the organization. . . . Part of the contributory responsibility for McGinnis' fall from grace is properly borne by the foreman and higher executive management. His discharge is unjust; strong disciplinary action is proper.

5. The strike of the brick-masons was completely inexcusable and deserves the highest censure but is not a factor in determining the justice of McGinnis' discharge. . . . The "wild-cat" strike in violation of the Agreement is completely without justification and properly censurable. Machinery for the peaceful settlement of grievances is provided in the contract. The Agreement is the

way of peace to which both parties pledge themselves. . . . The "wild-cat" brick-masons' strike that occurred on Nov. 12th to 14th was clearly a violation of the Agreement, illegal, and severely to be censured. . . .

It is important that both parties to a labor agreement recognize the fundamental truth that legalism is a subordinate consideration in operating under that agreement. The contract and the negotiating process on which its origin and application rest are in reality a way of life. If legalism is permitted to intrude and dictate action, the effectiveness of the document as a method of working together is needlessly crippled. This suggestion does not ignore the legal basis of the Agreement. Far from it, it merely relegates the question of narrow legalistic rights and implications to a subordinate role.

The action of Patrick McGinnis in striking his foreman on Nov. 12th was an act of insubordination that merited severe disciplinary action. The extreme disciplinary measure of discharge, however, was unjustly severe, since certain shortcomings on the part of both the foreman and higher management contributed to the situation. McGinnis is therefore subjected to a disciplinary layoff of three months beginning November 12, 1940, to and including February 12, 1941. The company is ordered to reinstate McGinnis in its employ as a brick-mason without prejudice with back pay beginning Feb. 13, 1941, to the date of his active reemployment.

Management found it difficult to swallow this decision, but complied with the order and reinstated Pat. The operating vice-president told us later that, in his opinion, the logic of the decision was indefensible. If McGinnis had killed the foreman, he argued, then according to the arbiter's decision the company would have had to pay him back pay, except for two months, until he would have been electrocuted, if the law had given him such punishment. The discharge of a worker is not a logical question or, as the arbiter pointed out, a legalism; it is a vital human act that runs to the heart of group relations, and requires treatment accordingly. The importance of the discharge question to industrial peace is demonstrated by the statistical, but nonetheless revealing, fact that two out of every five "wildcat" or illegal strikes engaged in by SWOC locals have been precipitated by the abrupt, arbitrary discharge of a worker. The discharge in most of these cases, of course, was the spark that set off a smoldering fire. Industrial peace can be promoted by throwing away this box of matches—the sole power of one individual to take the livelihood away from another—in favor of a set of rules providing that decisions on discharges should, in fact, be made by several persons to assure equitable consideration and treatment.

This principle has been accepted by most firms under contract with SWOC. The collective-bargaining contract between SWOC and the Carnegie–Illinois Steel Corporation, dated April 1, 1941, for example, provides:

Discharge Cases: . . . Management agrees that a member of the Union shall not be peremptorily discharged from and after the date hereof, but that in all instances in which Management may conclude that an employee's conduct may justify suspension or discharge he shall be first suspended. Such suspension shall be for not more than five (5) calendar days. During this period of initial suspension the employee may, if he believes that he has been unjustly dealt with, request a hearing and a statement of the offense before his superintendent, or the general superintendent, or the manager of the plant with or without the member or members of the Grievance Committee present, as he may choose. At such hearing the facts concerning the case shall be made available to both parties. After such hearing Management may conclude whether the suspension shall be converted into discharge or, dependent upon the facts of the case, that such suspension shall be extended or revoked. If the suspension is revoked the employee shall be returned to employment and receive full compensation at his regular rate of pay for the time lost, but in the event a disposition shall result in either the affirmation or extension of the suspension or discharge of the employee, the employee may allege a grievance which shall be handled in accordance with the procedure of Section 7—"Adjustment of Grievances." Final decision on all suspension or discharge cases shall be made by the Company within five (5) days from the date of filing of the grievance, if any. Should it be determined by the Company or by an umpire in accordance with Step 5 of the Grievance Procedure that the employee has been discharged or suspended unjustly, the Company shall reinstate the employee and pay full compensation at the employee's regular rate of pay for the time lost.

The arbitrary power of management, as in the matters of promotions, layoffs, and so forth, is replaced by a set of rules that prescribe in what manner an employee shall be discharged. The hasty, on-the-spur-of-the-moment decision to fire an employee is safeguarded against, and this regular source of conflict in union-management relations is eliminated. Management has to command respect for its authority by using it judiciously and not dictatorially. Each worker gains confidence that as long as he abides by the basic rules governing the loss of continuous service he will get his share of the "breaks." The job insecurity of the days when a single boss, with or without cause, could fire a man who had no recourse to any appeal is removed by the creation of a judicial process in industry through which it is determined whether a worker, suspended upon accusation, has forfeited his property interest in his job.

Workers should enjoy full freedom of opportunity for advancement and promotion.

Lawrence Nelson, general manager of a specialty-steel firm, is unlike most management officials we have met, because he knew and practiced the fundamental principles governing group relations before he entered into collective-bargaining relations with SWOC. He did not have to learn them, as have most management people, the hard way through strikes, lockouts, bitterly contested grievances, and arbitration decisions. He had learned them from his father, and as a worker himself in England and this country. A jolly, full-faced man in his mid-forties, Nelson is characteristically British and talks fast with slight traces of American invasions of his cockney accent. Nelson is the sixth generation of his family with the company, which moved from England at the turn of the century, and he has a son—the seventh generation—working in the mill. We have found

Lawrence Nelson better grounded in the fundamental principles of union-management relations than most management and union officials. His experiences and views on promotions, for instance, are penetrating.

"When I was breaking into the steel business as a young man," Nelson told us during one of our conferences, "I was working in the hot mill. I liked the chaps and got along splendidly with them. They were a fine bunch. My job at the time was a catcher. Though my Dad was an official of the company I had to work my way up the crew, and he left me strictly on my own. Well, the foreman in the department needed two more rollers and he promoted an older man and myself. I was pushed from a catcher to a roller—past twenty-six older men, some of whom had been waiting several years for an opening in a roller's job. I didn't like the idea, and told the foreman I could not accept the job and that he should give it to a more deserving man. I told the men I had done this, but they would not let me do what I thought was the proper thing. Their attitude was, 'Glad you got the break, Larry, but it's rotten.' I vowed to stop such injustice if ever I became head of a department of the company.

"I have never forgotten this experience. Every man in this mill gets his break when it comes his turn. I train all my own men. Nobody hires in here except as a laborer. When there's a vacancy we fill it from the labor gang. I set up a labor department for seniority purposes. A new man starts there and accumulates his seniority. When he is assigned to another department permanently, then his seniority begins anew there; but if ever he gets put back in the labor gang he gets credit for the time he originally put in there. We only lay off through the labor gang. For instance, if I have to cut out one of the hammer crews I don't lay them off; they go back to the labor gang, and the only men that get let out are members of the labor department with only short service records. I furlough them, and they get first preference whenever work picks up again. In a pinch I have hired skilled hammermen, hot millmen, and furnacemen; but I find it doesn't pay. Usually they're the type that don't stick, and my regular men don't like the idea. I have found it doesn't pay to detour a man in at the top. All the men below have been looking forward to someday getting a crack at a top job, and it only stifles them when you break in an outsider that cuts your regular men out of a chance for a better-paying job or one that carries more prestige with it."

He added, thoughtfully, "I follow the same principle with supervision. It used to be that you couldn't get a job bossin' in this mill unless you had the Union Jack draped around your bosom. It's not easy to break long-set traditions, but I have promoted around half the foremen and superintendents from among the Slavs, Italians, and other people of European origin. Of course, most were born in this country; but I have a foreman in the hammer shop who came to America after the first World War. I put him in charge because he was the best man for the job, and he also was the oldest man in point of service in the department. He has done well, and I don't think anyone else could get the co-operation from the men that he does; he's one of them, and commands their respect. Generally, I would say, every man in the mill feels confident that he'll get his break when his turn comes. If he can't do the job, then we have to pass him up for someone who can; but mostly the oldest men are the best fitted. Well, it all gets down to doing the decent thing. Men are the same all over. They appreciate fairness and equal treatment," Nelson concluded.

Our experiences bear out Mr. Nelson's. There should be no arbitrary step at which promotional opportunities for workers stop and outsiders are detoured in for the higher and better-paid jobs. When management violates this principle, a grievance, and frequently a strike, follows. A large steel firm bought out an independent tin-plate manufacturer, thereby immediately displacing thirty-one hundred workers, in the fall of 1940. The nature of the new orders the firm acquired by purchasing the independent tin-plate producer required the use of some of the latter's experienced supervisory personnel. This was especially true in the tin-assorting department, where one of the few groups of female workers is employed in the steel industry. To handle the particular requirements of the new customers, two foreladies from the assorting department of the old firm were hired. Customarily these supervisory positions had been filled from among the regular assorters, and the importation of these two "newcomers" provoked a grievance demanding that the new openings be filled from among the regular assorters. Management explained the reasons why it had departed from the established promotional scheme, but in vain. The girls went on strike, throwing in several other matters for settlement. On this point a compromise was worked out. Four, instead of two, vacancies were created; two of them were filled from the regular assorters, while the two "newcomers" were retained.

Male steel workers act no differently. In another steel mill the labor gang in the mechanical or maintenance department filed a general grievance. Management had hired two millwright helpers from the outside. The custom had always been that laborers in the mechanical department were promoted to helpers' positions for millwrights, pipe fitters, and others. No strike took place, as the grievance-adjustment machinery in this wireworks functions effectively. The case did not get past the superintendent of the department, who had the foreman take the outsiders off the jobs and promote two regular men from the labor gang.

The line of promotion for each well-defined group in an industrial concern should be clear-cut and remain inviolate. A crane operator on Bar-mill Hot-bed Crane Number One in a steel mill filed a grievance alleging discrimination in not being promoted to a vacancy on the soaking-pit cranes. He charged that younger men had been promoted to these higher-paying cranes in the previous year because they were not members of the union and were either good friends or relatives of the foreman. Management replied:

It is necessary to reject the Hot Bed Craneman's request despite his long service for the following reasons:

1. There are no vacancies on any of the soaking pit cranes.
2. There has been in existence in this mill for over twenty-

five years a known line of promotion on the soaking pit cranes as follows:

a. Motor Inspector Helper.
b. Motor Inspector.
c. Soaking Pit Craneman.

3. Present Motor Inspectors have been waiting for vacancies on the pit cranes in line with the established promotional sequence and have been catching extra turns on these cranes as the occasion arises and have established job training for these positions.

4. Present Motor Inspector Helpers have been waiting for opportunities to become Motor Inspectors in line with established promotional sequence.

It is felt that since this line of promotion has been in effect and is well known and since there are at present Motor Inspectors and Helpers who have been waiting hopefully for periods of years for the opportunity to obtain promotion to the next higher rated job it would be definitely unfair to these employees to place the aggrieved employee ahead of them in line of promotion. The aggrieved employee has been promoted from Bar Mill Bed Crane No. 2 to Crane No. 1 in line of succession, but it is not considered that he has established himself in the long established promotional line set up by years of precedent for an opening on the soaking pit cranes.

The management has offered the aggrieved employee and renews the offer to place him in line for promotion to the soaking pit cranes if he is willing to accept employment as a Motor Inspector Helper where he will become familiar with the special type of crane used in the soaking pits by doing the necessary repair work on the cranes and becoming familiar with the mechanism.

Should there be disagreement on the part of the grievance committee at the mill concerning the established line of promotion in accordance with the provisions of the contract, it is appropriate that negotiations be had locally in the interests of determination of mill units to which seniority factors shall be applied. It would seem apparent, however, that until there is mutual agreement on this subject which establishes new units for the application of the seniority factors the promotional sequence which has been in effect should be regarded.

The bar-mill craneman did not want to place himself in the promotional sequence as this would put him on a lower-paying job than he had. Naturally dissatisfied with the disposition of his case, on which the union agreed with management, he made an effort to change the promotional sequence. If he could establish a separate sequence for all cranemen and another promotional sequence for maintenance workers, his long service record would entitle him to the first opening on the soaking-pit cranes. His fellow workers, however, apparently felt that he was trying to use the seniority provision of the contract for his own selfish interests and did not go along with him. Another aspect of this case—promoting maintenance workers to production jobs—is discussed in the next chapter.

Like the increase or decrease of forces, promotion of workers within their respective promotional sequences is governed by a set of rules, commonly known as trial periods. A typical trial-period provision of a SWOC contract follows.

Vacancies: When a new created job or vacancy develops in a department, a notice will be posted on the bulletin boards advising all employees of the department and the plant, who are eligible as to skill and training, of the opportunity to make application for a definite job.

a. The applications of employees, in the department having the new job or vacancy, will be considered first; and after the eligible applications from the department have been exhausted, without filling the job, applications from other departments of the plant will be considered.

b. The applications for each job will be considered on the basis of the employee's qualification as to (1) length of continuous service in the department and (2) ability to perform the duties and requirements of the job in question. From among those employees eligible, the senior one shall have preference.

c. Should there be no applications that can qualify from the department, or other departments, for the job, the superintendent or foreman may select from the department an employee he considers qualified by skill and training and offer the job to him without considering length of continuous service.

d. When an employee has been awarded a job, there will be

a trial period of seven (7) working days for the employee to break in on the new job. Should the employee fail in the opinion of the superintendent or foreman to make good within the seven (7) day trial period, he will have a right to return to his former job. The employee, if dissatisfied with the opinion of his foreman, has the right to present his claim to the Grievance Committee.

e. When a vacancy develops from the promotion of an employee to another job in his own or another department, the vacancy cannot be filled permanently until after the seven (7) day trial period of the promoted employee has expired. Any job that is being filled permanently can be supplied temporarily for not to exceed fourteen (14) days without considering seniority.

Through these or similar rules workers secure full freedom of advancement and promotion—one of the principal reasons why they join unions in the first place. Al Risko, Bert Edwards, John Rider, and the anonymous thousands of industrial workers they typify took to the union out of a feeling of futility with regard to promotion. They look to their union to give them a "break" when advancements open up in their departments or crews, and, like the other motives for union membership, the satisfaction of this one is a prerequisite to peaceful and fruitful union-management relations.

There is no basic conflict between seniority and productive efficiency.

In losing the unrestricted freedom to promote or demote, transfer or discharge, increase or decrease, its working forces solely on the basis of ability, management contends without justification that productive efficiency is impaired accordingly. The greater part of America's basic industries for the last five years has been managing its working forces through a system of seniority rules—giving priority to workers with the longest years of continuous service—and the body of evidence on man-hour output shows that, instead of declining, productive efficiency has been rising at the same or greater rate than before the large-scale advent of collective bargaining and the introduction of seniority. Whether productive efficiency during the 1937-42 period has risen due to, or in spite of, seniority is beside the point; the significant phenomenon is that it has been rising steadily and, therefore, seniority rules inherently do not impede it. Nor is there any likelihood that productive efficiency would have risen any faster if there had been no seniority system in industry, because the growth in man-hour output in the last five years compares favorably with any similar period. This is so for two basic reasons.

1. Morale—that full measure of security on the job provided by seniority contributes to a greater productive efficiency from workers as a group.
2. Experience—time is necessary to attain proficiency on jobs, especially where skills are essential to productive efficiency, and consequently the oldest workers are most likely to be the ablest.

Let us look at these underlying factors more carefully. Morale is recognized universally as being invaluable to the attainment of optimum efficiency in industry. Seniority, properly administered, builds morale; it gives workers, as individuals and part of a group, a real sense of security and job protection. The suspicion engendered among a group of workers by arbitrary acts of management, the confusion growing out of the lack of specific rules governing promotions and layoffs, and the worry and insecurity caused by management's unrestricted power to discharge a worker peremptorily hardly contribute to a wholesome spirit. Seniority eliminates these causes of friction and introduces a large measure of fair treatment.

Specific instances are often cited by management purporting to show how unfair seniority works for a particular individual. These instances are of two varieties: either an ambitious worker with recognized advanced abilities is held back because some other worker has more years of service, or he is laid off for the same reason. The conclusion drawn from such examples is that productive efficiency is reduced, and if management were free to reward such recognized ability costs would go down and operations would be more profitable. Removed from their context, these examples seem to be convincing evidence against seniority and proof that there exists a basic conflict between efficiency and seniority. This line of reasoning holds that the basic objectives of unions in quest of security for their members and of management in pursuit of profitable operations are diametrically opposed to each other. More times than not the gains in output achieved by promoting a worker with outstanding ability, which runs against the group's sense of justice, are offset manifoldly in the loss of morale. In the interests of efficiency it may often be necessary for management to forego the small advantage of fully utilizing the services of an exceptional worker in order to achieve the greatest efficiency of the working forces as a whole. When left to its sole discretion, management is more likely to lose sight of the larger gain for the immediate one accruing from the use of the exceptional worker's services as it sees fit. Seniority sees to it that the larger gain—the morale of the group—is not sacrificed for temporary or short-term advantages. Though intangible, good morale, built upon equitable seniority rules, counts up in dollars and cents.

Seniority contributes to lower costs in other ways. Labor turnover is reduced by the introduction of job rights. *Business Week*[1] significantly reported when shortages in certain skilled workers began to develop in the defense program that:

> In surveying the national scene, Washington is inclined to regard Michigan as the "best performer," the region where labor competition has kept within the most reasonable bounds. To be sure, there are small job shops in the Detroit area that have suffered from pirating, but, on the whole, the state's record is considered exemplary.
>
> In trying to determine why Michigan has been less of a bad actor than her sister states, federal authorities point to . . . the thoroughly unionized condition of the state's principal industries.
>
> Unionism in itself is no insurance against pirating . . . the collective bargaining relationship between a union and an em-

ployer is usually embodied in a written contract which provides, among other things, seniority rules. And rigid seniority systems are considered about the best protection against pirating which a firm can get these days. A few cents more an hour is a much less persuasive inducement to a worker to change jobs if he has to sacrifice a seniority rating attained after years of service.

Employers who have tried to set up seniority plans independent of collective bargaining agreements find them less effective in deterring workers from shopping around for better offers than do employers who have incorporated seniority provisions in union contracts. The reason seems to lie in labor's general philosophy that "what the boss gives, the boss can take away." Hence the greater confidence in a seniority system bulwarked by a union contract.

So important is this consideration of seniority in unionized Michigan that some employers bent on labor raiding have offered workers not only higher wages but also seniority standing equal to that which the worker might have in present employment. In some instances, where terms like those have been offered and accepted, the employer has only made trouble for himself with his own workers. For example, an employer who offered ten years' seniority standing to new machinists had so many of his regular machinists quit and find jobs elsewhere he abandoned the practice.

The savings accruing from a lower labor turnover and the development of a stable working force are tangible, and this direct result of seniority—tying a worker to his job—of course, has a positive relationship to productive efficiency.

Secondly, if seniority does not contribute toward efficiency, certainly it does not impede it. One of the basic industries requiring a large proportion of skilled workers is the steel-foundry industry. A skilled pattern maker is required to make the patterns, and an equally skilled core maker and molder are essential in making the cores and molds for the steel castings. These key jobs in a steel foundry must be staffed with skilled craftsmen. Yet to do so does not require, as some management officials contend, that the foremen and superintendents retain the freedom to reward ability and place the best-suited worker on a job, unrestricted by seniority rules, in the interests of economy and efficiency. The implication of this contention—that seniority rules do not reward ability—is groundless. Ability on these jobs requires experience, and experience takes years. The ablest worker is most likely to be the oldest one in point of service; and a greater number of the ablest workers, or at least as many, will be advanced by following straight seniority—length of continuous service—than by permitting foremen and superintendents, human beings that they are, arbitrarily to promote or retain during a layoff those workers who, in their judgment, are the ablest. The number of able workers held back in promotions or laid off during slack operations because other workers outrank them in years of service will hardly exceed the number held back or laid off because a management official arbitrarily gives preference to a friend, relative, or member of the same fraternal order. We believe, and many management officials have confirmed our belief, that a more efficient working force naturally grows up under a seniority system than under a system where management is completely free to handle promotions, layoffs, and so forth.

Seniority, however, consists of more than mere length of service where union-management relations have reached maturity. Ability to perform the work determines a worker's seniority standing as much as does his length of continuous service. A common seniority provision in collective-bargaining contracts is the following one.

> In the case of promotion or demotion, or transfer, or increase or decrease of forces, the factors to be considered shall be continuous service and ability to perform the work. Where ability to perform the work is relatively equal, length of continuous service shall govern. Failure to agree as to relative ability shall constitute a grievance to be disposed of under the Grievance Section of this Agreement, it being understood and agreed that in the meanwhile the decision of management shall prevail.

Management officials frequently complain that the seniority provision of the contract, like the one quoted above, reads all right, but does not work out that way in practice. "All the union recognizes is length of service, and when we vary from this in a particular case the union promptly files a grievance," management explains. In 1938 we took up the cases of four workers who the local union claimed were laid off because of union activities, while younger men were kept on the job. While arguing the case, management showed us its records for the mill in question. Five hundred and forty-three workers out of fifty-three hundred had been laid off in the preceding seven months. In five hundred and thirty-nine cases management followed length of continuous service exclusively. In only four cases did the mill management feel that there was enough difference in ability to keep these men in preference to those it would have kept had it continued to follow length of service alone. Yet the union protested and charged discrimination; its conception of seniority was length of continuous service, and it recognized no other factor in determining a worker's seniority standing.

This attitude is typical of the more than one thousand SWOC local unions. At its 1940 convention SWOC, through its Wage Scale Policy Committee, declared:

> The second largest group of resolutions submitted deals with proposed revision of contract seniority clauses as related particularly to layoffs, reinstatement of furloughed employees, etc. The Committee feels that the seniority clause in the standard form of contract is ambiguous and permits management, where it is so disposed, to interpret the factors in such a manner as to be unfair and discriminatory toward Union members.
>
> The Committee recommends that every effort be directed henceforth in contract negotiations toward simplifying the seniority clause with length of service the chief factor to be observed.

Some SWOC contracts, mostly with smaller firms, define seniority as length of continuous service, with no other factors. The union's program, frankly, is to interpret seniority as length of continuous service and, where possible, to rule out every other consideration. Frequently management yields to the union's interpretation to avoid controversy, although the contract clearly permits it to insist upon ability to perform the work and other factors. This development in the administration of seniority provisions in collective-bargaining contracts is responsible for the conclusion, which we think is premature, that seniority is bound to conflict with efficiency over the long pull, since it eventually develops into a rigid, inflexible set of rules that recognize no other factors than length of service. But this turn in the administration of seniority is not of the union's own choosing; it has been dictated by management, and can be changed by management.

Workers, as individuals and part of a group, instinctively want others with recognized abilities to move on; this is the mortar of which the dignity of labor is built, and it goes against their natural grain to have to limit and restrict able fellow workers in the enforcement of seniority provisions of collective-bargaining contracts. Then why do they do it? The answer is simple.

The conflict between seniority and productive efficiency, where it exists today, basically is a conflict between union security and efficiency. Rigid, inflexible seniority rules are the symptoms of union insecurity, voluntary membership, the automatic application by management of union-contract benefits to nonunion and union workers alike, the anarchical freedom of union members to withhold their union dues whenever dissatisfied with a union decision, and the other evils of the "open shop." The halfway form of recognition that management has begrudgingly extended labor unions during the last five years is at the root of seniority rules that may interfere with productive efficiency. This fact is clearly observable. In the case of the four workers cited previously the local union admitted their greater abilities over the older workers who had been laid off, but demanded, and secured, their layoff for one reason alone. A variation from the continuous-service yardstick in one instance might open the way for management to use the ability-to-perform-the-work yardstick for purposes of discrimination against union members. When some workers belong to the union and some do not it is an impossible task for the union committee to consistently recognize ability in the determination of seniority standings, because this may entail a decision that a nonunion worker is better qualified than a union member. The only circumstance under which the committee can tell a member that a nonmember has preference over him is when the nonmember has a longer service record.

The union-shop form of recognition, as we discuss later, is not a cure-all, but, almost invariably, it creates confidence among workers that management means to give them fair treatment—from which develops a real sense of job security—and they are disposed to give their union committee authority to assume responsibility for the administration of seniority rules that recognize the importance of skill, ability, and efficiency as well as length of continuous service. Under these conditions a group of workers will not support for long a poor workman, a bad case, or a slacker. The importance of group morale and the natural factor that the oldest is most likely to be the best worker, when implemented by the real sense of security that flows from the union-shop form of recognition, determine the intrinsic nature of seniority. Instead of being impeded, productive efficiency is advanced by seniority rules whose objective, in the first instance, is job protection for the men and women working in America's basic industries. Economic betterment, an equally powerful union objective, is the concern of the next chapter.

Chapter VI: Distribution of Earnings

A prime objective of collective bargaining is the redistribution of the proceeds of production.

Of all the motives for union membership the economic one is the most difficult to satisfy. It is the ageless story of the people at the bottom of the economic ladder seeking more of the necessities and some of the finer things in life. The economic objective of organized labor is not higher hourly wage rates, but a higher plane of living for workers. Raises in hourly earnings are pursued as a means of redistributing the proceeds of production, of distributing to workers, who make up the bulk of the population, a larger share of industry's income. Thus workers' wage demands, based on the contention that the fruits of industry are divided inequitably between owners and workers, constitute a constant pressure for a larger share of the nation's annual income.

Industry, as represented by management, has an entirely different objective. It is higher profits. To achieve it, management, of necessity, tries at least to preserve the present division of the proceeds of production every time organized labor secures a wage raise. This is done by the use of two powerful weapons. One is the freedom to cut costs by the introduction of technological changes, and the other is to nullify each redistribution of industry's income that organized labor achieves through wage raises by passing the cost of it on to consumers in higher prices. The history of wages, prices, and technological changes in the steel industry from August, 1936, to September, 1939, graphically illustrates the basic conflict between the objectives of organized labor and those of management in collective bargaining.

This revealing economic history was presented to the Temporary National Economic Committee[1] by Philip Murray. He testified on April 12, 1940:

In 1936 and 1937 the Steel Workers Organizing Committee raised average hourly earnings for hourly, piece work, and tonnage workers twenty-six percent, or from 66.8 cents per hour in August, 1936, to 84.3 cents per hour in September, 1937 (both months being comparable in production). During this same period total monthly payrolls rose in proportion to average hourly earnings—a monthly payroll rise of a little more than fourteen and one-half million dollars, or from $52,200,000 to $66,800,000.

This was a substantial contribution to national purchasing power of which the SWOC has been justly proud. . . . However, the SWOC has been helpless to prevent the steel industry from taking it away through technological changes. . . . By September, 1939, two years later, when production returned to the same level of September, 1937, total monthly payrolls failed to likewise return to the level of September, 1937. In fact, total monthly payrolls in September, 1939, were virtually what they had been before the twenty-six percent increase in average hourly earnings, or $52,900,000. Thus from August, 1936, before the increase in hourly earnings, to September, 1939, total monthly payrolls merely increased by one and two-tenths percent, or to the same extent as production. In other words, despite the increase in hourly earnings, the benefits of technology are not being passed on to steel workers in higher total monthly payrolls. The new steel technology has not added to national purchasing power through increasing the industry's monthly wage bill; but, on the contrary, has cut down the national purchasing power of consumers to the extent of a nine percent increase in finished steel prices from 1936 to 1939. . . .

Briefly summarized, the period from August, 1936, to September, 1939, shows that the steel industry, through installation of technological changes, had done the following:

1. Maintained the same labor cost of production ($12.50 of wages per ton of ingots produced) despite an increase of more than one-fourth in hourly wage rates.
2. Eliminated fourteen million dollars from the total monthly pay envelopes of the steel workers from 1937 to 1939.
3. Raised productive efficiency by one-fifth.
4. Displaced thirty thousand steel workers.
5. Increased finished steel prices nine percent.

In other words, the steel industry is able to produce the same amount of steel with thirty thousand fewer workers. The steel workers who are currently employed are receiving more than twenty-six percent higher wages per hour, but at the expense of thirty thousand steel workers who have been displaced and are receiving no wages from the steel industry. . . . Through technological changes the steel industry has eliminated the effect of increased average hourly wage rates on the labor cost of steel production. . . .

Within two years after SWOC redistributed one hundred and sixty-eight million dollars of the steel industry's annual income, the industry recaptured it. The irony of this development is that these effects of technological changes had been set in motion before the birth of the union, and their consequences would have been even more disastrous if the union had not raised wages as much as it did in 1937. Remembering this remarkable feat of steel management, SWOC officials discounted both management's and government officials' claims that another ten-cent-an-hour raise was unjustified in light of the 1937 ten-cent wage raise, and that such a raise in 1941 would result in an inflationary panic. This view was all the more untenable when it is remembered, also, that hours per week were cut from forty-eight to forty in 1937, and still, by September, 1939, the industry could produce as much steel as in 1936 and with thirty thousand fewer workers—when the purpose of the seventeen per cent cut in the work week had been to spread employment. Suggestions that wages be tied to a cost-of-living index—assuming an accurate one could be developed—or to prices, or to the rate of production, therefore, are promptly rejected by organized labor because, in reality, they would result in thwarting the redistribution of industry's income. To tie wages to any of these indices would tend to freeze the present inequitable distribution of industry's proceeds of production.

In this connection the steel industry is typical of America's basic industries. Organized labor proposes to raise the plane of living of American workers, as it did in the spring of 1937, through substantial wage raises that distribute a larger portion of the industry's income to them. Then technological changes eat away at the increases thus gained, and the rising cost of living consumes some more of the increased plane of living. By 1941 the substantial redistribution of the industry's income achieved in 1937 is reduced to meager proportions. Once more organized labor takes a big bite out of industry's share of the national income for the purpose of elevating the plane of living of American workers and their families. Within nine months, from March 15 to December 15, 1941, four-fifths of the rise in real wages is consumed by a nine and one-half per cent increase in the cost of living, and further increases threaten to consume the rest of the ten-cent wage raise. Temporarily time-and-one-half earnings, in part, offset the debilitating effects of the rising cost of living, and the armament program postpones the introduction of technological changes that promise, when the program is completed, to weight the distribution of industry's income still more unfavorably against workers. As a consequence, demands for another substantial increase in wages are inevitable. Organized labor's obligation to its members is to pursue wage increases until the plane of living of American workers is raised as high as economically feasible, and the national annual income is distributed equitably and stays so distributed.

It has become evident to organized labor that the discharge of this obligation is impossible as long as union-management relations are confined to the level of the individual plant and competing company. How can the real wages of workers be raised permanently? What should be the share of the national annual income that goes to wage earners? How should it be determined? What is the highest economically feasible plane of living for workers? How is it to be determined? Is inflation to be fought by restricting wages, or by raising production so that there will be sufficient goods to be purchased with higher wages? How are the interests of consumers to be protected? These, and other, problems cannot be handled adequately in conferences between individual unions and companies; they require the co-operation of national unions in conference with equally representative organizations of management in the respective industries.

But industry-wide collective bargaining is only a partial answer for many of these problems. Still further steps are necessary within the framework of our democratic processes to resolve the conflict between the objectives of organized labor for a greater share of the proceeds of production and those of industry for higher profits. The national co-operation of management, organized labor, and government is essential to assure the success of our armament program and to meet the challenge of postwar economic, social, and political problems. Part Three of this book is devoted to a discussion of industry-wide collective bargaining and national democratic planning.

The springboard of such national efforts, however, is the local productive enterprise. This chapter is concerned with the mutual economic problems of unions and management that can be solved, in whole or in part, at this level, and with the development of patterns of joint co-operation for later use on an industry-wide and national scale.

Unions should participate with management in distributing the proceeds of each firm's production between its owners and workers.

Paternalism is no solution for the dissatisfactions of workers. They do not want anything given to them. The pleasure that management derives from giving things away should be confined to recognized philanthropic enterprises, members of the immediate family, and friends. Workers want to earn their livelihood; they want only what they feel they deserve, and their pride and adult dignity are hurt when management plays the part of father and gives them as gifts a paid vacation, wage raises, Christmas bonus, or something else which, in the first instance, workers feel they have justly earned. A recent president of the National Association of Manufacturers, himself quite a practitioner of paternalism, has seen the error of his ways and declared before a university audience in the fall of 1940, ". . . Employee-relations programs . . . which sprout quickly and are shallowly rooted wither and die as was the case with so many 'welfare' programs during the World War days. They were founded upon paternalistic motives and the American workman resents paternalism." The key to successful union-management relations in this regard is that workers seek through their unions and collective bargaining the opportunity, free and complete, to work out their own destiny in their own way. This ambition is wholesome and honorable, and for management to disregard it leads to strife and turmoil.

The era of collective bargaining into which American industry has been projected during the last five years put an end to the unrestricted freedom of management to decide what proportion of the proceeds of production shall be distributed to workers. This is now a matter for joint negotiations. We have noted in previous illustrations how costly it is for management to ignore its workers and their union in granting economic benefits. In the case of the company that ignored the union in adjusting wage inequalities, the union demanded, and successfully struck for, a paid vacation that, in the first place, it had no intention of seeking. One of the major contributions of organized labor to the nation's welfare as a whole is the extent to which collective bargaining has resulted in more of the tremendous incomes of large corporations being paid out in wages than was the case, say, in the first World War, when these mighty enterprises decided in their infinite wisdom how much of the money that they drained off from the national income should be returned to their workers. The wage-and-profit history of the United States Steel Corporation in the 1916-17 period, marked by the complete absence of unions or collective bargaining, contrasted with the 1940-41 period, graphically illustrates this.

In 1916 the corporation earned a net profit of two hundred and seventy-one million dollars, or fifteen per cent on its net assets, and in 1917 two hundred and twenty-four million dollars, or a twelve per cent return on investment—after all charges, interest, and taxes. Common labor was paid twenty-four and thirty cents an hour respectively in 1916 and 1917. SWOC prevented such an unhealthy economic development in 1940 and 1941. Net profits in 1940 were one hundred and two million dollars, or five and one-half per cent on investment, while in 1941—with the ten-cent-an-hour raise for nine months of the year—its estimated net profits were one hundred and ten million dollars, or a little better than five and one-half per cent on investment. Common labor in this same period enjoyed a raise from sixty-two and one-half to seventy-two and one-half cents an hour. *The New York Times*[2] reported at the end of the second quarter that "the wage increase of 10 cents an hour made by United States Steel Corporation effective April 1 was almost wholly absorbed by the increase in volume of business between the first and second quarters of 1941"; pay rolls were up twenty-two million dollars, but operating results were up twenty million. The corporation may complain that it was stopped, both by SWOC and Congress, from piling up a ten to twelve per cent net profit to take care of anticipated lean years after the armament boom, but this is largely discounted by the federal government's giving the corporation over a hundred million dollars' worth of new plant equipment. In the present emergency organized labor's participation in the distribution of United States Steel's earnings helped to prevent a runaway profit panic like the 1916-17 one and, at least for the time being, redistributed a small part of the nation's annual income.

Thus a single union added sixty-two million dollars a year to the purchasing power of two hundred and ninety thousand workers that the corporation in question had no intention of granting voluntarily. The strength of organized labor in the basic industries, shortly thereafter, secured similar wage increases from virtually every major corporation in the country. As a consequence of union participation in the distribution of these large corporate incomes, workers were better protected. How rising prices have consumed much of this increased purchasing power is another question; the significant fact is that the incomes of these corporations were distributed more equitably between workers and owners as a result of union participation.

Unlike the large corporations, many small ones were not draining off any, or very much of, the 1941 national income to be redistributed. In SWOC's experience these firms fall into two categories:

1. Those that were compelled to grant the ten-cent-an-hour raise, although their financial positions did not warrant it and in so doing they jeopardized their long-run positions, because of the absence of the union-shop form of recognition.
2. Those that granted lesser wage raises because they were not in a financial position to do more, and because the union enjoyed a secure status that permitted it and its members to approach the wage negotiations realistically.

The Peters Steel Company is in the first category. It is located in a noneconomic territory, remote from the major steel-consuming markets; it operates partially obsolete equipment and is dependent upon larger firms for much of its raw materials and semifinished steel. The ten-cent-an-hour wage movement in the spring of 1941 caught the company between rising material costs and frozen steel prices. An anticipated net profit of almost a million dollars for the year 1941 was cut to seven hundred thousand dollars by increased material costs. The ten-cent demand for three thousand workers, if granted, would leave a profit of a little over one hundred thousand dollars—less than a one per cent return on its capital investment. The cost of a strike with little expectation of settling it for less than a ten-cent raise would have eaten up this little profit. SWOC won a ten-cent increase for its members; the company made a net profit of eighty-three thousand dollars for the first six months. For the entire year of 1941 it expected to make about one hundred and fifty thousand dollars.

The attitude of the company's workers was that they wanted and needed the increase and it was up to management to find the money to pay it. The company president explained with tears in his eyes what granting such a raise would mean, but the men had no pity for him. Nor were they worried about what might happen to their jobs after the defense boom was over; they were concerned with the present. Like so many other firms, this one was reaping the results of its shortsighted policies of previous years. Before the men were unionized the company met every threat of unionization with a belligerent statement that if they organized the mill would be moved out of town. Demands for wage increases were invariably met with claims that the company, compelled to pay them, would go out of business. No substantiating evidence was advanced to support these claims, nor was any effort made to educate the men in the intricacies of corporate finances. When the company was making money and could well afford wage increases, like so many others, it cried "Wolf" and had the power to withhold a proper distribution of its income to its employees. Now that the wolf was really at the door, management cried "Wolf" once more; but to the employees it had a familiar echo—and it was ignored. SWOC was powerless to change the course of events. Management insisted that it would never force any employee into the union and that it was SWOC's job to sell itself to the employees. SWOC used the wage demand as an effective selling point.

As the present era of collective bargaining was emerging, management suddenly realized that "our employees don't know as much about the business as they should." Like a swarm of locusts, "Annual Reports to Employees" began to appear. They coincided with organized labor's demands for higher wages and, never having been issued before except in a few firms, gave workers generally the distinct impression that they were anti-wage-raise propaganda. A typical "Report to Employees" reads:

Every person wants to know more about the Company for

which he works, whether it is making or losing money and how much, whether the division between employees and investors is fair . . . the conventional balance sheet, and profit and loss statement, are not easy to understand. They are not designed to answer the main question each employee as an individual, and all employees as a group, want answered. This question is simple and very natural. How was the money divided that the Company received? The financial statement that follows is set up directly to answer this question:

1. For each $1.00 of profit, the Company had to sell $15.16 worth of merchandise.
2. For each $1.00 paid to stockholders in dividends, $15.93 was paid to employees as compensation for their services.
3. For each $1.00 of profit earned, $1.12 was paid in taxes.
4. Total earnings per common share amounted to $5.17. For each dollar thus earned, 39 cents was paid out in dividends, and 61 cents was left right in the business.

Coming in the midst of a unionization wave and demands for wage increases, reports like this one turned out to be a psychological aid to organized labor. Workers waved these reports in the face of management. "Who do you think you're kiddin'?" "Nuts," "Baloney," "Hooey," and other epithets greeted these company publications. Union organizers gathered them by the hundreds, piled them high on the speakers' rostrum at union meetings, and pointed to them as evidence that the company could afford a wage raise. "We'd rather have them put the money in our pay envelopes than into the printing of these booklets. You never saw any around here before we organized," they orated.

Participation in the actual process of distributing a firm's income, and not a report from management, is required to satisfy workers that they are receiving their proper share of the proceeds of production. Collective bargaining affords such participation, but the union-shop form of recognition is essential to the negotiation of wages on the basis of a realistic factual approach. The Peters Steel Company had to pay through the nose, and its employees were forced to jeopardize their jobs over the long-run, because their union was insecure. For example, if the union members had accepted less than a ten-cent raise, and then refused to work with an employee who refused to join the union because he did not get such a raise, management would send the union members home, demanding at the same time that the union live up to the no-strike clause of the contract. Naturally the union did not compromise its demand.

In the case of the Lincoln Steel Company, which falls into the second category, the union compromised its ten-cent-an-hour demand. Lincoln Steel was in no position to grant a ten-cent-an-hour raise to its five hundred and fifty employees in the spring of 1941. The price of tin, its most costly raw material, went sky-high. The little extra money the company was making on scrap was taken away by the setting of maximum scrap prices. The price of sheet bar, from which the company rolls tin plate on obsolete hand mills, threatened to rise a dollar or two a ton. But the selling price of its product was frozen at one hundred dollars a ton. Profits in the previous year, when material costs were lower, amounted to only sixty thousand dollars, and the ten-cent demand would have cost one hundred and ten thousand dollars a year. Management, on the basis of these facts, claimed it could not meet the ten-cent raise. The union called for an examination of the company's books. True, the company's profits did not permit the granting of such a raise; but the money was there to grant it. The company's "cash on hand" was well over the cost of the ten-cent-an-hour demand, and one member of the local union committee argued that the money should be used for this purpose. SWOC representatives explained that a large working capital was necessary to meet the requirements of the business and that the company's profit-making capacity, already pitifully weak, would be further weakened by the depletion of these funds.

"The money's there. It belongs to us. We took an eight per cent wage cut in 1939, and we're already below the industry.

By rights we should get the cut back on top of the ten cents. Let the company worry about how to pay it. I've got to worry how to pay my family's bills," this committeeman argued.

Frankly, we believe, SWOC could have forced it from the company, since it was not willing to engage in a strike under any circumstances. But the question uppermost in our minds was how long the company would be able to remain in business. Six months earlier one of the only other two remaining independent tin-plate firms operating hand mills went out of existence permanently, and its three thousand employees were abruptly cut off from private employment. The other firm was rumored to be on the auction block, with the jobs of its two thousand workers threatened, and a few months later the rumor turned out to be true. Without the authority and power inherent in the union-shop type of agreement, and the manner in which such an agreement affects the attitudes of workers, SWOC might have been compelled to insist on the ten-cent raise and rationalize its action on the grounds that the company is doomed anyway because of competition from the low-cost continuous-strip mills. Instead, SWOC faced the facts and acted accordingly.

Wages were referred to an impartial umpire. The arbiter granted thirty-five thousand dollars a year to be used for the purpose of eliminating wage inequalities. The union, by itself, worked out the manner in which this sum should be distributed. Wages of common labor, which had not been cut in 1939, were raised two and one-half cents an hour. Wage inequalities were eliminated completely, though wages were not raised as high as desired because of the limitation of the money available. The highest-paid workers—rollers earning more than two dollars an hour, who were cut fifteen per cent in 1939—received no adjustments. The union's schedule was discussed with management; several improvements were suggested and adopted, and finally agreed upon.

Active membership participation enabled the union to

equalize wages throughout the entire mill without creating any dissension; more than this, it eliminated most of the causes of dissension. The committeeman in each department met with his constituents; together they worked out what they thought would be an equitable solution to discrepancies in the wage structure. The committeemen, in turn, met with the local union officers and passed on their recommendations. The officers then met with their field director and a representative of SWOC's research department. From all this came the revised wage structure. Management found it, except for a few cases, in excellent shape. It was agreed upon and has resulted in a harmonious situation.

Wage equalization, as we shall see, is one of the most explosive jobs either unions or management, together or separately, can tackle—so explosive that in most firms it is still virtually untouched. The difference between Lincoln Steel and the average firm is accounted for by the form of union recognition, which enabled the union to secure the active participation of its membership in its relations with management. Workers join unions to get a voice in making the decisions that vitally affect them, and such a voice in economic matters is a path to industrial peace that cannot be by-passed, either by management or by unions.

The share of the proceeds of production going to workers is distributed, not only through wage payments, but through vacations with pay, shorter hours, and better conditions of work. Except for vacations these instruments to distribute the earnings of a productive enterprise are not designed to raise the income of workers already employed. Their primary purpose is to raise the plane of living of workers as a whole by spreading employment. Time and one-half for overtime, for example, is a measure to enforce the agreed-upon work week and workday. It is not a means of distributing earnings among workers. During the armament program it has been widely used for this purpose, and will be one of the most difficult problems facing unions and management in the postwar period.

The proceeds of technological changes, laborsaving machinery, and other factors contributing to lower unit costs of production should be shared equitably between owners and workers.

In its handbook *Production Problems* SWOC endorses the principle that owners and workers should jointly participate in savings resulting from mechanical or other technological changes. This is a hard principle to work out practically, since it is so difficult to measure the actual savings of such changes and to devise methods for distributing to workers their share of the savings and to preserve for later distribution to owners their share. Just how SWOC tries to administer this principle we illustrate by citing a typical case in full detail. The following formula was devised as the result of an accumulation of experiences with such cases, few of which, incidentally, were very pleasant.

SHEET MILL BOX ANNEALING CASE

March 12, 1940

THE CASE

The company has installed twelve Wilson gas-fired annealing boxes during the last three years. Each Wilson box has a capacity of 85 tons. As a consequence, the productive capacity of the sheet mill box annealing department has increased 33 1/3%, or from 12,000 to 16,000 tons per month. In view of this increased production, the company adjusted the tonnage wage rates downward.

However, the actual average hourly earnings of the helpers increased. From November, 1936, to March 16, 1937, the helpers averaged 78.6 cents per hour. During this period only a few Wilson boxes had been installed, and their effect on wages had not begun. To make this figure comparable with the following periods it is necessary to add ten cents to it, the amount of the general wage increase of March, 1937.

In March, 1937, the tonnage wage rates were adjusted downward. The group tonnage rate was abolished. In its stead a guaranteed rate of 75 cents per hour plus a small tonnage rate was installed. During the next nine months the helpers averaged 89.8 cents per hour, or an increase of 1.3% since the change; in 1938, 92.4, or an increase of 4.3%; and from January 1, 1939, to

October 28, 1939, 93.5 cents, or an increase of 5.5%. In December, 1939, the company offered an additional increase of four cents an hour on the average, which would bring the helpers' average earnings up to 97.5 cents per hour, or ten percent higher than before the substantial introduction of the Wilson boxes.

The company stated that the committee and men could decide themselves whether they wanted this four cents increase on a tonnage basis or on a minimum hourly guarantee plus a small tonnage rate.

DISPLACEMENT

There has been no displacement of workers up to the present time. However, when the entire production is done in the Wilson boxes nine helpers will be eliminated, reducing the force to sixteen workers. When operating at peak capacity two-thirds of the production is in the Wilson boxes and one-third in the old type coal-fired boxes. At the present time the company is not operating the old type boxes, but expectations are that they will work the greater part of 1940. During 1937, the old and the new boxes worked the entire year; in 1938, the old boxes worked only three months; but in 1939, the old boxes worked nine months. The capacity of the old boxes is fourteen tons each, and the company now has fifteen. The company has twelve Wilson boxes.

When the old boxes are finally eliminated, which will be within the next year or two depending upon how soon the company can afford to install enough Wilson boxes to take care of its peak production, there will be a total displacement of eighteen workers. These eighteen consist of nine helpers, as noted above, and nine pulverizers who are now attached to a different department and who pulverize coal for use in the coal-fired boxes.

COST OF EQUIPMENT

The cost of a Wilson box ranges between $21,000 and $22,000. The company has installed them for two reasons:

1. To reduce the cost of production for annealing a ton of steel sheets in order to be competitive, as almost all competitors do their present annealing in Wilson boxes.
2. To eliminate losses resulting from bad sheets which do not hold up for consumer use because of inadequate annealing.

The total cost of the twelve boxes is between $252,000 and

$264,000. The savings resulting from the installation of the Wilson boxes are as follows. On an average of 13,293,153 pounds per pay period, which is an exceptionally high average, the company's savings in wages, if there were no change in the average hourly earnings, would be $911 a pay period, or a savings of $23,686 a year. With an increase of 16.7% in average hourly earnings, as hereinafter recommended, this reduces the annual savings to $11,843 in wages. Added is the elimination of nine pulverizers at an annual estimated savings in wages of $13,500, or a total maximum savings in wages of $25,343 a year. In addition, there is an estimated savings of $10,000 a year in fuel costs resulting from the use of gas instead of pulverized coal. Thus the total estimated savings with a 16.7% increase in hourly earnings amounts to $35,343 a year. There is also a savings not immediately measurable that will accrue to the company by a reduction in rejections resulting from better annealing. While this saving cannot be exactly estimated, for purposes of calculations it is arbitrarily set at $25,000 a year [which later turned out to be quite conservative]. Thus the total saving accruing to the company is roughly $60,000 a year. On this basis it would take the company approximately five years to pay for the cost of its investment plus the interest on the money borrowed to install the equipment.

RECOMMENDATIONS

Precedent for Recommendations

In the reduction of costs resulting from technological improvements, there are two types of cases. A brief summary of these two types of cases follows.

In the case of technological improvements in an open hearth department which cost $750,000, sixty-two workers were eliminated at an annual saving in the payroll of $118,952. In addition to the reduced payroll, other savings were made amounting to $257,500 in fuel and other costs. Thus the company's total savings amounted to $376,425. The company's immediate savings were sufficient to enable it to write off its $750,000 investment and interest in less than two and one-half years. As a consequence of the improvements, production increased and the hourly earnings for different open hearth workers rose from ten to fifty percent. The company asked for a ten percent reduction in hourly earnings on the grounds that the men's earnings had increased 10 to

50% not as a result of their efforts, but primarily as a result of the improvements the company made. The company's request for a reduction in hourly earnings was rejected on two grounds.

1. The savings resulting from the displacement of workers and other reasons were sufficient to enable the company to pay off its investment in a reasonably short period of time.
2. The improvements enabled the workers to produce the same production in 133 days that formerly required 200 days, and as a result of the increased output per day they would receive fewer days' work per year, which would offset in large measure their increased hourly earnings over a one-year period.

The second case, which is more closely related to the case at hand, involved a wire drawing department. On three cold wire drawing machines, 16″ continuous, 6 draft, the company increased production 37%. At the same time it reduced tonnage rates so that the average hourly earnings of the workers increased only 7%. The company contended that this increase in hourly earnings was sufficient. After reviewing all the factors in the case, including the cost of the improvements, SWOC found that a 7% increase in hourly earnings failed to share equitably the profits of the improvements with the workers immediately involved. There were no workers immediately displaced; but the increased output per day, it was mutually agreed, would result in fewer days' work per year. As a consequence, it was mutually agreed that the tonnage rates would be adjusted so that the average hourly earnings of the workers would increase one percent for each two percent increase in production. Thus with a 37% increase in production hourly earnings were increased 18.5%.

The Recommendation

In view of the facts of this case, the formula for settling this case to the equitable interest of all parties involved is the one used in the settlement of the second case discussed above. It is therefore recommended that the case at hand be settled on the following basis.

1. The guaranteed hourly rate of 75 cents per hour should be maintained. The tonnage rate should be adjusted so as to provide a 16.7% increase in average hourly earnings, which represent one-

half the percentage increase in production. The average hourly earnings adjusted to the ten cents an hour increase of March, 1937, prevailing before the technological improvements in this case were 88.6 cents per hour. A 16.7% increase would thus result in an average hourly earnings for the helpers of $1.03 per hour. It is therefore recommended that the tonnage rate be adjusted to provide an average hourly earnings for the helpers of $1.03 an hour with a minimum guarantee of 75 cents an hour.

2. The union committee and management should work out a mutually satisfactory procedure for absorbing the nine helpers and nine pulverizers in the regular working forces when they are finally displaced from their present jobs. It is recommended that mutually agreeable procedures be worked out to absorb these displaced workers in the regular labor turnover of the company. Thus, for example, the displaced workers could be put on a preferred hiring list for the first openings that occur for which they are qualified; and while the displaced workers are on the preferred hiring list they could be given whatever extra work there might be from time to time until a regular place on the working force can be found for them.

The company offered four cents an hour; the union was demanding twenty-nine cents—that earnings go up in direct ratio to production—and the above recommendation, made by one of the authors, provided for a nine-and-one-half-cent-an-hour raise. The latter was accepted by both the local union and management. The one-dollar-and-three-cent-an-hour rate, now one-dollar-and-thirteen-cents, was, and still is, above the prevailing rate for this job in the steel industry—management and the union knew that when they set it. But it was not too far out of line with the other rates in the mill and so it was accepted.

In the open-hearth-department case mentioned in this recommendation the wages of the men rose in direct ratio to production. This has put their rates from ten to forty per cent out of line both with other rates in the particular mill and with rates for similar work in the steel industry. Our experience since has demonstrated that it was unwise to distribute all the proceeds of the technological changes in this case in the form of higher hourly earnings to the men immediately affected. It resulted in a glaring case of inequality —and is still one of SWOC's unsettled cases. This raises the question, "What should be done when the equitable distribution of its share of the proceeds of technological changes puts a group of workers' hourly earnings intolerably out of line with the rest of the mill and industry?"

The answer to this question, in our judgment, lies in the widespread wage inequalities existing in the wage structures of most mines, mills, and factories. We believe that each firm operating under a collective-bargaining contract should establish a wage-adjustment fund—although we realize such a proposal may well have to await the development of industry-wide bargaining. This fund should be agreed upon in amount at regular contract-negotiating conferences. Thus, for example, a steel firm would agree that it will set aside one hundred thousand dollars for the life of the one-year contract for the purpose of adjusting wage inequalities. During the life of the contract the amount of the fund may be added to in instances like the open-hearth case. Instead of having hourly earnings rise in direct ratio with production and consequently become intolerably out of line, the earnings of the open-hearth-department workers would have risen only to the extent that they would not constitute a wage-inequality problem for the mill. The total annual cost of having their wages rise in direct ratio with production would then be calculated. The difference between this cost and the amount their wages would have been raised would have amounted, say, to twenty thousand dollars. This sum would then be added to the wage-adjustment fund and, in turn, be distributed to other workers in the mill in the elimination of inequalities. The seriousness of the wage-inequality problem in industry demonstrates the wisdom of this proposal.

The adjustment of wage-rate inequalities should be exclusively on the basis of the merits of each case.

Of all the chickens unions stir up during the organizing stage, none come home to roost with a louder crow than the wage-inequality one. Management, to be sure, incubated the bird, but unions are responsible for making him crow. Until SWOC won its first collective-bargaining contracts its research department functioned almost exclusively as an agency to ferret out wage inequalities within plants and between plants. Quickly they were sent out to the organizers, who found the material very good agitational dynamite. Loud-speakers blared at the mill gates, "Who said a craneman is worth twenty cents more in Pittsburgh than in Chicago? Does a craneman eat any more in Pittsburgh? Does he have any more children to clothe? How about your mill? Is a millwright in the blooming mill worth eighteen cents more than a millwright in the electric-furnace department? No! No! A thousand times No! Join the union and bring justice to all workers." The only consolation management had as it stood by helplessly watching its employees sign their cards was that some day—if, by some miracle, the union won recognition this time—all these wage inequalities would be dumped into the union's hands. How well we know this, too!

For almost five years we have been trying to quiet the bird, but as fast as we satisfy the rooster in one place he turns up with a louder crow in another. Wage inequalities are as old as modern industry itself. The complete absence of a rational foundation for the wage structure; the unrestricted freedom of foremen to say to one of their employees, "I'll give you a nickel raise if you don't tell anyone else"; the subversion of the rewarding-employees-for-merit policy into a seething system of shop politics; and the several other practices contributing to wage inequalities have made them the serious problem that they are today. Management is finding them expensive to solve, and unions are finding them difficult to handle. Wage inequalities can be solved, but it takes money and joint union-management action.

Many firms—under union pressure more times than voluntarily—have tried to solve the problem with indiscriminate wage adjustments, but in vain. The Federal Iron Company met most wage-inequality claims presented by the union, in whole or in part, depending upon how much pressure was behind them. At times, as the cost started to mount, it got stubborn, but usually yielded when the men either threatened to strike or actually did. The industrial-relations director, when SWOC demanded the ten-cent raise in the spring of 1941, wrote one of us:

> This company cannot willingly agree to the 10¢ wage request, but this morning I offered officially on behalf of the company a flat increase of 7½¢ to all hourly rate employees. This figure gains added significance when it is considered in relation to the adjustments which have already been made. . . . As I shall presently relate the 7½¢ now proposed would bring up to 16¢ the adjustments which have been made for our older employees, and 12¢ as applied to the entire payroll since the last general wage movement in 1937. . . .
>
> This company's wage policy during the past four years has differed substantially from that of most others, in that individual wage rates have been adjusted from time to time, and this, in effect, has resulted in substantial wage increases. We have desired to continue that policy, but . . . if it has been unappreciated then it will be unwise to continue it. But if that is not the case, then the adjustments which we have made . . . leave no justification for the exorbitant request now being made. . . .
>
> Since the general increase in April, 1937, our wages have not been static, and although no general increase was effective the total individual adjustments granted since April 12, 1937, equal an increase of 8.4¢ per hour for present employees who were also with us in January, 1937 (306); or a general increase of 4.3¢ per hour for all present hourly rate employees (556). . . . This amounts to $51,660 a year or a five percent increase on our present annual payroll. In 1938 and 1939, of course, the percentage increase was much greater. . . .

The company, despite this strong protestation, granted the ten cents, because its basic approach to the problem of wages was one of appeasement. First, the company said it could not afford it and offered a nickel; this was raised to seven and one-half cents. Trained for four years to wait out management on wage adjustments, the local union waited on its general wage demand—and with complete success.

The irony of this company's apparently generous wage policy has been that, even today, its wage structure bristles with inequalities, the only difference being that the number of inequalities is lower and on a higher level than in 1937. Management, as elsewhere, took the position that "it's the union's job to sell itself to our employees." The figures quoted by the company show the extent of the union's success in this connection: one-third of the employees got raises in 1937 and 1939, almost one-half in 1940, and by April, 1941, the wage adjustments were running at the rate of seventy-five per cent of the number of employees.

Contrary to the impression of the firms' industrial-relations director, its policy in this regard was far from exceptional; it was typical of the firms with which SWOC has contracts. Average hourly earnings, for instance, in the basic steel industry rose three cents an hour between the ten-cent raises in 1937 and 1941. Several factors were responsible for this raise, but undoubtedly the adjustment of wage inequalities was one of the dominant ones. A policy of appeasement on wage-rate adjustments has no end, satisfies few workers for long. And management soon discovers that the money available for wage adjustments, on an expedient basis, runs out long before the demands. The Federal Iron Company, quite typically, found out after granting many adjustments without any wage-structure rationale that there was no appreciable decline in dissatisfaction over unequal wage rates for comparable work.

The development of a rationale upon which wage inequalities can be eliminated with some degree of permanency is essential. A sound wage-structure foundation is twofold: first, wage rates should be in line with those paid for comparable work in the district and industry; second, wage rates should be in a proper relationship to one another within each particular mine, mill, or factory. The problem is how to work out this policy practicably within the framework of collective bargaining. Our experiences have convinced us that wages have to be equalized in relation to other plants in the district and industry before the other half of the problem can be tackled successfully. This view is supported by the fact that unions and management, on the whole, have jointly tackled wage inequalities on the basis of plant-by-plant and industry-wide comparisons first, and that experiences on joint co-operation in eliminating intraplant inequalities are limited, to date, because the first half of the job is still largely unfinished.

It is natural for the two parts of the problem to be tackled in this order. Most firms like to feel that they are paying as much as their competitors and that they are paying the going rate in the community. Workers, on the other hand, are not satisfied unless they feel confident that they are getting paid at least the prevailing rate in the community and in the industry. In addition, the first half of the problem can be handled more easily by a union lacking the strength and security of a union shop than can the job of evaluating jobs within its own plant. The work of SWOC's research department, for example, is still largely in the field of job-for-job wage-rate comparisons, while the development of the time-study and job-evaluation part of its work is just beginning to assume sizable proportions—almost in direct ratio to the expansion of firms under union-shop contracts.

A typical job-for-job comparison case reveals that the technique is quite simple. Maintenance workers in a steel mill employing fifty-five hundred demanded a flat fifteen-cent-an-hour raise in the winter of 1940 on the grounds that they were underpaid in the industry and in relation to production workers. Management frankly recognized the inequity of electricians, for example, receiving only one dollar an hour alongside of production workers earning thirty cents an hour more, when the latter learned their jobs in a few months in comparison with the four years of apprenticeship served by the electricians. The general manager argued, however, that to wipe out this inequity in one blow was more than the company could absorb. He proposed for the moment that his company's maintenance rates be compared with the average for the industry. The union agreed with the proviso that those rates found below the industry average would be raised to the average, but those rates above the average would remain unchanged. The union and management each gathered rates from competing mills, jointly combined them into an average for each classification of maintenance workers, and raised those below the average. This cost sixty thousand dollars a year for four hundred and sixty-three workers. Since then these workers have been satisfied that they are being paid fairly in relation to pay for comparable work in the industry. Their "beef" now is that they are not paid properly in comparison with production work; this, however, is a problem requiring industry-wide attention.

The adamant refusal of unions to adjust downward any rates found to be too high is only partly related to the absence of the union-shop form of recognition. A basic part of organized labor's program is to resist wage cuts, on any grounds; this, in turn, is directly related to the major plank in its program—the raising of the plane of living. Frankly, rates on the high side are zealously defended to enhance the union's bargaining power. We have found the high rates to be a powerful lever for raising the base of the wage structure. Something can be done and unions are amenable to adjusting rates too far out of line on the high side, particularly when they are being paid by the lower-rated workers and not the company; but certainly a union is not free to adjust a member's rate downward when, as a consequence, he can immediately quit the union and agitate for other members to follow his example.

The greater the participation of workers through their unions in setting piecework and tonnage rates, in making time and motion studies, in determining work standards and job evaluations, the greater are the earnings and output.

The industrial-relations director of a large rayon firm in July, 1941, arranged for the local union committee from one of his plants to visit SWOC's office in Pittsburgh for the purpose of learning the practical methods through which

SWOC members and local unions participate in working out incentive wage plans. Joseph Scanlon, who is in charge of this phase of SWOC's work, spent two days with the committee, and took these leaders of a CIO textile local union to a few steel mills for firsthand observation. They acted as if they had stepped out of a hopeless industrial scene into a dreamland; the difference, actually, was between the arbitrary establishment of wage rates by management and union participation in doing this job. For all practical purposes this textile workers' union committee could have been the SWOC committee from any one of a majority of SWOC's local unions, because most of management still feels that this job is none of the union's business. Joseph Scanlon, who has had twenty-odd years of intensive and varied industrial experience, casually reported to us his two-day visit with the textile committee, and we quote from his report directly because it is so sharply to the point.

After several hours of frank discussion with the committee from the rayon company I got the distinct impression that if the management had tried its utmost to do everything the wrong way, it could not have equalled the success in that direction that it has attained. About a year and a half ago a stranger suddenly appeared in the plant. The employees had no idea who he was or what his function was to be. He, together with one or two assistants, began installing a merit rating system. Of course this was somewhat of a mystery to the employees. This naturally created a chaotic condition and a great deal of resentment developed. It was evident that even the supervisory force didn't understand it all and many of them were suspicious and resentful. Probably because of this bitterness and the advent of the union, this plan was discarded. However, the suspicion and bad taste remained.

Several months ago the same man who installed the merit rating system began making time studies of the operations in the pipe gang. There was no preliminary ground work, no explanations of the objectives—just a man of mystery with a stop watch. Some of the people being timed asked questions but were denied an answer. Recently the men on the pipe gang were informed that standards had been set and it was proposed that they work on an incentive plan. Suspicion, resentment, and distrust resulted.

Evidently it was at this juncture that the company's industrial relations director took hold and expressed a desire to approach this problem intelligently. Certainly I hope he carries on, for some of the tales of delays beyond the control of the pipe gang due to the lack of correct tools, even down to the utter impossibility to secure a proper wrench, signify the old economy of "save a dime and spend a dollar."

Witness this contrast. At the ABC Steel Company, the union was consulted before the company made any decision on incentives. A detailed explanation was given and a common understanding was reached. For the past two years four union members, including the secretary of the local union, have been working in the Time Study Department. All standards are checked and agreed upon before they are put into effect. After a trial period a recheck is made if the standards are unsatisfactory. The time studies and standards are an open book and can be inspected by all interested parties. No mystery, no secrecy—just a job to be done and one that can be done best with full union participation and understanding. The visiting committee was given a detailed explanation of every phase of this program. They were so enthusiastic about it that they were still in the mill at seven in the evening.

The next morning we visited the XYZ Iron Company. Here again the visiting committee found the union participating to the fullest extent in making time studies and setting standards. The job here is nearing completion. The union secretary and a member of the union negotiating committee are working in the Time Study Department. The visiting committee found the situation entirely to their liking, and freely expressed the conviction that if the problem of wage incentives and job evaluation received this sort of treatment by their management they would certainly participate and co-operate to the fullest extent in the program. As you know the committee left us with the enthusiastic determination to make every effort to have their company follow the pattern set at these two SWOC contract firms.

As a result of this experience I would like to make several observations. If the Industrial Engineers of today would tear the veil of secrecy and mysticism from the application and operation of their innumerable wage incentive plans, we might be able to achieve a mutually satisfactory acceptance of wage incentives. In most cases they remind me very much of the old tin mill roller who made a profound mystery of the art of rolling tin until someone eventually came along and discovered it was quite simple.

It seems to me that this question of installing a wage incentive plan should be handled as frankly and as simply as possible. In the past few days I have received several letters from our local union people on this subject. One letter from Connecticut tells us that the union is badly in need of expert advice and counsel from our office. They registered a protest because they believed their standards had been set too high and had resulted in a wage reduction. Thereupon, management informed them that since they were entirely ignorant of the technique of industrial engineering it wouldn't be worthwhile to even discuss the setting of standards with them. This is an insult to the intelligence of our people in the mills and factories.

Any wage incentive plan, any standard that has been set, that will not stand frank open discussion and complete explanation to the people concerned, leaves a lurking suspicion of unfairness and dishonesty. Why not tear loose this veil of secrecy, this air of mysticism and approach the problem as follows.

Management should go to its employees and say, "Now look here. You fellows are working on a straight hourly rate. Some of you are working faster than others and perhaps we are not paying you as much as you actually are worth to us. Again there may be others who if we furnished the opportunity for increased earnings might be able and willing to increase production. Now we want to make some time studies, but we are not going to do so unless we have your co-operation and participation so that proper standards may be set. If there are any errors in them, these errors will be ours and yours and together we can correct them. We shall arrive at these standards, not by timing the fastest or the slowest employee, but the average one. We shall credit you with a certain percentage of fatigue time. This naturally will depend upon the intensity, monotony, and physical requirements of your particular operation.

"We shall guarantee you a fair base rate so that security and stability of earnings will be protected. At eighty percent of this standard we shall pay you a bonus. Undoubtedly many of you will be able to make up to 125% to 130% of your base rate, but this does not imply a penalty on those who are unable to do this for naturally we know there is a vast difference in the speed, efficiency, and ability of our employees. Last and most important, each employee should tabulate all delay time that is beyond his control; for instance, lack of, or defective, material, tools, cranes, and so forth. We will deduct this time from your production time and pay you your base rate so that it will not interfere with the possibility of earning a bonus. We will charge all of this delay time as an expense against your department supervisor. Of course, this will keep him on his toes, and likewise will permit us to figure accurately whether or not, on the basis of delays registered, we can justify the expenditure of capital to eliminate delays which cannot be corrected otherwise. The more you make, the better we will like it, and we will not disturb the standards, for the more you produce and make, the lower our unit costs become. This we will put into an agreement with your union."

I believe this would put the proposition on an understandable basis and that our local union people, if approached in this manner, and invited to participate and co-operate fully, would look more favorably on the installation, or if the situation is otherwise, on the maintenance and improvement of wage incentives.

Less than two years ago Joseph Scanlon was operating a charging machine in the open-hearth department of a steel mill. This report is not a blanket endorsement of wage incentives, as Joe Scanlon strongly feels that flat hourly wage rates with measured production is the ideal method of distributing to workers their share of the proceeds of production. We discuss this in Chapter Ten. Instead, this report is a typical worker's attitude toward wage incentives after he has reconciled himself to their existence and the necessity of adjusting himself to working with them—at least for the time being. It is a blanket attitude that applies with equal force to merit rating, job evaluation, and other devices designed to place the question of wage payments on a more or less factual basis. Before examining the positive results from direct participation of workers and their unions with management in the job of setting wage rates, work standards, and so forth, it is first necessary to examine the negative results—in earnings and production—from the denial to workers and their unions of such participation.

At this point in our discussion we call upon outside authority to substantiate our views and experiences. The Western

Electric Researches,[3] conducted by Dr. G. Elton Mayo, of the Industrial Research Department of the Harvard Graduate School of Business Administration, and associates, in conjunction with the management of the Hawthorne Works of the Western Electric Company in Chicago, from 1927 to 1932, are the most significant body of evidence on the group behavior of industrial workers that has come to our attention. In every major detail the findings of these researches parallel our experiences. The unique feature of the final conclusions of these researches is that they are elementary truths that experienced people in industry, management, and union alike ignore or take for granted in too many instances. Two intensive experiments were conducted, one among six girls in a test room and another among the bank wiremen in an observation room. In the latter case it was found that:

1. An informal organization with a leader existed among the bank wiremen, whose observable purpose was protective in that the informal organization opposed "rate busters," "chiselers," and "squealers."
2. Although the employee participated least in the technical organization, he bore the brunt of most of its activities.
3. The communications system—the passing of data up the line and policies and data down the line—was observed to be a failure in both directions, up and down.
4. This informal organization gave the employees "a certain feeling of security," and the principal discovery of the research program was that the employees were "unconsciously attempting to protect themselves through their informal organization from real or fancied consequences of supervisory practices and technical innovations."

The researchers supplemented the bank-wiremen experiment with intensive interviews of a select group of employees to further "study the social relations of people actually at work on the job." These interviews revealed that "workers were banding together informally in order to protect themselves against practices which they interpreted as a menace to their welfare." Specifically:

1. They were against wage incentives.
2. They pegged production standards and enforced them.
3. They showed "preoccupations of futility with regard to promotion."

The bank wiremen and the employees generally at the Hawthorne Works of the Western Electric Company were not unionized at the time, 1927-32, nor are they now. Management, as a rule, when it finds such practices among unionized workers points the finger of accusation at the union, when, actually, these practices predate the union's birth by many years and are merely being carried on by the union because it has been unable to eliminate the underlying factors that compel workers to oppose group wage incentives and production standards. In fact, one of the earliest contributions of organized labor to productive efficiency is the way in which it alters the attitudes of workers to group wage incentives and lifts these self-imposed restrictions on output. More on this later.

The results of the test-room experiment were the converse of the bank-wiremen one. The six girls who participated in this experiment were given, at regular intervals, improved physical conditions of work with ideal rest periods. As was expected, production rose steadily with no observable increase in fatigue. Had the experiment stopped here, the conclusion, of course, would have been that the improved physical conditions of work were exclusively responsible for the increased output. The researchers, however, were not convinced that this was a sound conclusion and sought concrete evidence to uphold or disprove their views. This evidence was secured by taking away step by step, at the same regular intervals as they were installed, the several improvements in physical conditions of work and rest periods that had been given the six girls. Instead of declining, production continued to rise steadily. The obvious conclusion, naturally, was that the steady rise in output was not related to changes in the physical conditions of work, but to the development of an organized social group in a peculiar and effective relation with its supervisors. This was so, the experiment revealed, because:

1. It was fun in the test room for the girls, as they were not prohibited from talking to one another during working hours and for other related reasons.
2. "Employees must have confidence management is doing things for their welfare."
3. "Something in their experience of industrial life produced in a number of employees a conviction of personal inadequacy."

Had similar investigations been conducted concurrently throughout the whole of American industry, substantially the same findings would have been revealed. Management in each mine, mill, and factory that has seen its employees organize into a union in the last decade, or is seeing them do it today, can find evidence of the validity of the Western Electric Researches in its own back yard in the existence of a union among its employees—because for all practical purposes the findings resulting from these researches and the motives for union membership among workers are the same. These researches, therefore, constitute a study of the origin of labor unions; for example, they found that "although he participates least in the technical organization, the employee bears the brunt of most of its activities." As a direct result, an informal organization with a leader developed among the bank wiremen long before they participated in the experiment. The purpose of this informal organization was essentially protective, which made its activities negative; that is, the group through its leader opposed "rate busters"—members of the group who exceeded production levels—because of fear that management would set higher output standards and reduce their per unit earnings accordingly. Likewise "chiselers" were opposed, as they jeopardized the earnings of the entire group by slackening on the job. And, of course, the group opposed "squealers," because they tattled on its secret doings. The researches also found that this informal organization gave the employees a "certain feeling of security."

In this respect one of the directors of the researches observed that "these informal organizations much resembled formally organized labor unions." In fact, they are the forerunners of labor unions. In going about the task of organizing a group of workers in a given plant into a labor union, we have consciously sought out the leaders of these informal groups throughout the plant, interested them in taking a lead in forming the union, and found that their joining the union invariably caused the members of the informal organizations to follow suit. In labor-union parlance these leaders are called "the men with a following." Thus the leaders of the informal organizations take up leadership in a formally organized labor union, in part, because of "preoccupations of futility with regard to promotion," and the rank and file of the informal-group members join because, as the Western Electric Researches also reveal, "something in their experience of industrial life produced in a number of employees a conviction of personal inadequacy." The bank wiremen pegged output because they were denied a voice in making the decisions that vitally affected their everyday lives, while the test-room girls, as a result of having a voice in such decisions, continually raised output and apparently had no thought of engaging in restrictive practices. The factors in the lives of the bank wiremen that forced them to peg output were absent in the girls' work environment. Many other factors, of course, were at work in both cases—this we fully appreciate—but the denial of an effective voice in one case and its presence in the other constitutes, in our judgment, the dominating factor in these two experiments.

Do workers who engage in practices like the bank wiremen for the same reasons they did join unions to continue them or to free themselves from the compelling factors that in their nonunion state of affairs forced them to peg output, oppose group wage incentives, and so forth? Our experiences in this connection have been unanimous. Whether the informal organizations of workers in a plant continue their negative purposes in a formal labor union, or whether they are converted into positive and constructive channels, depends, in the main, upon the attitudes and policies of management. Give workers as a formally organized group a say-so in setting wage rates, work standards, job evaluations, and in making time and motion studies, and they will produce all they can within the limitations of physical endurance, health, and fatigue; deny workers such a say-so and they will engage in restrictive practices out of self-protection. The fact that in so doing they may impair their economic interests will not deter them in the slightest. Let us look at some typical cases that clearly tell this story; in the first case the negative purpose of the informal organizations was enlarged. In the second case the negative purpose was also enlarged, at first, but was then converted into a positive one.

Number One Company is a huge enterprise, much in the news these last few years. The basis of its operations is the assembly line. Its employees, as elsewhere in the auto industry, had organized into informal groups starting the first day the assembly line was put into operation more than a decade ago. Through their informal organizations workers on these lines had perfected ways and means of keeping production at certain levels, just as the bank wiremen did. Each year management changed the speeds and rates of pay of the assembly line; the men were not consulted. The new speeds and rates of pay were announced after management had worked them out through its own time-study department. Denied a direct voice in the establishment of assembly-line speeds and rates of pay, the men exercised an indirect influence through these informal groups. In 1936 and 1937 they formed a CIO industrial union, for which ninety per cent of the men voted in an NLRB election. Management opposed the unionization of its employees. Consequently they continued the negative purposes of their informal groups when transformed into a formal labor union; in fact, they enlarged them.

One of the purposes of the informal groups was to peg output. This had been done for years prior to organizing into a labor union, because, as previously noted, these workers were denied direct participation in the determination of assembly speeds and rates of pay. Management rejected the demand, arguing that if granted it would be an infringement on its prerogatives. Thwarted at the outset in changing the underlying cause of their restrictive practices on production, they continued to participate in setting assembly speeds and rates of pay through the indirect methods they had perfected over a long period of years. When expanded on a larger scale than under the informal organizations, the pegging of production became clearly observable to top management. Lower supervisory officials had known all about it, even co-operated with it, as did the minor management officials at the Hawthorne Works of the Western Electric Company.

Upon learning of these practices top management officials charged the union with sabotage, and for exemplary discipline fired the leaders in one department. The rank and file of these auto workers, who had followed these leaders for years, refused to work until they were reinstated. This power to stop production completely that workers acquire through a labor union is something they did not enjoy through their informal groups. Union spokesmen charged a lockout; management spokesmen claimed the union had called a strike. The dispute raged for two months and was finally settled on a compromise. Management would continue to set speeds and rates of pay by itself; but if any speeds or rates were unsatisfactory to a worker or group of workers, then the management would reset them in co-operation with the men and the union representatives. This was in 1939 and not all is in order in this company's plants now, nor is it likely to be until management clearly comprehends the meaning of the basic demand for participation of which restricted production is merely one manifestation.

Number Two Company, with a union-shop contract, now

enjoys the benefits of the positive and constructive activities of its employees' union, but first went through a year-and-one-half period during which its employees enlarged their negative activities before engaging in positive and constructive ones. The central point of difficulty was the establishment of piecework rates. Prior to the union organization management had set piecework rates itself and reduced them when the men exceeded their expected production and earnings. There naturally developed an informal organization among the men to hold production at certain levels, as the bank wiremen did. After they merged their informal groups into a formally organized labor union the men were able to make higher earnings on lower production because management had raised their piecework rates from twenty to sixty per cent to prevent them from organizing, but in vain.

Eventually management complained that production was falling off, and admitted its costs were out of line competitively because of the wage raises it had granted to stop the union. The men resisted management's request for a lowering of piecework rates. The management argued that they could maintain their earnings by raising output, but the men were interested in their earnings foremost. And if they could realize satisfactory earnings on a given output they were not interested in raising output to maintain them.

An agreement was finally reached guaranteeing piecework rates for a period of one year. The company's product changes yearly; management, employees, and the union establish the piecework rates each year by joint determination, and they continue unchanged until the following season. Knowing that their rates would not be changed, the men no longer restricted output. Production rose unbelievably; management benefited from greater output and the men from substantially higher earnings. At Western Electric's Hawthorne Works the researches revealed that "workers were banding together informally in order to protect themselves against practices they interpreted as a menace to their welfare." This is the way the employees of Number Two Company felt about piecework rates until the rates were guaranteed for a year and they had an effective voice in setting them.

The employees of this company have found satisfaction, by and large, for the economic, psychological, and social motives that impelled them to organize into a union. Behind the statistics on Number Two Company's production and its employees' earnings is an absorbing human story. From May, 1936, the last month before the union, through the year 1939 earnings in each department rose from a minimum of twenty-seven per cent to a maximum of one hundred and ninety-one per cent. By the fall of 1941 earnings had risen over May, 1936, a minimum of forty-two per cent to a maximum of two hundred and five per cent. Daily output rose during this five-and-one-half-year period from seven hundred units to seventeen hundred, or one hundred and forty-three per cent. Unit costs were down by almost a third, and the company's net profits have reached their highest levels in 1939, 1940, and 1941. In the depression year of 1938 the company stayed in the black.

There are six companies in this line of business, not one of which is within twenty-five per cent of Number Two Company's average hourly wage rates; but yet the latter is able to undersell them consistently. Five-dollar-a-day buffers have become twelve-dollar-a-day men. Six-dollar-a-day polishers have become seventeen-dollar-a-day men. They are typical of this company's thousand-odd workers. They have moved into better homes or built them in the last five years, and otherwise raised their living standards. They have found security on their jobs and greater prestige in their communities, and have overcome the personal frustrations and inadequacies induced by the preunion managerial policies that forced them to engage in essentially negative practices. Further, in their daily work they have found an outlet for their creative desires as they are free to make suggestions to increase efficiency, eliminate wastes, and so forth. As a consequence, production has risen steadily. This is not the diabolical speed-up brought about by force and compulsion; it is the attainment of a higher production by the willing and voluntary co-operation of a group of workers with management.

The company's slogan is "We don't care how much you earn, just so our unit costs go down." Because of a mutuality of interest, this policy has proved economically sound; the days that polishers, for example, make twenty dollars, the company's unit costs are the lowest. The company president says, "Not only have our work standards and wage incentives turned out to be more sensible and practical since our employees participate in making them, but once they are set, being self-set, they are adhered to willingly by the men and with a certain pride." What workers, like all folks, have a part in they not only understand but feel responsible for carrying out successfully.

This case is far from being an exceptional one in fundamental principle. The exceptional nature of it is the complete manner in which management, led by an astute, able president, has cashed in on full co-operation with its employees' union, and the union has secured maximum benefits for its members through full participation. Without a single exception the four hundred and sixty-six wage cases that have passed through our offices, either in final appeal to management or to arbitration, from March, 1937, to November, 1941, bear out the basic principles that this company's union history illustrates; namely:

1. Participation is essentially a constructive and positive undertaking, and workers are neither in the frame of mind nor in the position, except in a limited way, to co-operate jointly with management in decisions on wages and standards, or in reducing costs, or wastes, and so forth, until their union's status is secure and permanent through the union-shop form of recognition.
2. Greater results in production and earnings—to workers in wages and owners in dividends—are achieved when wages are set, jobs are evaluated, and work standards are determined jointly by management and

workers through collective bargaining than when management does these things solely and arbitrarily.

Further evidence of these principles is found in *The Iron Age*, a trade journal in the steel industry, which reported on February 6, 1941:[4]

One reason munitions contracts being manufactured by Massachusetts firms have not been speeded up is said to be a feeling among workers that if they make more than $40 or $45 a week on piece work, the rate setters would cut the pay rate. If piece rates were frozen at current levels for the duration of the emergency, it is said, output could be tuned up at least 25 percent.

Knowing his workmen, a Springfield, Mass., manufacturer of fire arms with British government contracts recently enclosed the following notice in pay envelopes:

"Smith & Wesson wants to do everything possible for defense, and to that end asks all employees to help. Production is needed. The company in order to assist in defense work announces that no reduction in any piece price or day rate will be made on such work. Make all you can and the more you make the better we will like it. Harold Wesson, president, Smith & Wesson, Inc."

We have not inquired into the results of this pay-envelope announcement. But if it has not produced the desired results it is not because *The Iron Age* preface to it is inaccurate. It is because the employees, lacking a union, collective bargaining, and direct participation in these vital matters—or, if they have a union and collective bargaining, lacking the security of a union shop—did not feel free to walk through the door Mr. Wesson opened for them.

Joint union-management co-operation on such elementary matters as wage rates, job evaluations, and setting work standards develops a pattern of co-operation that can be used later for more fundamental matters and on a broader scale. When collective bargaining in a local industrial establishment reaches maturity it is then possible for the union and management to co-operate to increase efficiency, reduce wastes, and otherwise cut costs of production. This is the concern of Part Two of this book.

Before union-management relations can reach such a state of maturity, however, it is first necessary that the principle of the union-shop form of recognition be incorporated into the collective-bargaining contract. Hence we turn our attention to this question in the next chapter.

Chapter VII: Necessity of Union Shop

Membership in the union should be a condition of employment.

Leaders of industry and finance for more than a half century resisted the democratic idea that workers have the right to organize, bargain collectively, and have a voice in the operation of industry in practice. For a management official to believe in this democratic idea, except as a theory, was considered a heresy. Now that this simple and elementary idea has been accepted by these leaders almost universally, they resist the correlative and equally simple and elementary democratic idea of the union shop. The definition of the union shop is that membership in the union shall be a condition of employment in any given bargaining unit where a majority of eligible workers voluntarily belong to the union, that management may hire whomsoever it pleases provided, always, that after an agreed upon period of time all new workers shall join the union, and that all workers shall pay their dues and otherwise continue in good standing in the union under penalty of discharge. Just as the idea of bona fide collective bargaining was considered a heresy until a few years ago, so at present is the idea of the union shop considered by a majority of management. Yet the union shop will have to be removed from this category and become a working policy before industrial peace can be attained and union-management relations can begin to reach full development.

Like the half century of resistance to the idea of unions themselves, so the present opposition to the union shop is contrary to the fundamental concepts of democratic principles as well as to the practical requirements of operating a productive enterprise. The leader of management in the "Little Steel" strike of 1937 knew what he was talking about when he based his opposition to SWOC on the ground that recognition of the union would lead inevitably to the acceptance of the union shop and the checkoff. He called it the "closed shop," a term we detest because it is used as an epithet and, as we point out later, it has a marked distinction from the union shop. Both ideas—organizing a union and having it recognized on a union-shop basis—are correlated; the first cannot be accepted indefinitely without the second. The only alternative to the union shop is the ultimate disintegration of the free labor movement. A union in a given bargaining unit cannot exist either peacefully or indefinitely with part of the working force union and part nonunion. Over the long run either the union will attain one hundred per cent membership or become completely ineffectual.

In this chapter we examine the democratic origin and basis of the union-shop idea first, and then its imperatively practical necessity. Mr. Arthur Henry, vice-president in charge of operations of one of the larger steel firms, is a sensitive, cordial, understanding man in his mid-forties. He is tall, gray, and thin-faced. The way he expresses his views gives them a sincerity and credence that few corporation spokesmen achieve in arguing their side of the union-management relationship. In the spring of 1938 the SWOC contract-negotiating committee, consisting of one union representative from each of the firm's nine plants, two SWOC field directors, and the authors, requested the union shop. Mr. Henry, quite typically, objected. His reasons, though the ones customarily expounded by management, are as fine a statement of them as we have heard.

"My situation is not exactly like yours," he began; "the objectives before us are our only ones. We have no long-range or social objectives—that's not our job; it might be yours. Our objectives are different from yours. My job is to operate these mills as efficiently as we can, and to produce the largest possible return to the investors. Naturally we are concerned about the welfare of our employees and, within certain limits, have always looked after them, but this is not one of our primary objectives. We recognize that your objectives are to protect the interests of our employees, and we have not tried to make it any harder for your union than we have had to. Your suggestion that we compel the minority of our employees who are not in your fold to join the union is un-American. We used to fire employees for belonging to unions, and that was wrong. Now we make no distinctions between employees because of membership or nonmembership in the union. To fire an employee, which is what your suggestion would mean in the final analysis, for nonmembership in the union, we feel, would be as bad a practice as our now discarded one of firing an employee for holding a union card."

Mr. Arthur Henry paused to exchange a smoked-out for a fresh cigarette. But no one on our side took advantage of the pause to interrupt. He continued:

"As I see the union's task, it is up to you fellows to sell yourselves to our employees. I do not think it is our prerogative to tell an employee he has to join the union. That's his business. We can readily see where conflicting unions inside our mills would be injurious to our interests, and to this extent we have co-operated in keeping the door closed to all unions but the Steel Workers Organizing Committee. But I do not see how we can go any further. Our employees have the right to join or refrain from joining the union, and it is not our freedom to infringe on this right by either encouraging or discouraging union membership. Your contention that the majority-rule principle should be translated into a state of affairs where union membership should be compulsory because a majority have joined the union of their own accord, or lacked the strength to stay out under certain union pressures, as the case may be, frankly is challenging. And I have given it much thought. My conclusion is that your contention is not valid in this case, any more than it would be for the Democrats to contend that us good Republicans should be compelled to join their political party because, for the moment, it is the majority party.

"There are things from time to time that we will do for the sake of expediency. But on matters of principle, about which we feel strongly, we will not compromise for the sake of expediency or anything else. One of these things is coercing employees to join a union. Under no circumstances will we do this. It is an inalienable right of employees to work and this right should not be impaired by the requirement of union membership. If your union chooses to force this issue," he concluded, "we are ready to fight it out and let the strong side win. In the past under pressure we have had to change what we considered to be our principles, and this might turn out to be the case in requiring the company to compel membership in the union—I don't know. But I do know that we will fight your union on this issue at present, although I realize that, win, lose, or draw, we will resume making steel."

SWOC did not choose to force the issue in the year 1938.

Significantly, Mr. Henry did not object to the union shop on practical operating grounds; in fact, he conceded that the company's best relationships with the union were in the mills most strongly organized, and stated that he preferred to deal with a strong union rather than with a weak one. He expressed the hope that all of his employees might join the union, since it would then be better for all concerned. But, he added, there was nothing the company could do toward this end, because to compel membership in the union was un-American and nondemocratic. He felt so for three basic reasons.

1. Compulsory union membership would deny workers their inalienable right to work.
2. The majority-rule principle is not valid in the case of union membership.
3. By the same token that it was wrong to fire workers for union membership it is wrong to fire them for refusing to join the union; that is, it is coercion to force an individual worker into union membership against his will.

Let us examine these concepts of democratic principles. The alleged inalienable right to work is a myth; of the precious few inalienable rights workers enjoy, the right to work is not one of them. The great lawyer and logician Clarence S. Darrow many years ago wrote a pamphlet, *The Open Shop*,[1] in which he analyzed this alleged right. We do not know how long ago he wrote this pamphlet. The pages of our copy have turned brown like a scorched white shirt collar, but the timeless character of the views expressed on them is in sharp contrast to their physical condition. We quote:

So long and vociferously have the enemies of trade unions declared for the open shop that no doubt many of them really believe that they are fighting for some principle of liberty and justice and not to serve their selfish ends. Mainly their arguments consist in various statements of the assumption that every man has an inalienable right to work when he pleases, for what wages he pleases, and for whom he pleases. The word "inalienable" sounds well, for it is taken from the Declaration of Independence but it has no meaning in this connection. An "inalienable" right is one which cannot be taken away, and it is obvious that under present conditions no such right exists. In fact, it is stoutly contended for by the very men who have taken away every opportunity that would give a laborer a right or chance to work. Man cannot labor without an opportunity to apply his hands to some of the bounties of nature, to some material from which things are made, and still the inalienable right to work is insisted upon by those who have taken all the coal, and ore, and lumber; who control all the factories and railroads, all the land, and every means to which man might apply his toil.

There can be no inalienable right to work without a place to work, and neither the government nor those who declaim the loudest or insist the most, have ever furnished the laborer a place to toil. To this class the inalienable right to work means simply the inalienable right of the employer, without let or hindrance, to go out in the open market and bid for laborers on the hardest terms or, rather, to so order that industrial world that all men and women and children must bid against each other for a right to toil. No organized government and no powerful body of men ever really made any demand or enforced any means that would give to every working man an inalienable right to work. All the rights a laborer has under the law, or under present industrial methods, is the right to go from employer to employer in search of work.

His right to work depends entirely upon his ability to find someone who has the means and inclination to hire him, and no matter how willing or anxious he cannot force himself upon an employer, but he may be denied this inalienable right upon any reason or pretext no matter what. The great mass of working men to-day have practically nothing but their hands. Where are they to go to enforce this inalienable right? No one knew better than the masters of industry that they may be denied this inalienable right upon the master's will, and could trade unionism be destroyed the will would be harder and more arbitrary, and the right to work far less available than it is to-day. The inalienable right to work is a bit of birdlime, used to catch the unthinking mass, and society and all industrial life must be made over, or, at least, radically changed before such a right is anything except a far-off dream.

Clarence S. Darrow talked of "trade unions," while the passing years, the growth of industrial unions, have given this term a specialized meaning and stripped it of its all-inclusive connotations. He spoke of a laborer having only his hands to apply to the bounties of nature, while advancing technology has outmoded this conception of the functions of workers in the productive process. But these, and others, are mere detail; they have their place in their own time and die. The fundamental tenets of Clarence S. Darrow's views, however, apply with the same force—in fact, with more force—today than they did in his own time. A measure of the validity of a man's views is their capacity to live from generation to generation, to survive even the most fundamental changes in the political climate and the technology of mass-production industry. The timeless character of Darrow's views on the alleged inalienable right to work is demonstrated in the case of the Atlantic Coast shipyard which the federal government was compelled to commandeer in the summer of 1941. The outlines of the Atlantic Coast shipyard case are brief and simple.

The union requested the union shop because it represented

a majority of the company's employees. The company rejected it. Whereupon the case went before the National Defense Mediation Board, which upheld neither position and recommended a compromise maintenance-of-membership recognition clause. It follows.

> In view of the joint responsibilities of the parties to the National Defense, of their mutual obligations to maintain production during the present emergency and of their reciprocal guaranties that there shall be no strikes or lockouts for a period of two years from June 23, 1941, as set out in the "Atlantic Coast Zone Standards," incorporated herein and made a part hereof, the Company engages on its part that any employee who is now a member of the Union, or who hereafter voluntarily becomes a member during the life of this agreement, shall, as a condition of continued employment, maintain membership in the Union in good standing.

This recommendation was not unanimous; the employer representative on the panel of the board dissented. The leaders, or at least the public spokesmen of the employing group, promptly made their views on this recommendation known, with the full implication that all leaders of industry and finance, management, and employers were expected to fall in line. This is not a conjecture on our part; we have entered into union-shop contracts, for example, with one hundred and seventeen firms, employing more than one hundred thousand workers, on a private, semiconfidential, or oral basis, because they fear reprisals from customers, bankers, or others in the industry if they publicly accept the union-shop principle.

The shipbuilding company involved made the first public declaration.[2]

> . . . This company is unwilling to consent to the union's demand that we shall contract that the continued employment by this company of any employee who is now or in the future may become a member of the union shall be dependent upon his remaining a member of the union in good standing. In plain language, this means that this company shall be obligated to discharge any employee simply because for reasons of his own he

sees fit to withdraw from the union or discontinue paying union dues. This constitutes the only issue of importance in the dispute over which the strike has been called.

The policy of this company is that the right to work in our shipyard shall not be dependent upon membership or nonmembership in any organization. . . .

A few days later the National Association of Manufacturers issued a pronunciamento.[3]

. . . The strike at the . . . shipyard . . . focuses the attention of the whole people upon the basic underlying structure of our labor law as it affects the right to work. Before this country witnesses once again a return of that inviolable right to every workman, union member or not, a new bill of rights for American industry, workmen and management, must be written.

If the government of this country seeks to preserve fundamental American principles, it cannot tolerate . . . [the] demand that every worker belong to a union to work for national defense.

On the same day the Chamber of Commerce of the United States issued its declaration, lest there be any doubt about the unanimity of opinion on this issue among industry, finance, and management officials.[4]

. . . the closed shop or any equivalent thereof is un-American and monopolistic and interferes with the individual freedom granted to all our people under the Constitution of the United States.

Any man should be able to work lawfully when, where and how he pleases; and any man, company or corporation should be able to hire anyone to work in a lawful pursuit. This should be so whether the individual belongs or does not belong to any lawful union. . . .

If the people as a whole permit any group to define or limit the scope of action or the rights of any other group of American citizens in a different way than their rights are established by law then we will cease to be a free people.

The right to work is equally sacred with the right to quit or strike. . . .

The board's recommendation of the maintenance-of-membership clause had been made originally by the labor representative on the board's panel and the public's representative—Judge Walter P. Stacy, Chief Justice of North Carolina. The contention of these pronunciamentos about the "inviolable right to work" did not move this learned member of the judiciary from his original recommendation. The chairman of the board, also a distinguished member of the bar, supported the recommendation, and a few days following the publication of these two pronunciamentos he declared:[5]

> . . . There is no restriction of the worker's choice as to whether he will or will not join the union.
>
> It has been suggested that this clause does restrict the worker's freedom of action in some measure because when he has joined the union he cannot get out. But a few words will show that this is in reality a restriction which he has chosen to impose upon himself, and self-imposed restriction is the essence of freedom. Every man who joins the union agrees to be bound by its majority action, and those who are now members of the union have voted by overwhelming majority for a union shop which would make their jobs depend upon their union membership. New employees who may hereafter voluntarily join the union will know before hand that if they join the union they will have to remain members for the two-year duration of the shipyard contract. . . .

Apparently they felt, along with organized labor, that, as Darrow said, "the inalienable right to work is a bit of birdlime, used to catch the unthinking mass." The doctrine of the right to work, as preached by management, is either a clever piece of propaganda or a dastardly distortion of economic fact and democratic principles, depending upon one's viewpoint. At each stage of organized labor's progress this fallacious doctrine has been thrown out by management to confuse the public and defeat the legitimate aims of organized labor. In 1937 the auto and steel strikes, for example, were denounced as interference with the "right to work" of the American workman. The next year, when workers were being laid off by the hundreds of thousands, the "right to work" doctrine was mockingly thrown back at management by union spokesmen. In 1941 a government agency recommended a maintenance-of-membership recognition clause to a subsidiary of the largest corporation in America, and again the false doctrine of the "right to work" was spread across the nation's newspapers. The leaders of this corporation knew only too well, as Darrow declared years earlier, that the only right workers have is "the right to go from employer to employer in search of work." Their use of this false doctrine is ironic and, of course, insincere.

It is insincere because it implies that management is a champion of the individual rights of workers when, of course, it has not only ignored but denied these rights. The policy of management—which the leaders of this huge firm have helped formulate during the last forty years—has denied workers their right of free speech and assemblage. The record of civil liberties in industrial America before the rise of the CIO is well known. This policy likewise denied workers the freedom to exercise their right to join a union of their own choosing, and fired and denied employment to workers who exercised this right. The record in this regard is also well known. With this background, management has the indignity to assert that its objection to the union shop is predicated upon a sincere concern for the individual rights of workers. The insincerity of this position is obvious upon an examination of the right which management professes to protect—the right to work. It is a fabrication and a sham. The only right workers had before the rise of the CIO in the mass-production industries was the right to seek a job, and, as Darrow observed, this right could be denied "upon any reason or pretext no matter what."

The extent to which organized labor has limited the reasons and pretexts upon which management could deny employment to workers or discharge them is the extent to which it has given reality to the right to work. Organized labor has established the right to work unhindered by discrimination for union membership. We have seen how unions, through seniority, have protected the right of workers to keep their jobs unhindered by arbitrary discharge, favoritism, or petty discrimination. Step by step organized labor has given substance to the right to work; but it has not established it as a pure right, because in modern economic society it is always conditioned upon an employer providing work. Consequently, compulsory union membership does not deny workers their "inalienable right to work"—because they enjoy no such right and, therefore, cannot be denied something that they already do not possess.

It is organized labor, and not management, that is the champion of the rights of workers. Each time it advances a step in this direction, management charges organized labor with attempting to deny the right to work to workers. But the use of this false doctrine in the case of the union shop is ironic, since the idea of the union shop was first conceived and practiced by management during the long, violent, anti-union period when it sought to deny workers the right to organize.

The union-shop idea is simply that union and nonunion workers in most instances cannot work alongside of each other indefinitely for practical reasons. The "yellow-dog contract," now illegal, provided that, because (1) management did not recognize labor unions, or (2) believe in or practice collective bargaining, and (3) its employees were not union members, it was a condition of employment that no employee could belong to a union. Management, then, used its arbitrary powers of discharge to enforce these contracts, whether they were written or just understood, that any employee who joined the union would be fired when it was learned he had joined, or it was suspected he had joined or might join. Management's enforcement of the dictum that union and nonunion workers should not work side by side was complete. The "blacklist" was devised; this simply provided that once a worker was fired for union membership, union agitation, or suspected union membership no firm in the district, frequently in the industry, would give him employment. This policy naturally flowed from the basic opposition of management to organized labor, but it was also conceived and practiced for practical operating requirements. Associate OPM Director Sidney Hillman aptly pointed this out to the House

Judiciary Committee of Congress[6] early in 1941. A Congressman asked, "Now, my understanding of an open shop is a place where union and nonunion men work together. Is that true?"

"Oh, no, Congressman," Mr. Hillman replied, "they just work in the same place. They don't work together."

Members of labor organizations favor the union shop for different but nonetheless potent practical reasons; they cannot afford to work with nonunion workers for reasons of self-preservation. Unionists do so only temporarily as a matter of expediency—until the first opportune time to bring the nonmembers into the union fold or replace them with union members. On this point Clarence S. Darrow's[7] words are conclusive.

> The reason why a union workman does not choose to work with a non-union workman is plain and evident and founded in the protection of himself and his fellow craftsmen. . . . Instinctively men love the company of others of their kind. . . . The man who desires the society of his companions must so conduct himself that his associates are content to live with him. If he sees fit voluntarily to so arrange his life that his fellows do not desire his company he must accept the consequences, however unreasonable society may be. Whether the boycott is just or unjust, equitable or inequitable, has no bearing on the case. In this world men are not crucified because they are good or bad, but because they are unlike their fellows. Trade unionists for centuries have believed that they are upholding the right of man, the welfare of their class; that without their organization their liberty and independence would be lost; they have come to regard the nonunion man as one who not only refuses to stand with them, but who is unloyal to his class, a traitor to his kind. They look on him as a man who seeks to undermine and destroy his fellow workman, and from the nature of things there is a great gulf between them and him. This is not a fact in trade unionism; it is a fact in human nature, and is as deep as the right of self-defense. For in the last analysis, it is self-defense.
>
> The employing class has exactly the same feeling toward one of its members who gives his influence and strength on the side of the union workman, and who refuses to stand with them in

their opposition to the demands of labor, that the trade unionist has toward the one he calls a scab. Neither is loyal to his class. Both pay the penalty of their disloyalty to their class; they are cut off from the friendship and association with others of their kind. . . .

Trade unions in this regard are not unlike any other class. The doctors and the lawyers, the brokers and the bankers—in short, all sorts of trades and professions—organize for their own protection. Everyone knows how doctors and lawyers regard those members of their professions who will not be bound by their rules as to charges, advertising, and generally such conduct as they term the ethics of their profession, which in its analysis is the establishment of such rules and regulations as, in their opinion, tend to the improvement of their own condition. Of course, doctors and lawyers, like trade unionists, will stoutly insist that these rules and regulations benefit the public more than their own craft or profession. Perhaps this is true, but, whether true or not, the instinct of self-preservation causes each member to regard one who willfully stands outside as an enemy to his craft. . . .

If it is right to protect American workmen against the cutthroat competition of Chinamen and foreign contract labor, then the same logic makes it right to protect them against unjust competition at home, against the aggressions of the vicious workman, the ignorant workman, the weak workman, the woman and the child. It matters not whether law makers have ever carried legislation to this point. The reason for the one is the same as the other, and the workman has the same right to make his own rules and regulations and to protect it by contract in the one case that he has in the other. . . .

Man has not a right to apply his energy to the bounties of nature until the master gives him a chance to work, and so long as this right is so monopolized that he must look to the employer for a job, he is forgetful of himself and recreant to his class, if he fails to impose all reasonable restrictions and conditions, and exact all just terms in the service that he sells.

Since Darrow's time employers generally have recognized unions; but, where such an act was cause for social boycott in his time, granting the union shop today brings down on management's head the opprobrium of its competing associates. Though we have union-shop arrangements with fully thirty per cent of the steel firms, not a single one has dared, as yet, to acknowledge publicly that it has entered into such an agreement with SWOC. The telling way in which management coerces its fellows was demonstrated during the Atlantic Coast shipyard case. We had negotiations under way with three separate companies that were agreed on signing a union-shop contract at the time this case was publicized. The management in each of these firms had taken courage from a large automobile company, but no sooner did the heads of America's biggest financial and industrial empire give up a shipyard before yielding to a modification of the union shop than these companies ran for cover. Sheepishly the chief negotiator for each firm came to us, begged that we release him from the agreement on the condition that he would give SWOC a private confidential letter embodying the union-shop form of recognition. One of these negotiators said, "With the Manufacturers Association, the Chamber of Commerce, and all the trade journals denouncing the union shop, we can't afford to go out on the limb. You understand."

Management's policy is that all firms must resist the union shop together or each firm will have to concede it individually. This is a pure and simple policy of self-defense. We saw it in operation in the Atlantic Coast shipyard case. The meaning behind the high-sounding words contained in the pronunciamentos of the company involved and the two large employer organizations was, "Don't give unions the union shop. We are giving up a profitable shipyard to prove we mean business. We are not responsible for what happens to you if you vary from this policy." And it had its effect, as evidenced by the three firms previously mentioned. Yet in exercising this right of self-preservation the leaders of industry attempt to deny the selfsame right to organized labor. Certainly if it is proper—and we believe it is—for industry to coerce its fellows to conform to its accepted policies, then it is right for organized labor to engage in equally vital acts of self-preservation.

The self-defense policy of union workers is, "If we don't

hang together, we will each hang separately." As management finds it essential to self-defense to "coerce" those who may stray from an antiunion-shop policy, so, likewise, do union workers find it essential to self-defense to "coerce" nonunion workers into the union fold. In arguing the union shop with a management official who is prominent in high society circles in Pittsburgh, one of the authors remarked, "Whether or not you grant the union shop, union members will continue to exert social pressure on nonmembers to get them into the union." He laughed; the idea that workers might exert social pressures against members of their group who failed to conform to the group's attitudes seemed ridiculous to him. In his own group, of course, social pressures are rigidly exerted—a daughter who marries the chauffeur just has to move across the railroad tracks with him. That a nonunion worker might have to drink his beer at home instead of at a bar frequented by union workers, to this man of high society, was laughable. Maybe he thought workers exert social pressure only with their fists and he was laughing at the idea of calling a street brawl "social pressure." More likely, however, he felt social pressures were subtle practices that his group in society engaged in exclusively, when actually, of course, they are a vital part of the habits of every social group.

But there is a significant difference in the way in which management and union members exercise their respective policies of self-defense. A small minority of industrial leaders —only a very small percentage of the manufacturing establishments in America, for instance, belong to the National Association of Manufacturers—formulate the basic policies affecting union-management relations, and "coerce" the vast majority of industrial firms to abide by them. Union members, on the other hand, exercise their self-defense policies within the framework of democratic principles. They do not seek to "coerce" with the penalty of discharge any worker into union membership in a given bargaining unit until a majority of eligible workers have voluntarily become union members. Then a majority—in accordance with the democratic principle of majority rule—seek the right through the union shop to "coerce" a minority of their fellow workers into union membership at the penalty of discharge.

The philosophy of the union shop, therefore, is rooted in the basic democratic principle that governs our political life; namely, the rule of the majority. The only thing that is revolutionary—to management—about the underlying principle of the union shop is that it should be fully accepted in our industrial and economic life as well as our political life. Mr. Arthur Henry is typical in his belief that the majority-rule principle of our political democracy is not valid when applied to industrial democracy. The New York *Times*, for instance, disputed the defense of the Atlantic Coast shipyard maintenance-of-membership-clause recommendation made by the chairman of the National Defense Mediation Board on this ground:[8]

> . . . His attempt to prove that the provision does not restrict the freedom of the individual worker, that it would be a "self-imposed restriction" and therefore "the essence of freedom," is unconvincing. When he declares that under this provision "each worker is allowed to determine for himself whether or not he shall belong to the union" he neglects to add that he is not allowed to determine for himself whether or not he may quit the union. If Mr. Davis [the board's chairman] were not allowed to leave a political party, a church or a club which he had once joined, except on the penalty of losing his livelihood, he would hardly consider the arrangement "the essence of freedom."

The fallacy of this analogy is self-evident. The democratic principle upon which the union shop is based has already been accepted by management in every fact of employment except union membership. We recently had the case of a skilled machinist in a shell-manufacturing plant who was laid off because he had a social disease. Management denied him his individual "right to work" in consideration of the general welfare of all of its employees. The union agreed, and refused to take up the machinist's case until he secured a clean bill of health from an established community clinic. Hence the right of a majority of the employees in a given bargaining unit to decide that an individual employee shall be laid off because of the state of his health is accepted by management. On the question of health and sanitation the welfare of the majority is widely recognized, and is not disputed. On the other facts of employment, however, the general welfare of a majority has not been so unanimously acknowledged, because it is less obvious. But, except for union membership, it has been as unanimously accepted by management.

The "right" of an individual worker to set his own wage has been abridged wherever the institution of collective bargaining has been established. Not many years ago it was widely defended by management but not by workers, since it did not benefit them in the slightest. In signing a collective-bargaining contract management accepts the right of the majority of its employees, through their union, to decide upon the wage for each individual one. The union members make this decision at a union meeting, and bind all employees by it. Management does not contend that individual workers should continue to have the "right" to set their own wage in direct negotiation with it. In fact, management looks upon its contract with the union as a means of protection against general wage-raise demands from individual workers during the life of the contract. The individual worker gladly gives up his valueless "right" to set his own wage with management for the effective union right of setting his wage through the bargaining power of a majority of his fellow workers. Thus the general welfare of all employees, no less than in the matter of health and sanitation, requires that a majority shall have the right to set the wages of each individual one, because if each individual employee set his own wage—as was done prior to the union—then none would be able to set it as high as a majority can through a union that has bargaining power equal to that of management.

It is a condition of employment that workers shall abide by the wage for their respective jobs that a majority set in negotiation with management. It is likewise a condition of employment in the matters of the workday and work week and time and one-half for overtime. The individual worker is not free to bargain with management that he will work a longer day or week without overtime. Nor can he demand a shorter day or week. Neither can he agree to work, say, for time and one-third instead of time and one-half for overtime that has been established by a majority of his fellow workers in their union contract. And, further, the individual worker must abide by these terms of employment at the penalty of discharge. He cannot walk home from work at the end of six hours because he is opposed to the eight-hour day without losing his job. He cannot work a ten-hour day at straight time, because the union will not allow it. In this connection management accepts the right of a majority of its employees to decide how long each individual one shall work per day and per week, and at what overtime rates of pay. What is equally important is that Congress and the federal government and many state governments likewise have accepted the principle that the welfare of a majority of workers requires the establishment of minimum wages and maximum hours.

Thus the "right" of management and individual workers to agree upon whatever terms of employment may be mutually acceptable is abridged by federal legislation. Furthermore, this legislation accepts the right of a majority of the employees in a given bargaining unit to set, in negotiation with management, a lower work week than required by law, to which each individual worker is bound. The same principle is accepted in unions negotiating minimum wages in excess of those established by law. On the questions of health and sanitation, wages, workday and work week, and overtime pay, then, the principle of majority rule is universally accepted in American industry.

In the determination of seniority rules only the interests of a majority of the employees can be protected. If departmental seniority, for instance, is written into the contract, it is inevitable that some employees with long years of service in departments that become slack will be laid off while younger ones are kept in other departments. By the same token if plant-wide seniority is written into the contract, it is inevitable that younger employees in certain departments will be laid off in preference to older ones from other departments who may transfer into their jobs during a period of curtailed operations. In a nut-and-bolt factory we had the case of an individual member with three years of service in a single department who waged a one-man strike. Management and the union had agreed upon plant-wide seniority. The member, having only three years of service, opposed the union policy since in slack times he would be laid off. He took it up at a union meeting, but a majority voted against him. He protested to both the union and management, but learned that he did not have the individual right to negotiate his own seniority rules in conflict with those determined by a majority of his fellow workers. Whereupon he conducted a one-man strike, and picketed the plant for several days. He even took a gun to a union meeting and shot the union president—almost fatally. To be certain, he was discharged for refusing to abide by the rule of the majority. In so discharging him, management accepted the right, as does industry as a whole, of a majority of its employees to determine the seniority rules that apply to each individual one.

President Franklin D. Roosevelt in a personal letter requested the employees in a large aircraft firm to forego their vacations during the summer of 1941 and accept vacation pay instead. In one of the firm's plants under contract with SWOC the union conducted a poll among its members. All but three voted "Yes." These three had to abide by the vote of the majority. This democratic principle governs on all facts of employment but union membership. And it is enforced with the power of discharge. It is a condition of employment in every industrial concern under a collective-bargaining contract that all employees must abide by its terms of employment. Failure of any individual employee to abide by any such term makes him subject to discharge.

It is inconsistent, therefore, for management to deny the principle of majority rule on the question of union membership. Yet a large shipbuilding firm gave up its yard before accepting this principle applied to union membership. In so doing, it ignorantly or maliciously—it matters not, for the one is as inexcusable as the other and the effects are the same—inserted a full-page advertisement in many newspapers throughout the country when the federal government took over the shipyard.[9]

> . . . This change in the management of the shipyard has been brought about solely because of the unwillingness of this Company to accede to the demand of the Union that we should discharge from our employ any worker, a member of the Union now or hereafter, who failed to pay his Union dues or otherwise failed to maintain his membership in the Union in good standing. We could not conscientiously agree to dismiss our old, faithful and tried employees on such a ground. We felt that the only test of employment should continue to be the proved capacity, zeal and fidelity of the workman, irrespective of his membership or nonmembership in any organization.

Like all other firms operating under collective-bargaining contracts, this shipbuilding firm has accepted, as we have seen, the principle of majority rule for every condition of employment that is embodied in the contract. Union membership is the only remaining fact of employment not so covered. The union asked that it be included in the 1941 contract. The firm refused. And a government agency said, "Let's compromise. You don't have to discharge any employee for refusing to join the union; only those who, having joined voluntarily, refuse to continue in good standing with the union." The firm then gives up its shipyard, and replies, "We [can] not conscientiously agree to dismiss our old, faithful and tried employees on such a ground." Yet the firm has already agreed to dismiss any one of these employees for failing to abide by the majority decision of its employees on wages, hours, seniority, vacations, and so forth. In addition, the firm has the indignity to say that "proved capacity, zeal and fidelity of the workman" is the only test of employment, when abiding by the majority will of its employees on wages, hours, and so forth has already been accepted as tests of employment. Consequently, in refusing to apply this democratic principle to union membership that it applies to every other fact of employment, the firm's position is neither logical nor just.

Management generally cannot contend—with either logic or justice—that it is unfair, un-American, or nondemocratic to abridge an individual employee's "right" to be nonunion in a given bargaining unit where a majority of the employees are union members. The general welfare of a majority of employees requires one hundred per cent union membership, because their welfare is dependent upon the strength of the union. And the union's strength is determined by the all-inclusiveness of its membership. Union workers look upon the nonunion worker, as Darrow so clearly says, "as one who . . . refuses to stand with them . . . as a man who seeks to undermine and destroy his fellow workman. This is not a fact in trade unionism; it is a fact in human nature, and is as deep as the right of self-defense. For in the last analysis, it is self-defense." The union shop, therefore, is demanded by organized labor not alone on democratic principles but to promote the general welfare of its members.

Industrial democracy is predicated upon the principle of majority rule in no less a degree than is America's political democracy. Congress wrote this principle into the National Labor Relations Act. It has been accepted by the federal government, the Supreme Court, and management on the question of union representation. In any given bargaining unit, the act provides that the union chosen by a majority of the employees shall be the exclusive bargaining agency for all employees eligible for union membership. There is no minority representation. The defeated union, if the victor has a contending union on the ballot, loses all standing with management as a bargaining agency. Even those employees who may vote for no union at all have to accept representation by the majority union. This is so for practical reasons. A productive enterprise cannot be operated peacefully or successfully with more than one bargaining agency for the same group of workers. Management itself is most vigorous in stating that it cannot afford to have two or more conflicting unions in its mines, mills, and factories. It is, therefore, a fact of industrial democracy, written into the law, that it is a one-party system of democracy. In this respect it varies from our traditional two-party system of political democracy. No doubt this factor has snarled the sincere opponents of the union shop into the fallacious analogy of comparing membership in a union with membership in a political party. We make the distinction of "sincere opponents" because this false analogy is used by many opponents of the union shop with the same malicious intent as is the false doctrine of "the right to work."

Republicans do not have to join the Democratic party, or vice versa, when it becomes the majority party in Congress. Within each Congressional district, to be sure, the minority voters are unrepresented in Congress; the victorious Congressman represents all the voters in his district. But the minority are thus not denied a voice in Congress. From at least some of the Congressional districts, Congressmen are elected who represent the views of the defeated minority voters in a majority of the districts. Consequently the minority within each district can express its views and exert its influence through its party's Congressmen, even though they may not come from its particular district. The opposite is the case in industry.

It is practical for only one union to represent any given group of workers. The minority nonmembers cannot express their views or exert their influence through another union, because neither the law nor management recognizes a minority union. All workers in a given unit have to be represented by one bargaining agency. Thus the only way the minority workers can express their views and exert their influence is through union membership. They are bound by the action of the majority in any event, and to have a voice in making the decisions of the majority the minority or nonunion workers have to join the union. In cases where SWOC local unions lose an election conducted by the National Labor Relations Board, we usually advise our members to join the victorious union to protect their interests. This does not necessarily deny them their particular views which led them originally to choose SWOC in preference to the victorious union. Within its councils they can express their views and, as frequently happens, after an interval of time they persuade a majority of their fellow unionists to change their local union affiliation to SWOC. But to secure a voice in industry the minority must join the majority union. Membership in the union as a condition of employment, therefore, is an essential requirement of industrial democracy in order to assure all workers a voice in the determination of their conditions of employment.

Police powers or disciplinary powers are vested in the union in direct proportion with the amount of responsibilities it assumes. The union assumes the responsibility to see that no stoppages of work occur, that all workers adhere to the contract machinery to settle grievances peacefully, and that wages and other vital cost factors are pegged generally for the life of the contract. To fulfill these responsibilities the union must have sufficient authority to discipline those workers who, for example, may stop work in violation of the contract. Because supreme power is divided between management and the union, the majority-rule principle operates differently from the way it does in a political democracy—where supreme power is vested in one agency, the government. Here, if the Republicans are elected, Democrats do not have to join the Republican party, because the state or government has the supreme power to enforce the laws passed by the Republicans. But it is necessary for the minority nonmembers to join the union or else the majority, through the union, lacks the power to see that the minority abides by the rules. For example, nine hundred of a thousand workers vote for SWOC. The one hundred that vote against it refuse to join. If they stop work the entire one thousand workers are affected. Management holds the union responsible for enforcing the contract; but it cannot discipline nonmembers, since its authority is confined to members. Thus in order to discharge its responsibilities for the maintenance of industrial peace the minority workers must be required to join the union at the penalty of discharge.

Lastly, it is a basic principle of industrial democracy that those who share its benefits must assume the responsibility of securing them. This principle has its counterpart in a political democracy; namely, those who enjoy its freedom must assume the responsibilities of it. The city taxpayer, for instance, who votes against the victorious candidate for mayor, whose program advocates increased taxes to build a new city hospital, must pay the additional taxes to erect the hospital. Failure on his part to pay such taxes, if persisted in, results in the recalcitrant taxpayer losing his property. All the employees in a given bargaining unit, as we have seen, are bound by the collective-bargaining contract. The wage increases, shorter hours, and other benefits secured by the majority in the contract are enjoyed likewise by the minority. The union has to pay hall rent, postage, grievance committeemen for lost time, and other operating expenses. To meet these obligations every member must pay the taxes (union dues) levied by and for the support of the union. All the workers in a given unit derive equal benefits from the union and, therefore, they should all share equally in paying the cost of its upkeep. This is possible only through union membership, because the union cannot collect dues from workers for whom it bargains but who, in turn, are not members of it. Union members also, on occasion, have to strike to win gains. This often means that the union has to assess its members to win the strike. The benefits of the victory are shared in equally by the minority nonmembers. Consequently, it is a requirement of industrial democracy that all of its beneficiaries assume their share of the burdens.

The virtual revolution set in motion by the organizing activities of the CIO was the overthrow of an autocratic form of life in industry and the substitution in its place of a democratic form. The basic principle of democracy—majority rule—has been extended to every field of union-management relations except union membership. Industrial democracy will not be really achieved, however, until this principle is extended to union membership, because it is based on the participation of all workers in a given bargaining unit. This is not possible as long as a minority of workers fails to subscribe to and accept the fact of citizenship in industry. Mr. Arthur Henry objected to compelling workers at the penalty of discharge to become union members—citizens of industry—on the ground that this is as wrong as was the firing of workers for union membership. The fallacy of this objection is obvious. The union worker was fired by management without the consent of a majority of its workers and for the express purpose of denying the majority the right to organize. This was wrong, since it was done to perpetuate an autocratic form of life in industry. The purpose of firing a worker who persists in refusing to join the union in an industrial democracy is the very opposite. Union members seek one hundred per cent organization to protect their general welfare and establish a democratic way of life in industry.

The analogy of comparing union membership with membership in a political party, as we have seen, is likewise unsound, since industrial democracy functions through a one-party system. All workers are represented by one union, and they are not citizens of industry until they belong to it. The principle of majority rule cannot be denied in one area of union-management relations except at the peril of industrial democracy. Hence it is a vital path to industrial peace for free America that this principle govern throughout the entire union-management relationship, as it does throughout our political democracy.

An important part of the foundation of industrial democracy, therefore, is the union shop. It has a marked distinction from the closed shop. In the latter, management must hire union members. In a union shop, management may hire whomsoever it pleases provided, only, that after an agreed-upon period of time all new workers shall join the union. The very reason why the building-trades unions, for example, insist upon the closed shop is why industrial unions do not seek it. The latter are only too glad to leave to management the freedom to hire whomsoever it pleases, because there are too few jobs to be distributed to too many job seekers. Yet this is the reason why the building trades need the closed shop—in order to protect their members and their standards. To them this is important since their respective members are all the same type of craftsmen. The opposite is the case in industrial unions; their membership consists of a diversity of workers—skilled, single-skilled, or unskilled.

It is doubtful whether management could ever get industrial unions to share the responsibility of hiring. To have to tell an unemployed worker, "Sorry, no work today; not hiring just now," is too unenviable a responsibility for industrial unions to desire or seek. Furthermore, they do not need a voice in hiring to develop and maintain their full strength, because the union shop gives them about all the strength needed to preserve and advance the general welfare of their members. That here and there in an isolated instance an industrial union has sought, or even secured, a voice in determining who shall be hired does not alter this in the slightest. Most experiences indicate that such a union would gladly and for good reason return to management the exclusive power to do all of the hiring.

The objection to giving unions the right to secure the discharge of a worker who persists in refusing to join the union because, here and there, a union may abuse this right has no relation to the democratic right of a majority of workers in a given unit to establish membership in it as a condition of employment. This objection has no more validity as a reason for opposing the union shop than would an objection to allowing individuals of sound mind and body to drive an automobile because, here and there, one might abuse the right to drive a motor car on a public highway. The abuse of a right has no relationship to its validity, only to its preservation; as the union shop, like all rights, will not survive continued or excessive abuse. Workers have a right to the union shop to the same extent that they have the right to a union. Whether they will prove worthy in the basic and mass-production industries of keeping the union shop once they have secured it remains to be seen on the basis of their conduct and integrity.

Rights in a democracy are usually strengthened when abused. This is not one of their weaknesses. When a right is abused it eventually comes to light. The fact that it is publicized either strengthens the right or eventually reveals that those enjoying the right are not entitled to retain it. A scoundrel, for example, is revealed to have controlled an established drug firm for more than a decade. He did it by overvaluing, among other things, the firm's inventories. This was brought to light, and the practices of certified accounting firms in checking into the physical existence and worth of inventories have been immeasurably improved. Huey Long abused the rights of political democracy. It was exposed and, though his native state still suffers from many defects as a democratic state, the rights of democracy are not being abused as they were in Huey Long's day. Certain Southern Congressmen are sitting in Congress by the vote of less than twenty per cent of the citizens in their districts. This is due to the abuse of the poll-tax system or its very existence. It is being exposed, and will eventually be corrected. While, in contrast, abuses under a nondemocratic form of government, not being subject to public scrutiny, lead to endless abuses. Of course, confidence that the universal acceptance of the union shop in industry will work for the general welfare of workers and owners, like confidence in any other democratic principle or democracy itself, requires a faith in the individual and group intelligence and integrity of the common people. We have such faith; our fears grow out of the denial of democratic principles in vital segments of American life.

This leaves one remaining principal objection to the union shop, that it constitutes "coercion" in some form. One of the authors spoke on this subject in New York City in 1939 before an audience of more than a hundred management executives. An hour question period followed the initial talk in which every conceivable objection to the union shop was thrown at the speaker for reply. One by one he answered them. Finally a persistent questioner took the tense and provoked audience by storm. He calmly asked, "Granted all you say is correct, and certainly nobody in this room has successfully challenged your arguments for the union shop, but isn't it coercion to force a worker to join the union?" The audience bellowed, obviously relieved that, at last, the whole fabric of reasoning in support of the union shop had been shattered. But its relief was short-lived. The speaker simply replied, "Of course, it's coercion. That's what all the argument is about: the right to force someone to do something against his will. But this is not a legitimate objection to the union shop, as coercion is the fundamental basis of organized society. In fact, civilization can be said to have attained maturity when men became intelligent enough to order their affairs and compel the recalcitrant man, the ignorant man, to submit to certain compulsory rules for the common good of all men. I cannot drive through a red light, although I have enough good sense not to carelessly drive through an intersection; but, because other men lack such sense, for the common good I am coerced into stopping for a red light, although no cars may be coming from the opposite direction. The essential difference between a democracy and, say, Hitler's government is that in the former a majority do the coercing, or if the action is unanimous it is self-imposed; while under Hitler the minority is doing the coercing, and though an action may be generally approved by the people it is forced on them from the top."

The audience, convened under the auspices of the National Industrial Conference Board, adjourned somewhat subdued but, significantly, still opposed to the union shop. In the intervening three years, however, more and more industrial firms have accepted the union-shop idea. A large automobile company has shown the way. Others are following, and before long the union shop will be accepted as universally as collective bargaining now is, not alone, if at all, because of its democratic righteousness, but for imperatively practical considerations to which we now turn our attention.

The union shop is a necessary prerequisite for constructive union-management relations.

For three weeks in 1940 a strike in a steel mill near Pittsburgh filled the newspapers. The company president said it involved an "irreconcilable difference of opinion." In conference with us and in the public press he argued that great American principles of life were at stake and that "on the matter of a union shop we are standing upon a principle which we cannot yield." Finally, like the sudden change when the sun shines through the clouds after a severe thunderstorm in midsummer, he signed a union-shop contract. One of the authors could not resist the temptation to lean over the desk and ask this company president as he was in the act of putting his signature to the contract, "Tell me, what's become of your principles all of a sudden?"

"Hell, Clint," he replied, "I'm a steel man, not a political-science teacher. You'll have to ask my attorneys about that."

In another case, management stood out for eleven weeks against the union shop, publicly arguing that "we would be violating the individual rights of our employees if we told them they would be required to join the union." This firm had been particularly militant in its opposition to SWOC and, after a fifty-year record of complete disregard for the rights of its employees, this great concern for the individual rights of a minority of its employees seemed hypocritical—a vast majority had voted for SWOC in a government-supervised election. The real purpose for opposing the union shop was revealed by one of the top officials of this firm, who told a common friend, "I'm not going to let a really strong union in my plant. If I do, then I'm likely never to be able to get rid of it." SWOC won the union shop; in fact, SWOC would never have waged a long and costly strike on this issue in the year 1939 if it had not been convinced that without the union shop management would have succeeded in getting rid of it.

In still another case we were arguing the union-shop issue when the plant manager interrupted, saying, "We have to keep this America." The manager's remark was challenging to one of the authors, who went into a lengthy elaboration of the democratic basis for the union shop. The plant manager seemed a little startled with the elaboration, apparently had never thought the issue through clearly, and did not reply. Instead he turned to the company president. "Perhaps Mr. Williams better answer that question, as it's company policy." Taken by surprise, the president sat up in his chair, and stated bluntly, "We're agin it. We run an open shop. There's no use further discussing the matter." This ended the discussion, and we did not get the union shop.

It has become evident to us that management as a whole is not fundamentally opposed to the union shop on principle or democratic grounds, and will not accept it for these reasons. Its opposition is mainly, if not entirely, upon cold, hard, practical considerations. Management did not want unions, in the first place, to have a voice in operating its mines, mills, and factories, and for this reason opposed the self-organization of its employees. Once they organized unions, management did not want them to have much of a voice in how things should be done. But gradually it becomes apparent to management that a strong union—one whose membership is all-inclusive—contributes more toward successful operations than one whose principal occupation is with self-preservation—getting and keeping members, collecting dues, pressing grievances, and so forth. Thus it is essentially for cold, hard, practical considerations that management universally will eventually accept the union shop.

Certainly the union shop, or any other democratic principle, would have no virility, or cause for acceptance, unless it is wholly practical and urgently needed. This fact is implicit in the history of American democracy. Virtually every extension of democratic principles in American life, since the first amendments to the federal Constitution which embrace the Bill of Rights, was accepted for reasons of practicality and necessity. The cause of public education was long advocated by organized labor on democratic grounds, and eventually accepted—after much resistance—for practical and necessary considerations. The National Labor Relations Act is another example. It established as a matter of law the principle of collective bargaining, not alone on democratic grounds, but also for practical and urgent reasons. It is clear from the history of the development of democratic principles in our country that a proposition, no matter how well grounded it may be in democratic principles, has first to be demonstrated as practical and necessary before being added to the American Way of Life. Thus, while pressing for the union shop on democratic grounds, organized labor is taking advantage of every opportunity to demonstrate its essentially practical character.

Throughout this discussion the shortcomings of collective bargaining have been readily apparent, but, as we have pointed out consistently, these shortcomings are not so much those of collective bargaining itself as those of collective bargaining with unions whose members or potential members enjoy the anarchical freedom to join, withdraw, or refrain from joining the union as their fancy strikes them. In refusing to grant unions more than the barest minimum of recognition, management encourages the belief—which is widespread among union members in American industry—that it is still opposed to collective bargaining and unions and is only waiting for an opportunity to cast both aside. This, in turn, perpetuates in office militant, uncompromising local union leaders. They make it all the more difficult for management to work out equitable seniority rules that have enough flexibility so as not to impede productive efficiency. They likewise make it almost impossible to handle grievances on their merits, which is such an essential of industrial peace. We have seen how union grievance committeemen, operating under a voluntary union-membership contract, are under constant pressure to consider factors other than the merits of grievances. It has also been obvious that management can hardly work out with a union whose membership is purely voluntary the difficult problems of inequities in its wage structures.

The shortcomings of collective bargaining that have been apparent throughout this discussion are most undesirable, but under a limited form of union recognition they are almost inevitable. It is as if taxpayers had the privilege of ceasing to pay taxes if Congress does not pass a particular bill in which they are interested. Management's policy, "It's up to the union to sell itself to all of the employees," has cost industry millions of dollars and workers and owners untold amounts in industrial turmoil. Wages, seniority, and the other problems of union-management relations can be handled much more efficiently and equitably under the union-shop form of recognition. Let us look at a few typical instances.

A steel firm replaced its hand-style sheet mills with two-high, semiautomatic finishing mills. A serious seniority problem immediately arose. Of the two hundred-odd skilled hand-mill workers displaced, only thirty-one were needed to man the semiautomatic mills. Management and the union had the problem of selecting this small number from among the more than two hundred displaced workers. During the ninety-day period between the abandonment of the hand mills and the completion of the new ones, these men were laid off except for a few who were absorbed in other departments of the mill. The union and management agreed that each would submit a list of men who would go on the new mills a week before they were ready to operate. Neither side would see the other's list until both of them were submitted. Those men on both lists would immediately go on the new mills, while the grievance machinery would be invoked in the case of those about whom there was disagreement.

The union leaders diligently prepared a list, and those men with the longest service that the union felt were not fully qualified to operate the new mills were given a hearing and told why they would have to be passed up in favor of younger men better qualified. They picked twenty-two men on the basis of their service records and nine on the basis of ability. When the union submitted its list to management, the latter submitted its list. They were identical except for seven men. Management said, "It's all a question of judgment. Maybe the union has made the better choices. Anyway it worked the problem out with all the men affected, and they will be more satisfied with the union's selections than ours. So we will give the union's list a ninety-day trial." All but one made good.

An analysis of this case reveals the essential differences between collective bargaining on a purely voluntary membership and that on a union-shop basis. In the first instance, such co-operative union leaders probably would not exist. Further, even if they did, they could hardly have departed from the strict union policy of picking the thirty-one employees with the longest service records. And, if they tried, then those employees with long service records who would be passed up for younger men would raise so much turmoil inside the union's ranks that its unity and dues-paying membership would be seriously threatened. Hence, if this steel firm had not been operating under a union-shop agreement, it no doubt would have been plagued with grievances unless it selected the thirty-one oldest employees. In this event it then would not have been able to utilize the most able employees and the efficiency of the new mills might have suffered accordingly. In addition, the company might have had a strike over the technological change. As it was, the union members had confidence that management was making the change out of consideration for the company's long-run welfare. Not being concerned exclusively with the problems of self-preservation, the union leaders had time to acquaint themselves with such problems. And, not being fearful of losing dues-paying members, they were able to stand up and tell their members the facts no matter how unpopular they might be.

In the case of Mr. Arthur Henry's company's relations

with SWOC, the inability of a union enjoying only partial recognition to assume full responsibility on vital questions is clearly demonstrated. During the 1938 depression Mr. Henry tried to regularize employment for the fourteen thousand employees of his company (six thousand had been laid off) remaining on the pay roll. He wanted to give them all an average of four days of work a week. This involved transferring men from a slack department to one that was temporarily busy, instead of recalling laid-off men from these departments for a short period only to lay them off again.

The idea appealed to us. It gave those men working part time fuller employment. Since it usually took several weeks before temporarily recalled employees could get back on relief and WPA, it saved them this inconvenience—which, in many cases, was a serious hardship. But the furloughed men would have no part of it, nor were the men remaining on the pay roll enthusiastic about the idea. The former revolted against outsiders, men from other departments, taking their jobs temporarily—they feared it might become permanent and they would never get back their old jobs. The latter disliked the idea because of the criticism coming from the furloughed men when they met on the street. To both groups, of course, the prospect of being permanently frozen out of one's job by the operation of such a policy stared them in the face. SWOC field representatives tried to explain that when the mills picked up again every man would go back to his old job on the basis of seniority. But the nature of SWOC's relations with the company had prevented the development of the kind of confidence necessary for workers to trust to the company such a risk with their jobs. Had the union enjoyed a union-shop contract, our experience indicates, such confidence would probably have existed in the company and SWOC would have been able to sell the policy to its members. In several companies where SWOC had the union shop this policy was adopted and worked to the satisfaction of almost every worker as well as management.

Mr. Henry also tried to get SWOC to agree to a policy of allowing foremen, who were not needed because of the reduced working force, to do production work. We recognized the desirability of preserving management's organization. Mr. Henry argued that it was absolutely necessary that he keep his management personnel intact, lest he lose some good men to competitors. We did not even try to sell this idea to our members; they had joined the union to protect their jobs and on no grounds would they share work with bosses. The amount of lost time the men would have suffered, as Mr. Henry pointed out to SWOC local union committees, was negligible. Rarely would the work that foremen might do result in laying a man off, and only in a small number of cases would men work three instead of four, or four instead of five, days. The committees unanimously replied, "How do you suppose we could get new members or hold our present ones if any single one of them lost as much as one hour's work to a boss!" During 1938 and 1939 this was one of the most frequent and bitterly fought grievances we encountered in the industry. Even with a union shop, SWOC's members may have the same attitude toward this idea; but, at least, SWOC could go to them and explain the underlying reasons for preserving the managerial organization. Any attempt to do this in 1938 and 1939 would have brought, as it did in a few cases where we tried to explain the long-range advantages of the idea, the rebuke, "You sound like a company man. That's our work and we're goin' to see that no boss takes it from us."

Finally in the spring of 1941 one of the authors proposed to Mr. Henry the adoption of a union-shop contract. "Basically," he wrote Mr. Henry, "most of the irritations and difficulties experienced grow out of the doubtful and insecure status of the union. The nonunion men continually act as a catalytical agent on our members, which produces friction between the local unions and management, work stoppages, and other bitter and unpleasant experiences that, I firmly believe, would be eliminated, or reduced to a vanishing point, by granting SWOC a secure, permanent, and unquestioned status." This proposal led to a personal conference with Mr. Henry. "I agree with you, Clint," he said. "I would prefer that all of our employees belong to the union in each mill. That would simplify your problem and mine also. But it's all up to you. It's against the company's principles to coerce workers into the union."

Then he reflected for a moment, and added, "If you get the big fish in the industry to grant the union shop, maybe we will be able to do something about this question."

Though Mr. Henry firmly believes in his convictions, he is also a practical operating man. His four years of collective bargaining with SWOC on the basis of partial recognition had convinced him that the union shop is a practical necessity in developing constructive union-management relations.

A word about the checkoff. It is a device used by management for years to collect various obligations of workers. The federal government uses it to collect social-security taxes from workers. Each pay period management deducts from workers' pay envelopes such items as cash advances, group insurance, restaurant bills, rent, company-store bills, safety shoes, and various other obligations that workers incur from time to time. The only instance when management makes a big point of refusing the checkoff is when unions ask that it be used to collect the monthly dues of their members. This is not done on logical grounds, since obviously management cannot accept the checkoff device for every other obligation of its employees and deny it for union dues without revealing an underlying motive for such discrimination. The refusal of management to grant the checkoff of union dues is merely a barometer of its basic attitude toward unions. To us—and also to most other unionists—opposition to the checkoff of union dues reflects a management attitude that looks upon unions and collective bargaining as unavoidable evils, to be recognized for the time being until the opportune moment arrives to destroy both. As management increasingly realizes that a return to nonunion days is a vain dream, the discrimination against union dues in the use of the checkoff device, no doubt, will be removed. The checkoff is only a side issue.

The union shop is the big issue confronting management and unions today. From it stems most of our industrial disputes. It is unfortunate that the armament program developed before union-management relations had passed through the transitional period from partial union recognition to the union shop. Constructive relations can be built only on the solid foundation of strong unions and well-organized management. The trend is irrevocably toward strong, democratic, and responsible unions; it cannot be stopped. The needs of the armament program are too critical to delay this trend by impractical and nondemocratic resistance to a full and complete form of union recognition. It is coming as surely as death and taxes, and management had best adjust itself to this fact graciously and quickly. The only alternative—the ultimate complete annihilation of the free labor movement in the United States of America—is an impossible one, since the country is not likely to turn from the conduct of a foreign war to the conduct of a civil one.

We are hopeful that this issue will be resolved peacefully, because the lines of conflict on the union shop are no longer drawn strictly between unions and management. Most operating-management officials we negotiate with daily are in favor of the union shop, and a large number of them have granted it on an oral or unpublicized basis. The area of conflict now is mostly between unions and practical-management officials on the one side and top industrial and financial leaders of American industry on the other. The latter's traditional and natural resistance to the extension of democratic principles in American life is being broken in the case of the union shop, because it is opposed to their own best interests and runs counter to the practical requirements of running America's industrial machine. The men they have hired to run their enterprises tell us, "We have to sell the money men. Management is sold on the union shop. We believe it is only a matter of time."

The union shop may be an instrument for either constructive or negative union-management relations, depending chiefly upon management's outlook and the caliber of union leadership.

Industrial peace is a means toward achieving the goal of optimum efficiency and full employment and production, and not an end in itself. Collective bargaining in too many instances has settled down to "a negative business, there is no give-and-take, but mere force and yielding to force; mere taking advantage of one another's weaknesses," as a prominent author observed recently. This has led a nationally known industrial engineer to say with much justification that "practically all labor leaders, and I may add practically all industrialists, look upon the union wholly as a mechanism for adjusting grievances. As long as you have the organization set up for the adjustment of grievances and emphasize that, you cannot use it for more constructive purposes." It lies within the power of management to have it otherwise.

We testify personally that the denial to unions of the union shop limits their scope of activities, restricts the assumption of certain industrial responsibilities, and circumscribes the constructive possibilities of collective bargaining. The outlook of management, its purposes and motives, are judged by unions primarily upon management's attitude on the union shop. We cannot afford to trust implicitly a management that adamantly refuses to concede the union shop after our local union (or unions) in its plant (or plants) has enrolled a majority of eligible workers on a voluntary basis. Nor can other labor leaders, except at the peril of their union's life. A management that withholds from the union full and complete recognition puts the latter on the defensive, compels it constantly to be prepared for an eventual strike for its very existence.

Nothing short of the union shop can take the union off the defensive, and this does not do it automatically or immediately. Organized labor, from the viewpoint of its own security, cannot disarm emotionally and psychologically in a struggle for its existence until management, by word and concrete action, views the union as a permanent and constructive part of the business enterprise. We appreciate that the union-management marriage, in the first instance, frequently was a shotgun affair, that one party went through the marriage ceremony against its will. It is only natural that the party forced into the marriage hesitates to embrace its unwanted partner enthusiastically. But respect—full and complete—can grow with the years, as well as hate. Imaginative management and courageous union leadership can see that it is respect and confidence, and not hate, that the years of association develop. The token of hate to the union is opposition to the union shop, and the token of respect is, of course, the opposite. It takes two parties, however, to make a happy and fruitful marriage; and after management has kept the union at arm's length during the early years of the forced marriage, the latter is a bit hesitant once management fully embraces it lest the result be strangulation instead of fruitful endeavors.

After management has granted the union shop, the responsibility is largely with the leaders of organized labor as to whether union-management relations continue along essentially negative lines or blossom out into co-operative and constructive undertakings. In the long run the dynamics of the basic and mass-production industries force out the militant and uncompromising union leader and replace him with a constructive one once the union-shop principle has been made a permanent feature of collective bargaining. But meanwhile there is a large gap that can be filled only by the courageous leadership of the top officials of organized labor. It is their job to show their subordinates and members that the union shop is a device to engender respect and confidence, not hate and intolerance; that the defensive approach to industrial problems is no longer adequate; and that the requirements of union members and officers run beyond the elementary tasks of protecting seniority rights, adjusting wages, and improving working conditions.

The national officers of the Steel Workers Organizing

Committee, along with a dozen-odd other international unions of an industrial-union character, have made this job an integral part of their program. The union shop is no panacea for the problems incident to industrial peace, productive efficiency, full employment and production; rather, it is a prerequisite to the attainment of these goals. Without the union shop we cannot, nor can labor leaders generally, guide union members toward participation in achieving greater productivity, full employment and production. That labor leaders in particular cases have not done this is not an argument against the union shop but a reflection upon the caliber of top union leadership.

Collective bargaining eventually reaches a point of economic saturation, more quickly, of course, in marginal and high-cost firms or in firms that have not yet been affected by the newer technologies of production. At this point the union has but two alternatives. One is to continue to fight with management over the distribution of current earnings. The other is to co-operate with management in increasing production so that there will be larger earnings to be distributed to all persons dependent upon the enterprise for a livelihood. Without the union shop the latter alternative is closed to a union. Inadequate leadership may postpone the adoption of the latter alternative after the union shop has been made a basic part of the union-management relationship, but the dynamics of the basic and mass-production industries, the pressure of economic and other factors, will in the course of time lead the union to the adoption of a co-operative policy.

This is so for more reasons than the fact that the failure to co-operate with management for greater production blocks the union in advancing its members' economic welfare. Workers join unions, among other reasons, for an outlet of their creative desires. Like other human beings they possess essentially constructive ideas, and union membership without the union shop frustrates the discovery of practical channels for the outlet of workers' inherent creativeness. The freedom and security of the union shop awaken organized labor to the possibilities of full co-operation in the productive process. Philip Murray summarizes these possibilities thus:

> The basic problem confronting our economy today is the need to increase its social income, to raise the National Annual Income. In no other way can unemployment be reduced, and standards of living raised to higher levels. Collective bargaining can make a contribution to the solution of this basic problem, provided, of course, that leaders of industry and labor recognize its full potentialities. Such recognition should lead to the elimination of the causes that force collective bargaining to develop into a tug of war. And with the elimination of these causes, collective bargaining should gradually develop into a mechanism that will release the full brain power of management and workers on our productive processes. When this is done the maximum production of which our productive processes are capable will be realized, and the trend toward lower production and standards of living will be reversed.

The price of such union co-operation is the union shop. It buys more than industrial peace. Workers and their unions realize that production is the basis of all earnings. Management, in the main, takes the sole responsibility for production. When management has the vision and courage to share this responsibility with its workers through their unions, then, and only then, will full production be achieved. The necessities of the armament program make such a vision and courage on the part of management mandatory for the national safety and welfare. The use of labor's brains as well as brawn in the productive process will result in more tanks, planes, guns, and other implements of war, and more domestic goods now, than America is currently producing. Likewise, in the postwar period the full and complete participation of organized labor in the productive process will result in a greater use of America's industrial machine than would otherwise be the case. How greater productivity can be achieved in the local productive enterprise, and total military and domestic output attained in industry generally, are the subjects of Parts Two and Three, respectively, of this book.

Part Two

WAYS TO PRODUCTIVE EFFICIENCY

Chapter VIII: Responsibility for Productive Efficiency

Management's assumption of sole responsibility for productive efficiency actually prevents the attainment of maximum output.

Unity of purpose and action are so necessary for the success of the industrial part of America's war program now, and the preservation of our free society in the postwar period, that the creative side of union-management relations requires full development. All during our experiences in the steel and allied-metal industries we have found both parties, more times than not, seeking to co-operate with each other but not knowing just how to go about it. Workers have a passion for efficiency, detest needless wastes, and love to work in an orderly shop, mill, or mine where production flows smoothly. Where these conditions do not prevail, workers are full of ideas and practical suggestions on how they can be brought about or, where they do prevail, how they can be improved.

Why don't they come out with their thoughts? What's holding them back? Here is the problem. Management too often resents the expressiveness of workers in a way that stifles the communication of helpful production ideas. Normally the individual worker who expresses his ideas is promptly shut up, his creative instincts are frustrated, and he finds little chance for self-expression in his daily work. Management has long felt productive efficiency to be its sole concern. Consequently, a common attitude has developed among industrial workers over the years that it is useless or harmful to pass on to management the benefit of their experiences. This, in turn, has resulted in only partial productive efficiency, and scientific investigation and experienced observation show that few productive enterprises in American industry attain the maximum output of which their men and machines are capable. The problem, then, is to create the kind of relations between management and organized workers that bring about an interchange of ideas and suggestions on how to increase efficiency, eliminate waste, and otherwise reduce costs. Only in this way can the full benefits of collective bargaining be achieved.

Just why workers normally do not pass on their experiences to management is dramatically illustrated in a one-act play presented and acted by steel workers at one of their summer recreational and educational camps. The theme of the play is particularly significant because it is the joint product of several score of workers from as many different mills or plants; it reflects their common experiences. The title of the drama is *The Innocent Upsetter*. The characters are the upsetter (who is a new employee), the foreman, the plant manager, the company president, and an invisible board of directors. The play is presented in *Our Town* fashion.

"I discovered a way to hook up three of these machines so a fellow can operate them and get out three times the number of bolts that he can now produce on one machine," the upsetter observes to his foreman just a few weeks after he enters the shop.

"Nuts," the foreman replies; "you're paid to run one upsetting machine, not to do the thinking around here."

A few hours pass.

The foreman to the plant manager: "Boss, I think I've got a way to treble the production of our upsetters."

Listening patiently, the manager answers, "Doesn't sound practical to me. You see that the men produce on the one machine they've got—that's your job." . . .

Next morning in the president's office.

"Chief," the manager begins, almost out of breath, "I've been in the shop almost all night, and I got a great idea in the upsetting department," etc., etc.

The president cuts him off short and sends him out of his office thoroughly chastised.

Pulling his hair, wringing his hands, and pacing the floor, the president suddenly grabs his hat and coat and rushes out—almost knocking over the commentator, who is returning to the stage.

"Well, folks," the commentator drawls, "you'd think he is going to have a baby, I mean his wife is; but no, that's not the case. You see, it's like this. He's running off to a meeting of the board of directors to sell them the idea of giving one man three upsettin' machines instead of just one. He's going to tell them it's all his idea, that he worked on it for months and only figured it out because of his long years of practical experience and great technical training. I bet he's even going to get a big bonus for showing the directors how efficient he is in running their shop." . . . And on he drawls. . . .

The following Monday morning in the president's office.

The president to the factory manager and the foreman: "Boys, I've done it. Got the money for a dozen more upsettin' machines from the board. They're already on the way from the factory, and will be here late tonight. You [pointing to the manager] see that they are unpacked carefully, and you [pointing to the foreman] see that room's made for them in the department."

Heads bowed, they leave the office. The president calls them back. "And, yes, we won't need all the upsetters. Better let half of them go tonight. That's all. Get a move on ya." . . .

Last scene, back in the department.

Foreman to the new upsetter: "Guess they're going to get three machines for each man all right. But they won't be needin' you round here no more. This is your last day. Your pay will be waitin' for you at quittin' time."

The drawling commentator returns.

"Well, folks, you see it's like this. A new fellow's gotta learn his way around these parts. He can't afford to be so free with his ideas. Never can tell when one will swing right back and knock him plumb outta his job. A fellow's gotta learn to keep his mouth shut at the right time. Yes, sir!"

One of the authors recited this play at a conference on management and defense. A company president said the theme of the play was not typical, and denounced its recitation as the kind of thing that breaks down confidence in management. A personal talk between him and the author afterward developed the fact that he seldom went into his plant and was dependent upon his subordinates almost entirely for information on what happens there. He was sure a free interchange of ideas went on daily between his employees and their supervisors, but admitted that he did not know this of his own knowledge. When he returned home, apparently he found the play fairly typical of his shop—a few weeks later one of his subordinates ordered a dozen copies of SWOC's handbook *Production Problems*, which sets forth a program to achieve what he mistakenly thought existed in his shop.

Management someday will have to get over its "I can't be wrong" attitude, and get down to the business of producing goods jointly with workers as intellectual equals—not as so many unavoidable parts of the productive process. Management officials no longer can afford to operate on the basis that they know it all, and that if anyone else knew more about their work than they do such a person would have their jobs. Instead, they need to conceive of their qualification as being the ability to benefit by the knowledge of everyone under their supervision and to add such knowledge to their own. The idea that workers are hired to follow instructions only, and not to do any original thinking, constitutes an impediment to productive efficiency. The case of Joseph O'Toole illustrates this observation.

In the operation of an open-hearth furnace, a heat will sometimes develop a "boil." Unless it can be worked out or guided to the rear of the furnace, it breaks through the front and the molten metal pours out on the floor. This is costly and dangerous. Every effort is made to prevent it. At the time an epidemic of "boils" had been plaguing the department and the superintendent, a graduate of an outstanding university in metallurgy, had applied all his knowledge to solve the problem, but it was beyond him. For weeks Joe, a charging-machine operator, tried to tell him how to kill a "boil." The superintendent would not listen.

During a shift when the superintendent was out of the mill a "boil" developed and threatened to break out through the front of the furnace. Joe decided to put his idea to practical use. He loaded a four-thousand-pound box of ore on his charging machine and drew it up before the door of the furnace. Just then the superintendent arrived on the scene. He ordered Joe away, told him that he was a fool and would get "burnt to a crisp." The first melter in charge of the furnace favored trying Joe's idea. The superintendent said nothing doing. Finally, as the "boil" was almost at a head, the melter ordered the super off the floor. The super could fire him later, he said; but he was in charge at the moment and, come what may, Joe was going to get a chance to see what he could do, because "We've been losin' too many heats and my pay envelope has been showin' it."

The infuriated super returned to his office. Joe brought back the box of ore. A man was stationed over the furnace with a cold-water hose. At the split second the metal started for the door, Joe dropped the box of ore in the mouth of the furnace and speedily withdrew his machine. The man above poured cold water on the box, "freezing" it so tight that the metal could not get by and had to reverse its direction. The "boil" was broken; the heat continued and was tapped without the loss of a minute's working time or an ounce of steel. For a month the super would not talk to Joe, who had so humiliated him. They are good friends today and, though they meet frequently, this incident is never discussed. The trouble, in this case, was not with the super but with his elders. Somewhere along the line he had acquired the idea that he was intellectually superior to those who had neither a college degree nor a position on management's side. The persons responsible for putting this idea in his head did him a gross injustice, since the man on the job day in and day out knows more about its intricacies than anyone else. In their franker moments management officials, college-trained in the physical sciences, admit that they learned the steel "game" in their early years from the men in the mills. A standard procedure in most steel firms, before giving them responsible positions, is to route newly hired college-trained technicians through the different departments of the mill, where they pick up some knowledge of the practical side of the business from the men who spend their entire lives there. Here is an immense reservoir of human knowledge that remains virtually unorganized in every systematic way.

The gap between workers and management that must be bridged in order to tap this unused body of technical knowledge is an organizational one. Workers, their creative desires frustrated under the military type of management which usually precedes union-management relations, are anxious to pass on their experiences and ideas. Few have Joe O'Toole's courage; they just keep their knowledge bottled up within themselves. Management's social disregard for their welfare over the years has resulted in the prevailing attitude among workers that it is useless to pass on their knowledge because, like the Innocent Upsetter, they will neither get credit for it nor be protected against potential loss of earning power or job tenure. It is therefore impossible for management to bridge the gap with individual, unorganized workers, since they lack the organization to assure them proper credit for their ideas and an equitable share of the benefits resulting from them. In fact, the underlying philosophy of union-management co-operation designed to improve productive efficiency runs counter to the social group attitudes of workers that have developed from generation to generation. As a consequence, organized workers need the security of the union shop before they can afford to assume joint responsibility with management for productive efficiency. Even then bold, intelligent labor leadership is required to convert the group attitude of workers from disapproval to approval of participation in speeding up production. Disapproval of such participation does not mean that workers fail to realize that their welfare is inextricably tied up with optimum efficiency, but that in the past, and in too many instances at present, they have been denied an equitable share of the proceeds of increased production.

Instead of generously awarding to workers all the brawn while appropriating to itself the possession of all the brains, management should begin to put into practical effect the idea that workers possess something besides strong backs. The business of producing steel, autos, and other goods is more than a technical problem; it is as much, if not more, a human one. Management has no monopoly on knowledge, except as it wields its power to frustrate the use of the knowledge of workers. General William S. Knudsen was once a bench mechanic. All workers cannot rise to the corporation's presidency. But all workers, in varying degrees, possess some knowledge of producing goods. Management officials who realize this and have the vision and courage to work out practical ways with their employees' union to fully utilize the brain power of everyone, from board chairman to common laborers, come closest to achieving optimum efficiency. By utilizing the full brain power of American industry's working forces it is possible to mold collective bargaining into an instrument which may well reach a pinnacle of productive efficiency never previously attained.

The participation of organized workers in management provides an outlet for their creative desires, as it is essentially a creative and co-operative undertaking.

Men and women by themselves, machines alone, orders for finished products on the books, capital itself, and raw materials in the yard—all these elements of production separately amount to nothing more than what they are in themselves; but when they are properly co-ordinated, a final product—something entirely new—is created. The co-ordinating element in this production process is management, a creative undertaking by its very nature. The managers of industry naturally enjoy a means of self-expression in their daily work, because it is essentially creative and gives their personalities dignity and their lives a meaning. For them, in the main, their jobs are a pleasure. When they brag about working fifty, sixty, or seventy hours a week, management officials are to be neither honored nor pitied, but envied.

There is something lacking in the lives of individuals who put more pep into punching out their time cards and rushing home from work than they do in their regular eight-hour day and forty-hour week. We work the long sixty- and seventy-hour week, and we love it. We are organizers. We help workers of all ages and origins get together and create a new social mechanism—the labor union—which, in turn, molds a final agreement or policy out of the conflicting emotions and opinions of workers and management. The fact of going home from work is not exhilarating to us; our wives find us uninterested in hectic, energy-letting dances, picnics, and parties. We have put our innermost thoughts and energies into our regular work. This is mostly true of individuals engaged in essentially creative undertakings. But it is not typical of industrial workers; they look forward to getting away from their regular work with a vengeance.

One of the compelling motives for union membership is the desire of workers to give their personalities dignity and their lives a meaning. They join unions to become something more than a check number that is ordered around as a piece of material is forged. They crave to be recognized as human beings, to be treated with respect, to be given the opportunity to find satisfaction in their daily work through the free play of their inherent creativeness, and to win the praise of their fellow workers and secure personal recognition and advancement for their ideas and their ability to think. Collective bargaining, as it is currently practiced in most productive enterprises, fails to satisfy this motive for union membership except in a limited sense. Protecting a worker's job, getting him more money and better working conditions, and haggling over grievances largely satisfy the economic and social motives for union membership, and the extent to which workers have a voice in these matters partially satisfies their psychological motives for joining unions. But not until union-management relations become essentially constructive will workers find full satisfaction for their inherent creative desires; nor will management attain optimum efficiency, because creative participation of workers in making the vital decisions with management is the key to full production.

Failure of management to comprehend this fundamental principle is retarding armament production at the level of the local productive enterprise, and has been since the outset of the armament program in 1940. SWOC's reward for pointing this out in the summer of 1941 to the management of a propeller plant of a large airplane manufacturer was the following newspaper story.[1]

> . . . "Mismanagement is rampant and inexcusable," Golden charged. He declared that in the past eleven months a total of 2,195 propellers have been scrapped—an average of 200 a month—because of management inefficiencies and poor quality of materials.
>
> The Federal Bureau of Investigation and Army and Navy Intelligence officials have been deeply concerned about the heavy loss of propellers through scrapping and at one time it was feared saboteurs might be at work in the plant.
>
> SWOC tenders its union-management plan as a solution to this problem. . . .

The facts in this case are typical of the standard of productive efficiency in plants primarily producing armaments. So, unfortunately, is the reaction to the union's proposal that its members can help do a better job of producing airplane propellers, tanks, shells, etc. On June 7, 1941, one of the authors wrote the vice-president of the propeller division of this aircraft firm.

> The defense program is losing from four to five hundred airplane propellers a month at your ——— plant, and one out of every four propellers produced is being scrapped monthly.
>
> This is due to inefficiencies and mismanagement that the union can assist in correcting through union-management cooperation. Our Research Department has made a thorough survey of this problem, and we are prepared to do our part to raise propeller output and cut down scrap propellers.
>
> The inefficiencies and wastes uncovered . . . constitute a lengthy report, and . . . I shall mention only a few of the larger factors that are retarding output. . . .

Welding Rod—SWOC has had a piece of the poor quality welding rod analyzed and it can be corrected. . . . This poor quality rod results in a drop from three propeller blades every eight hours to one and three-quarter or two blades per welder. Sixty welders have signed a petition, which is in our possession, complaining that "we are continually being forced to use bad rod in the welding of propeller blades."

Heat Treating—This is a potential bottleneck in the plant that will restrict output in raising the production of the welding and other departments. SWOC has canvassed the district and found close to the ——— plant unused heat treating facilities that are available. The double job of normalizing and heat treating done in your dip furnaces, of course, accounts for the low production at present. Several years ago the plant in question, which is not more than ten minutes away by truck, did heat treating of propellers for the predecessor company that owned the ——— plant before your firm purchased it. In reaching higher levels of output some of this work may have to be farmed out. At any rate the attainment of 400 to 500 more propellers monthly need not be thwarted by this possible bottleneck.

Scrap Propeller Blades—In the last eleven months, from July, 1940, through May, 1941, 2,195 propellers have been scrapped. . . . It would take a work stoppage of many weeks to lose this many propellers. Toward the end of last year the members of our union . . . at the suggestion of your management interested themselves in the low level of output. In January, 1941, they helped raise production by sixty-six percent over the previous month. This raised production to its highest peak, but gradually it has been slipping back to the old lower levels because of the gross practices of mismanagement that, in the absence of a union-management cooperation program, the union is helpless to prevent. In fact, in order to get suitable welding rod so output in the welding department can be raised by one-third, the welders have to sign a petition, which, at this moment, has failed to correct the condition. A joint union-management production committee could take care of such matters promptly. . . .

Wage Equalization—A welder on one side of a jig receiving a wage seventy percent above a welder on the opposite side must drop his production in order to stay with the lower paid welder. An exceptional case of this kind is understandable, but this is typical and common practice. There are twelve different wage rates for welders, ranging from $0.65 per hour to $1.18 per hour. . . . Nothing has been done by management to correct this obvious malpractice. . . . The 400 to 500 propellers the defense program is losing monthly can hardly be produced as long as this cancer is permitted to continue to eat at the morale of both the lower supervisory management and the production workers. . . .

Approximately 100 employees are given individual wage adjustments every two-week pay period. This has kept the plant in a constant state of uproar, and only the most strenuous efforts of the union have preserved the industrial peace. No other firm among the 717 companies under contract with SWOC pursues this long outmoded method of handling wages. . . . We submitted a bonus wage system to modernize the management's methods of handling wages. . . .

The challenge in this letter was not accepted. The company vice-president said it was "damnable." The strike-hysteria campaign of the press was not abated by this constructive proposal, but was increased by hints of "saboteurs." The government officials to whom a copy was sent never acknowledged it, and local government inspectors tried to stop the press from publishing it. The accuracy of the letter was not questioned. Instead, management immediately farmed out the heat treating of a large portion of its output to the company mentioned in the letter. The suggestion on welding rod was adopted. In our collective-bargaining conferences, of course, the wage inequalities and wholesale pay-period wage adjustments were corrected, but management made it plain that its employees were hired to work and not to tell it how to produce propellers. Except for the immediate suggestions contained in the letter, all of which came from men in the plant, the technical knowledge of this plant's thousand workers has gone unused.

The price for this knowledge, naturally, was the union shop. Without it workers do not feel secure in advancing their ideas freely, nor does their union have much extra energy or time to devote to matters other than those pertaining to survival. To this aircraft firm the union shop was too large a price to pay for higher efficiency, and the idea of workers participating in operating problems so infuriated the management that it was blinded to the possibilities of union-management co-operation. One of the authors told this case to a group of New England management executives. The president of a rival aircraft firm followed him on the platform, and explained the entire case away on the grounds that the hollow-blade steel propeller was a relatively new product and its production had not been mastered yet. This explanation, of course, is all the more reason why the participation of workers is necessary to the speedy attainment of mass production in implements of war.

Far from being exceptional, this propeller plant is typical of plants newly converted to the production of armaments. On the production of its thousandth army tank in the summer of 1941, a railroad-car plant adapted for this purpose held a huge celebration. The impression created that tank production was going ahead full speed was false, since the inefficiencies existing in this plant were almost unbelievable. The local SWOC director tried to point this out to the company president, and to sell him the union shop so that the union members could help raise output—daily tank output could be doubled. The president was not interested; he acknowledged output was lagging seriously, but felt that in due time efficiency would improve. In the case of a newly built shell plant producing thirty-seven-millimeter and larger shells, idle or lost productive time was still fifty per cent at the end of the first year. The parent company owning this plant was the one that gave up its shipyard before it would concede the principle of maintenance of union membership, let alone the union shop. These cases, in part, explain the meager production record of American industry in the first year of the armament program. Not all the cajoling of patriots, or the fervent pleas for co-operation emanating from government and industrial circles, can raise the productive efficiency of America's armament plants a fraction as much as can the simple device of giving workers direct participation, mentally as well as physically, in helping management get on with the job of producing tanks, airplanes, shells, and other implements of war.

The evidence that such participation is vital to production is overwhelming; it can be found in virtually every industrial enterprise. The case of a small steel firm in eastern Pennsylvania is illustrative. On February 15, 1941, one of the authors wrote the chairman of the board of directors, saying:

> I am prompted to write you on behalf of SWOC by a . . . news story . . . stating,
>
> The ——— Steel & Iron Company, which employs 650 persons, announced today that stockholders would vote Feb. 20th on liquidation of the concern to prevent "additional losses." . . .
>
> On behalf of your employees I wish to offer your company the services of our organization and the accumulated knowledge and experience of your employees . . . to save your company from liquidation. . . .
>
> Our chief concern is the welfare of your employees, who are members of our organization, most of whom will suffer if the plant is abandoned, and many of whom are advanced in years beyond the age that they can reasonably expect to secure other gainful employment in private industry.
>
> In regard to the feasibility and practicality of this union-management cooperation program to save your firm from going out of business, we shall be glad to refer you to the presidents of several other firms in the steel industry, firms with similar problems as your company. These firms have found the program successful, and in three particular instances the companies were saved from bankruptcy.
>
> As evidence of our good faith and the ability of a union-management cooperation program to produce tangible results in your plant, I am enclosing a list of several practical suggestions, emanating from your employees, showing how productive efficiency can be improved, wastes can be eliminated, and the costs of production otherwise reduced.

This list of suggestions is a revealing document. It represents largely the combined brain power of the six hundred and fifty workers in the plant. Excerpts from the suggestions follow:

On the sixteen inch mill the hot bed is in poor shape. As bars cool they come out wavy. The bed was originally ruined by the practice of piling stock on it when the mill wasn't operating. . . . Because of the condition of the hot bed "wavy" bars have to be run through the straightening machine twice instead of once. . . .

Various stock sizes are piled on top of each other instead of being placed into proper bins ready for delivery. As a result orders have to be "dug out" and special gangs are hired for this purpose.

One inefficiency leads to another. We used to have thirty-five men in the shipping department. Now we have over ninety. Fifty men could do the work if it were properly directed. . . .

Steel from scrap, such as axles and shaftings, is supposed to be classed as "B" steel. They mix it with fresh billet steel in filling orders that call for "A" [open-hearth] steel. Customers complain, and business is lost.

When we are working steel on the machines we never know when we will run into hard [scrap] steel. As a result dies made for working soft steel break. In one day about two hundred dollars' worth of dies were destroyed. . . .

The heads on an order of rivets were cracked. We said they were no good. We were told to "send them anyway." They came back. The company paid the freight both ways.

Several truck loads of navy rivets were sent to Philadelphia. The men said they were cracked. They came back.

The management won't listen to our suggestions. . . . This report is only an indication of what could be done to increase efficiency if we had a chance to help out.

In these plain words this group of workers spoke out in the dying days of their company. A half year earlier they had joined SWOC as a haven of refuge from the threatened abandonment of their plant. Under their newly organized union's protection, these six hundred and fifty workers at last felt free to speak their piece. Their thoughts and ideas had been bottled up inside of them for years. But it was in vain. At the time when the steel industry was being called upon to expand capacity this small steel firm went out of existence permanently. Direct participation of workers at this late date hardly could have saved the company; but had these workers been given the opportunity to contribute their practical production ideas years earlier, the fate of their company might have been different—at least it might have survived long enough to serve America for the duration of the war.

The statement that the creative participation of workers in production raises productive efficiency and, in turn, total output represents a challenge to management, because it is a basic criticism of its production record. Management tries to deny it, but in vain; the evidence to the contrary is overwhelming. Before discussing the fruits of union-management co-operation, let us look at an instance of worker participation that has developed naturally without the benefit of a formal program. Such an instance, indeed, is the exception which seems to prove the rule that, by and large, workers do not enjoy a say-so in technical matters that so vitally affect their daily lives. In the open-hearth department of a large steel firm the furnace crews and the men in the pouring pit do more than the hard, exacting physical labor of melting and casting steel; they also do much of the mental labor in figuring out how to produce the largest quantity of the best steel at the lowest cost. And the closer they come to this ideal, the more wages they earn. But, equally important, they derive considerable personal satisfaction from their daily work. The results speak for themselves. Yields average ninety-two per cent, charging time three hours and fifteen minutes, heats eleven hours from charge to tap, output thirteen and one-half tons per hour, fuel consumption thirty-one gallons of oil per net ton—the envy of any open-hearth superintendent. To hardheaded steel-management officials this may read like a fairy tale, not that it is untrue but because it is exceptional.

We found the men using their heads all of the time, not that they are an unusually brilliant group but because they enjoy the opportunity of putting their ideas into effect when demonstrated to be workable. The president of the local union, a first helper, took us through the department. Customarily a management official escorts us through a visit to a steel mill. Each man was proud of his job. Not a single one complained about having to earn his living in "this damned hot hole." A first helper showed us how he operates his furnace. His nickname was "Red." He let us examine his records. The preceding two weeks his furnace yielded .937 and averaged sixteen and one-half tons an hour. "That's a mighty good operation," he proudly emphasized. Then he opened up all four doors to his furnace, gave us a pair of goggles to peer into the boiling mass, and explained the inside of this burning caldron. He turned off the oil, and the boiling mass became easier to observe. Then he turned it on again. A flame shot across the big furnace with a tremendous force. "That's a real sharp flame," Red observed, obviously glowing over the power to control such a terrifying thing. "If I could get ahold of Hitler with the end of that flame, there wouldn't be no more trouble over in Europe." Red's attitude was typical; he showed us his furnace with the same pride as a man shows his friends through a new home.

The superintendent of this open-hearth department is busier, in many respects, than his counterpart in a mill where the men just follow instructions and management does all the thinking. To win and then maintain the respect of his employees this super has had to keep one step ahead of them. They advance so many intriguing ideas, many of which are adopted, that he has to throw new ideas at them to keep in the running of things. And he does. He has the added task of sifting out all the suggestions advanced by the men, the responsibility for explaining why any one of them is impractical, and the more difficult responsibility of helping the men try out an idea that seems workable. Examples of this are plentiful; every man went out of his way to show us what he had contributed to the department. The case that we remember most distinctly is that of a clean-up laborer working, at the time, for five dollars a day.

His job was to keep the furnace floor clean. After each heat is tapped, the front door bank is pulled out on the floor. The laborer's job was to help shovel this dirt into wheelbarrows for removal. It was, of course, hot and molten and frequently could not be shoveled away fast enough before the next charge. As a result it hardened in the tracks of the charging machine, sometimes making a buggy jump the track and thus causing expensive lost time. These delays were not rare and reduced the department's tonnage in direct proportion to which they lengthened the charging time. For years this hazard was accepted as part of the job, and we have observed it as a cause of lost time in other open-hearth departments we have visited in the industry.

This clean-up laborer corrected it in his mill. He is a short man in his late forties with a tremendous torso. His nickname is "Little George." He suggested that a flat iron box with three sides a foot to eighteen inches high be placed underneath each door when the charging-machine operator knocks the front door bank onto the floor. This box would catch most of the dirt, Little George argued; a crane could carry it away; and all the hard labor of shoveling it up would be eliminated, as well as the lost time resulting from scrap buggies jumping the track. The superintendent ridiculed the idea for several months. "Hell," he argued, "the trouble now is that, with the charging machines, the hot-metal cranes, the backwall machine, and what not, there's too damned much equipment on the floor now. What Little George should do is figure out how we can do without some of this equipment and then we'll cut down lost time around here." Several of the higher-paid men supported Little George.

The superintendent would not think of taking out the dirt boxes now. They catch all but a few wheelbarrowfuls of the dirt, and these are quickly shoveled up. Little George was promoted to a newly created job, called boxman, paying ten cents above labor. He directs the cranemen in placing the boxes underneath the furnace doors and taking them away filled, and helps a small crew of laborers in cleaning up the little dirt overflowing from the boxes. He is proud of his suggestion. He benefited from it and was given credit for the idea. The men call the boxes "Little Georges." The extent to which creative participation in production raises a worker's social prestige and gives him personal satisfaction and a vital sense of belonging and being important, is one of the underlying motives for union-management co-operation. The opposite, by the same token, is true—denial of such participation robs workers of the opportunity to find a meaning for their lives and dignity for their personalities in their daily work. By treating workers as just another element in production, instead of as human beings moved by identical creative impulses as itself, management has paid dearly through lower productive efficiency, higher costs, and the immense waste of the brain power of the large body of workers who, by virtue of their daily work, know more about the intimate details of production than anyone else in the industry.

These conclusions are confirmed not only by SWOC's experiences but by scientific investigation. The Western Electric Researches, which we have described earlier in this discussion, found that a desire for self-expression is usually present in every individual in an industrial enterprise and, consciously or unconsciously, each one constantly seeks some way to express himself, except, perhaps, industrial workers who have been numbed by years of hard toil and repression. The six girls in the test room, whose output rose steadily despite alternatingly favorable and unfavorable changes in the physical conditions of their work, enjoyed a means of self-expression that they never found in their regular department. Although their supervision was greater than in their regular department, they felt relief from "the constraint of supervision" and were able "to work freely without anxiety or fear." The girls' "views were consulted and in some instances they were allowed to veto what had been proposed." Such a voice in their working conditions inculcated in the girls a feeling of responsibility to demonstrate that what they had agreed to or proposed was right; as a consequence, the rise in productive efficiency left management and the researchers stunned. In addition, the girls found their daily work to be "fun" instead of drudgery, and the cumulative effect of these factors was the "social development of the group itself with leadership and a purpose." The finding of this experiment was that the steady rise in output was not related to changes in the physical conditions of work, but to the development of an organized social group in a peculiar and effective relation with its supervisors.

The finding in the bank-wiremen experiment was that productivity not only failed to rise but in specific instances was held down because the wiremen were compelled "to respond to technical changes which they did not originate." Their physical conditions of work were not changed, nor were they given any more voice in determining operating practices than they had enjoyed normally. They went on working as usual, and productivity remained stationary. The bank wiremen found no more satisfaction in the experiment than they had in their regular work. The experiment did not provide them with a means of self-expression as it did the test-room girls. The negative and protective purpose of the informal organization of the wiremen continued throughout their experiment, while in the case of the girls the purpose of their informal group was converted into a positive and constructive one. The explanation for the difference in the purposes of the respective groups lies in the fact that the one participated in making technical decisions while the other did not. This explanation is illustrated by a case of union-management co-operation of one of SWOC's local unions with a submarine-motor-plant management.

For more than a year the plant was on the verge of being closed permanently. The general manager had been in charge of its operations for more than a generation; his method was to produce by authority. Orders were given as his fancy guided him, and anyone who questioned their wisdom, or the manner of his giving them, had to carry them out or seek a job elsewhere. The men naturally banded together over the years into informal organizations in each department to protect themselves. These informal organizations, as in the case of the bank wiremen, secured considerable co-operation from the minor supervisors. When confronted with the necessity of abandoning operations at this plant, the top officials decided to replace the old general manager and give the plant a trial for another year. Shortly before this took place the men had organized into SWOC.

The new general manager was the direct opposite of his predecessor; his method was to produce through the co-operation of his employees. The local union leaders, who had been the leaders of the informal groups that preceded the formal organization of the union, rejected a plea of the new manager for a wage cut but offered to co-operate with him to raise production. Jobs for which twenty hours had been set as the standard under the premium system established by the old general manager, for example, were completed in five and one-half hours under the new manager—with all premiums or incentives eliminated. Suggestions came in from the men on methods designed to make operations more efficient. The results were apparent within six months: the company's efficiency rose by fifty-three per cent; six months later the company announced the plant would be kept in operation indefinitely, and it is now engaged in a vital phase of the war program.

The findings reached in the test-room and bank-wiremen experiments are confirmed by this case. When these submarine-motor workers were denied a voice in the determination of their technical and other conditions of work, they reacted like the bank wiremen. They made no contribution to productive efficiency but, in specific instances, actually retarded it. However, when they were given an opportunity to determine, in part, their technical and other conditions of work, they reacted like the test-room girls. They made more than a fifty per cent contribution to increased output. The new general manager gave expression to the combined brain power of these submarine-motor workers, which had been frustrated by the old manager. The possibilities that the findings of the Western Electric Researches, confirmed by SWOC's union-management co-operation experiences, hold for raising armament output now, and domestic-goods production now and in the postwar period, are staggering.

Certainly the implication in all this that industrial management is not as efficient as is generally assumed—in fact, is as inefficient as fifty per cent in large sectors of industry

—seems unbelievable; yet it is largely true. The manager of an industrial concern in Ohio frankly confessed:[2]

> There is no business in this country that is operating more than 50 percent efficiently. Until you get the men to realize that they are partners in the business with the men who own it and the people who manage it, you have not made an approach to eliminate this 50 percent of inefficiency.

The experience of this management official, Mr. John D. Gordon of the Taylor–Winfield Corporation, Warren, Ohio, is confirmed by Mr. Sanford E. Thompson, industrial engineer by profession and former Lieutenant Colonel, Ordnance Department, U. S. A., who declared at a conference on management and defense in November, 1941:[3]

> It is a bold statement, but it is based on experience in both industry and war that, total productivity of war material can be increased at least 20 percent by raising the management methods of most of the plants to the standard of the best plants. This means the availability for more production of one-sixth of the men employed. It means, since speed is governed by the slow producer, a great advance in time of completion of the vital elements of our program.

SWOC's experiences support these statements. A large firm under contract with SWOC spent a year, through a union-management committee, conducting a study of each operation. The purpose was to establish a sound basis for overhauling an outworn and inequitable piecework-wage system, but its principal result was the finding that only thirty-six minutes out of each hour were spent in productive work. The rest of the time, forty per cent, was lost time, and surely all but twenty-five per cent of this lost time could be used for productive work. This firm, operating at only three-fourths of possible efficiency, has consistently returned over five per cent to its owners for the last twenty years. This case is typical of a large segment of American industry. In every plant or mill where SWOC's union-management co-operation program has been tried out, the tangible results have been an increase of at least twenty per cent in efficiency;

and in several instances it has exceeded fifty per cent. While this may appear to be a reflection on the particular companies co-operating with SWOC, actually it is merely a measurement of the difference between productive efficiency dependent solely upon management's ingenuity and that dependent jointly upon the brain power of management and workers.

In 1921 Herbert Hoover, then Secretary of Commerce, signed a report on "Waste in Industry,"[4] prepared by himself and sixteen other engineers of the Federated American Engineering Societies, based on a careful investigation of management practices and methods. The report held both management and workers responsible for waste and inefficiency in industry, but by far the larger share of the responsibility was assessed against management. The report stated that "over 50 percent of the responsibility for these wastes [all types of waste] can be placed at the door of management and less than 25 percent at the door of labor." Further, the report found the widest differences in the efficiency with which plants are operated in the same industry. The greatest uniformity was found in the textile industry, where the best plant was only fifty per cent better than the least efficient. But in most instances there was much less uniformity in performance. For instance, in the metal trades the management of some plants was reported as being more than four times as efficient as that of some others. The report, covering nearly two million workers engaged in the metal-trades industry, showed that in the fifteen representative plants selected for the study the estimated waste averaged twenty-nine per cent for all, and ranged from six per cent waste for the best plant to fifty-six per cent for the worst one.

The current performance of American industry indicates that the conclusions of Mr. Hoover's report apply with as much, if not more, validity at present than in 1921. Colonel Thompson, now a consultant to the Secretary of War, believes so too. Management generally recognizes this, though few management officials have the courage of Mr. Gordon to state it publicly. Evidence of this recognition is found in the adoption of suggestion boxes by many firms to solicit the help of their employees. These boxes, as we discuss later, are hardly a substitute for the creative participation of workers. The doctrine, embraced by many management spokesmen, that American industry has achieved a satisfactory goal in productive efficiency is as ridiculous as the assertion of the automobile manufacturer who advertised his 1912 model as his "last car because a better car cannot be built." By the introduction of union-management co-operation in American industry an entirely new era of productivity may be unfolded, because the limits of output are almost boundless when the great creative force that has been bottled up inside of American industrial workers becomes harnessed to America's production facilities.

The problem to which we now turn our attention is how to reconcile the authority of management to the natural desires of workers for a voice, directly and effectively, in determining how production can be increased, wastes eliminated, and costs of production otherwise reduced.

Union-management co-operation to reduce costs, eliminate wastes, increase productive efficiency, and improve quality represents a practical program that provides workers with effective direct participation in the creative phases of management.

Labor unions have their origin in the desire of workers for self-protection—against arbitrary acts of management in layoffs, promotions, wage distributions, speed-ups, and other matters that vitally affect them. Their original purpose is defensive and their psychology is negative; unions resist practices of management deemed injurious to their members' welfare and oppose, or at least question, such acts and proposals of management. This essentially negative approach, about which management complains so bitterly, can be converted into a positive one by the simple twin devices of assuring the union's security and providing workers with participation in the matters against which, in the first instance, they organized. One of these is the speed-up.

Making human beings work beyond endurance is a means

that does not justify its end. The cost of the increased production in human drudgery, unhappiness, illness, and deaths is far too great from either an economic or a social viewpoint. With this organized labor and management are in unanimous agreement; both oppose the speed-up. However, it is more than a physical problem; the speed-up is a psychological problem. The term is used by workers in a derogatory sense, as an epithet, and it is attached to managerial practices that do not necessarily overtax their physical, mental, or nervous endurance. In fact, certain union leaders whose viewpoint is that the interests of workers and management, in whole or in part, are irreconcilable denounce SWOC's union-management co-operation plan as a "vicious speed-up." Their prejudice warrants them in denouncing the plan as a scheme to make workers toil harder and, of course, further enrich the owners of industry. This, to be sure, is what the speed-up is in unregulated practice. Management in a wire mill, for example, installs new dies which enable it to increase the speed of the wire-drawing machines thirty-three per cent and, at the same time, cuts the tonnage-wage rates of the wire drawers so that their earnings rise only seven per cent. They go on strike against the "speed-up and cut in wages." Contrast this with the regulated speed-up in a rail mill under union-management co-operation.

Rail output was ten tons an hour when the union and management set up their co-operative plan. Gradually output rose to eleven, then to thirteen, and finally to fifteen tons per hour—an increase of fifty per cent. It was not the result of arbitrary action of management. The men helped management achieve this speed-up; actually, they were mainly responsible for it. Though they are producing fifty per cent more than before, their work is not any harder—many of the men say it is easier now. The rails come through the mill regularly, lost time is reduced to a minimum, mill changes are not so frequent, and as a consequence the men do not have long periods of idleness followed by an hour or two of hectic work to catch up. They did not strike against this speed-up, because it was not arbitrarily imposed upon them by management. They did not strike against a wage cut, since they shared in the benefits of increased output to their satisfaction. What accounts for the difference between these wire drawers and rail-mill workers? Actually the thirty-three per cent increase in production did not tax the wire drawers beyond physical endurance. Yet they struck against the increase and tagged the two most effective union castigations on it, "speed-up" and "wage cut." SWOC corrected the wage-cut phase leading up to the strike; their earnings were raised one per cent for each two per cent increase in output. But the actual speed-up factors leading up to the strike could not be solved, not because of physical reasons but for psychological ones. If it had been for physical reasons, the union and management could easily have worked out production standards that would not overtax the wire drawers' endurance. The difference between the wire drawers and rail-mill workers is one of mental attitude.

Fatigue is closely associated with mental attitude. Take an example from everyday life. A young frustrated man is working at his bench, nervously looking at his watch every two minutes, impatient with the slow passage of time until the quitting bell rings. It rings. He is off to the washroom, changes into clean street clothes, runs to his auto, and starts off to pick up a buddy. They have their bags already packed in the auto, the tank filled with gas, and without delay take to the road for a three-hundred-mile-distant point to have a good time for the week end. The owner of the auto drives all the way, at an average of fifty-five miles an hour. When he arrives he is naturally tired, but not exhausted; in many ways he is more relaxed than before he left his workbench. Contrast his physical, mental, and nervous condition with a presumed experience a week later. His buddy, who is waiting in the auto for him at quitting time, puts a gun to his ribs and forces him to drive to the same point at an average of fifty-five miles an hour. They arrive, but the driver is neither refreshed nor relaxed as he was the previous week; he is exhausted, a nervous wreck. One week this driving feat is a pleasure; the next week it is a speed-up of the most vicious sort. The physical requirements of the two feats were the same, but not the mental or nervous ones.

Thus there are two fundamental differences between the speed-up in its conventional sense and the speed-up as a result of union-management co-operation. Workers participate with management in the latter form of speed-up, for it is something of their own creation; and, secondly, they share equitably in its fruits. The wire drawers, in our judgment, would not have characterized the thirty-three per cent increase in production as a speed-up if it had been either the result of consultation with management or the expression of their own ingenuity—preferably, of course, the latter. This speed-up likewise would not have been described as a "wage cut" if, in the first instance, management had shared the fruits of it equitably with the wire drawers as it did after the strike. Admittedly the difference between an increase in production representing a speed-up to a group of workers or a satisfying creative experience is an intangible one, but one that is not beyond the practical reach of management and unions. And the term "speed-up" is not irrevocably consigned to the union vocabulary of cuss words. The title of Philip Murray's plan to achieve total steel output, through the participation of SWOC on an industry-wide and national basis (which we discuss later), is "How to Speed Up Steel Production."

Union-management co-operation is an integral part of the basic policies of the Steel Workers Organizing Committee enunciated in its official handbook *Production Problems*, the substance of which, as summarized by the *Reader's Digest*,[5] is:

> The steel workers' union stands for the progressive policy of security and plenty for all. In order for all to have more, we need to produce and distribute more, not less. Greater production, guided by efficient management, means lower cost per unit. Lower costs tend toward lower prices. This enables our people

to buy and use more goods. This, in turn, makes possible putting our unemployed back to work. With little or no unemployment, the bargaining power to labor is increased, resulting in higher wages. Higher wages coupled with lower prices mean a higher standard of living.

When asked for a wage increase or a reduction of hours, an employer may say, "I can't afford it; it would put me out of business." What then? Is the union to try to enforce its demands? Or is it simply to do nothing?

There is something that often can be done about it, something that has been done in dozens of cases. Suppose the union could say to the employer, "We will show you a way to save money enough to grant the wage increase," or, "You can make changes in working conditions that we want, and yet have lower costs than you do now." If the union could say such things, it would have additional bargaining power. It would have something valuable to offer the employer in exchange for what it wants.

Almost any shop or mill is full of wasteful practices. There are many workers in any establishment who could off-hand give the management hints as to how it could save money and put out a better and cheaper product. If a systematic study is made, a great many unsuspected ways of making economies can often be discovered. . . . It may take time to educate most employers to such [a program]. . . . But nothing is to be gained by trying union-management cooperation before both sides are ready to accept it in good faith.

One of the pitfalls confronting union-management co-operation in the railroad industry and in textiles was the insecurity of the union. Each firm engaging in co-operation with SWOC has been successful, and one of the reasons is that this pitfall is eliminated by the insistence of SWOC on a union-shop contract. After this condition is met, SWOC insists upon the fundamental principles set forth in the following agreement, because the absence of these principles, in whole or in part, constituted some of the shortcomings of similar ventures in other industries.

PREAMBLE

It is herewith declared to be the joint objective of the union and the company to increase efficiency, eliminate wastes, and otherwise reduce costs of production for the mutual benefit of all parties dependent upon the ——— Company for a livelihood.

PROCEDURE

There shall be created a Research and Planning Committee consisting of five representatives of management and five representatives of the union.

This committee shall meet semi-monthly. Minutes shall be kept of all meetings of the committee and shall be available for the examination of all interested parties.

The duties of the committee shall be to solicit from the employees of all ranks suggestions designed to increase efficiency, reduce production costs, and eliminate wastes; to review them; to adopt those that are practical and feasible; and to explain to the employees whose suggestions are not adopted the reason or reasons why their suggestions are not accepted.

The management and the union shall share equitably any benefits so obtained through regularized employment, better working conditions, increased earnings, lower costs, and other feasible ways.

Nobody is to lose his job as a result of any improvement that is installed. If ways are discovered to do more work with less labor, they are to be put in gradually, and then only with the consent of the union and the management. They shall be installed in such a way that no discharges are necessary—as for instance at a time when sales and output are increasing, or in the regular labor turn-over.

The work of the committee shall be truly joint in every respect. All facts and plans affecting the cost of production are to be revealed to the Research and Planning Committee, and its understanding and consent shall be obtained at every step.

The committee shall be guided in its general work by the basic principles outlined in the handbook, PRODUCTION PROBLEMS, namely.

1. Standard costs for each department, or where necessary for each operation, shall be devised for the purpose of measuring the effects of the committee's work on reducing operating expenses.
2. The handling of grievances shall be distinct from the work of the committee, and the committee, or any of its mem-

bers, will in no way entertain grievances or other matters not connected with cost reduction.

Management opposes this agreement primarily on the ground that it is an encroachment upon its prerogatives. A well-known consulting engineer, Morris L. Cooke,[6] does not think this objection is sound for the following reasons:

Management today may include thousands of employees—all agents of the stockholders—ranging from the president . . . down to the lowliest gang boss. . . . It has been a treasured theory that those of us who have the authority—by virtue of title, salary, or what have you—to make decisions, actually do make them; whereas, as a matter of fact, most well-rendered decisions grow wholly out of the assembled facts. When these preliminaries to a decision have been well conducted, usually only one wise decision is possible. The making of decisions, of course, is not a function reserved for the top. They are being made constantly at all levels in an industrial organization.

The workers—the organized workers—want and should have an opportunity to contribute their ideas and data and have them considered with any others. If the management begins to exclude suggestions, where can the line be drawn? Who wants to do a thing in the wrong way if a better one can be discovered? In the great majority of cases suggestions are not made to annoy, but because of a wholly commendable human instinct to be useful. The sad fact is that when given the widest opportunity to suggest and therefore broaden one's field of usefulness only a relatively small percentage will avail themselves of the opportunity. For generations the workers have been told to do as they were told and only that. Workers absolutely need the stimulus and backing of a labor organization if they are to make suggestions.

Obviously the job of management in charge of operating intricate business enterprises today is to secure from each individual, from laborer to board chairman, the best service of which he is capable, mentally as well as physically. Union-management co-operation is an aid in this job. The control of the business remains in the hands of management. The union exercises only such authority as may be necessary to discharge its responsibilities. "I can go away for a couple of weeks and expect to return and find everything in shape," the president of a company practicing union-management co-operation told us, "because the union and the plant management are a kind of natural check and balance on each other, like the Supreme Court on Congress." In no way does management surrender any of its prerogatives, since nothing can be done without the consent of both parties. Instead, the scope of its prerogatives is enlarged. The freedom of management to make technical or other changes under ordinary circumstances, for instance, is subject to the approval of its employees, who may strike against a change they dislike. Union-management co-operation actually makes this management freedom more real by securing, through understanding, the approval of workers to specific changes in advance of their installation. The objective of the program is to develop machinery that provides workers with creative participation in the productive process, and in actual practice the prerogatives of management have become more secure though, to be sure, less sacred and exclusive.

The acid test of any program, however, is the results, and this is the concern of the following chapter.

Chapter IX: Fruits of Union-Management Co-operation

Union-management co-operation tends to make management more efficient and unions more cost-conscious, thereby improving the competitive position of a business enterprise and increasing the earnings of both workers and owners.

The results of union-management co-operation, ranging from a twenty to more than a fifty per cent increase in efficiency, are likely to be misunderstood unless measured against the background of the extent to which ordinary collective bargaining—merely over wages, hours, and working conditions—makes management more efficient. This is an unpleasant fact for management to acknowledge. The National Industrial Conference Board[1] reports that the "hourly output of a typical manufacturing worker" has risen forty-two per cent between 1929 and the middle of 1941 with sixty per cent of this rise taking place since 1934, the year that witnessed the advent of unions on a large scale. Even if this steady rise in productive efficiency is accounted for exclusively by other factors, collective bargaining has not impeded it. That collective bargaining has been a key factor in this growth, however, seems clear.

Management immediately becomes self-analytical when its employees organize into a union. Something has gone wrong, and efforts are made to find out just what and correct it. Personnel departments, which were denounced a decade earlier as window dressing, are installed. The persistent grievances of the union members keep top management acutely aware of what is going on in the plant. Wages are raised; a new ventilating system, for example, is put in at a cost of fifty thousand dollars, and other improvements are made. Costs begin to mount. Management becomes alarmed about its year-end financial report. Steps are taken to offset the costs imposed by the collective-bargaining contract. Price increases accomplish this only partially. Attention, then, is turned to the plant. A system of budgetary control is installed. Wasteful practices are carefully watched. New cost-cutting machinery is purchased. Excess supervision is slashed. Working crews are cut. Frequently in its search for ways of getting back the cost of the union demands management becomes overzealous. And the men strike against "one man having to do two men's work." The old crews are returned. This "wildcat" strike adds further to costs. Management exerts itself more vigorously to preserve its earnings position. Finally a year passes and management is happily surprised; the financial report turns out to be unexpectedly good.

To be sure, many firms find the first year of union relations reflected adversely in profits; but usually the next year or two changes the picture. Union pressures for cost-raising concessions put management on the alert, and a little-expected by-product of collective bargaining is more efficient operations. The evidence is overwhelming. Management need look no further than its own records. Compare the unit cost of production on the day they signed their first union contract with the present day, and nine out of ten, perhaps even more, of the firms that entered into contracts during the last decade will return the verdict that the unit cost—or, at least, the manufacturing cost before taxes—has declined. The collection of this data from the eight hundred and twenty-eight firms under contract with SWOC has been slow because cost-of-production figures are closely guarded secrets; but of the two hundred and sixty firms from whom we have this data, over ninety per cent uniformly show a declining unit cost of production since the first month of contractual relations with SWOC. The unit costs of the steel industry as a whole are almost at the same level as five years ago despite a twenty-cent-an-hour wage raise in the meantime, the reduction of the work week by eight hours, the imposition of heavy overtime payments, the elimination of countless wage inequalities, and other costly adjustments of union grievances. Thus one of the results of ordinary collective bargaining—quite incidental to the main union objectives—is more efficient operations.

It is only against this background that the results of union-management co-operation can be judged accurately. When the incidental benefit of union pressures for more concessions is a steady rise in efficiency it should be no surprise, then, to find substantial results accruing from a program in which the avowed objective of the union is to raise output and cut costs. A twenty, thirty, or fifty per cent increase in efficiency, therefore, does not necessarily reflect inefficient management before union-management co-operation. Rather, the unity of effort growing out of such co-operation reflects a singleness of purpose that brings actual performance closer to a maximum production and optimum efficiency. Unfortunately there is no magic formula to produce this singleness of purpose. It is the product of group reactions, and develops in its own way in its own environment. Neither union leaders and members alone nor management alone can achieve it, because, by its very nature, a singleness of purpose by two traditionally contending groups is a co-operative human endeavor.

Few management officials seem to realize this. SWOC handbooks and speeches by SWOC officials dealing with union-management co-operation have produced a common reaction. That of a die-casting-company president is typical. He informed us that SWOC's union-management co-operation program met with his full approval and he wanted to adopt it. One of the authors visited both him and the union officers. They had the erroneous idea that we would come into the plant, put the program into effect—and that efficiency would rise the next month. Such an attitude, no doubt, is the result of the advertising of professional engineering firms that say, in effect, "Hire us and we'll do a job for you in raising output." The essence of this kind of approach is that management, instead of solving its own problems, turns them over to someone else. Two SWOC representatives spent several days explaining to the die-casting-company president and the union officers and members that the basic philosophy of union-management co-operation is that workers, through the mechanism of their union, and management get together to solve their mutual problems. Furthermore, it was explained, the greater the output and the lower the costs, the more fully these problems can be solved. The idea that their problems could be solved by turning them over to someone else, they finally realized, was not the underlying approach of union-management co-operation.

Workers and management in each plant have to work out their own destiny in their own way. This die-casting firm and its CIO union went ahead with the program, plant by plant. The structure and machinery devised was at some variance with what we have experienced under our own SWOC programs, but the underlying philosophy was the same. Instead of dissipating their energies fighting each other, or waiting for management to call in outside engineers or for the union to call upon a sister union to help solve their problems, these union workers and their management joined hands to tackle their problems by themselves. After the program had been inaugurated the company president told a magazine editor:[2]

> I'm elected by the stockholders and the union representatives are elected by the employees. Stockholders and employees have interests in the profitable operation of the company. We are in a competitive field, paying the highest wages in the industry and if we are to continue to make money and pay high wages we have to increase production by more efficient management. We think that we are going to have it under our plan.

It is too early at this writing to judge the results of the plan; but we feel confident they will be as substantial as others in SWOC's experience, for the plant management has the right approach. The superintendent of one of the plants said, "I can't be everywhere in the plant and the foremen can't supervise every operation. It's the men on the floor who can save the most money for the corporation—the stockholders, the supervisory employees, and the workers themselves."

Not all of the inquiries from management result in the creation of a union-management program. A bedding firm read about SWOC's experiences and wanted to co-operate with its employees to raise output and share the benefits equitably. But the union was against the idea. It had a union-shop contract; but the national officers frowned on the program, and the local did not accept the challenge of management to increase its members' earnings by increasing output. Such a lack of vision on the part of the national union leaders may prove the undoing of their union or, at least, unduly limit the value of the union to its members and the industry.

In the case of a paint company SWOC was requested by the top officers of the chemical division of the United Mine Workers of America to assist its local union in formulating a program for one of the company's plants. A SWOC representative found the plant management hesitant. Several days of conferences finally evolved an agreement that followed the pattern of SWOC's union-management co-operation proposal. The superintendent became enthusiastic about the prospects. The plant was closed completely for two hours at five-thirty in the evening to permit all workers to attend a general membership meeting to act on the proposal. The adoption of the plan was voted unanimously. All that remained was for the company president to sign the agreement. He positively refused to do this, maintained that the union had been instrumental in decreasing efficiency and that any co-operation it might give belonged to him without an agreement of any kind. One of the reasons the employees favored the program was because it gave them the chance to show the president, who held himself aloof from operations, what was wrong in the plant. When costs rose, the president always blamed the union. He had never become acquainted with it and apparently believed implicitly the information brought to him by plant officials, who blamed their mistakes and shortcomings largely on the union members. The program did not materialize because the company refused to agree that the benefits of increased production would be shared equitably. And the union naturally refused to go ahead without this essential assurance.

Difficulties of this kind, however, usually are overcome and the program gets established. The firms whose first enthusiastic interest in union-management co-operation fails to materialize are those who think it is simply a formal thing. They get the impression that we have a key that opens the door to higher efficiency. We explain that the key to such results lies in their own plants; it is something intangible, yet it is also something definite. It is a co-operative spirit that grows in only a particular type of social environment. The union-shop form of recognition helps create such an environment, but does not do so entirely. Something else is needed; this is confidence and mutual trust and respect. Management has to earn this by word and deed. To get optimum efficiency from men and machinery is like getting the highest yield of corn from an acre of land—like the farmer, management has to work at it day in and day out. After explaining this to a company president who had come into his office fresh from seeing the results of union-management co-operation in a neighboring plant, one of the authors saw a fifty-thousand-dollar-a-year executive lose his enthusiasm quickly.

"Well"—he paused a long second—"Clint, that ain't no bargain. The union shop is not easy to swallow, but you don't even guarantee it will produce results. It's like buying a pig in a poke. You can't run a sound business without knowing what you get for your money. Your co-operation sounds all right and they're getting good results across the creek from me, but it isn't sound business to give something, like the union shop, without some assurance you'll get something profitable in return."

"I'm not so sure about that," the author replied; "it's not such good business to own a plant that is not, according to your own admission, producing the results of which its potential capacity is capable. You know when you buy a farm you get no assurance it will produce results. All you get is the land to till. The results are up to you, you know."

The president, comforted by his thought, blurted it out. "Hell, Clint, buying a farm ain't good business."

Union-management co-operation is not yet operating in

his plant, but a forerunner of it is being practiced by his management and the SWOC local union. They are jointly making job evaluations, eliminating wage inequalities, and setting work standards. A natural outgrowth of joint co-operation on this particular problem is co-operation on more fundamental matters.

Threatened bankruptcy and abandonment of the plant present to workers and management alike a common misfortune and challenge, and quickly overcome the resistance of each to union-management co-operation. It is under such pressure that SWOC's early efforts have been undertaken. When the Federal Steel Company, employing a thousand workers, was on the verge of going out of business in August, 1938, the union proposed a program to reduce costs, and the men returned a percentage of their wages as a loan. The conditions existing when the company accepted the union's offer to put operations on a competitive basis, at the time, seemed to preclude a successful outcome. Steel prices had been cut in June, freight charges formerly paid by customers had to be absorbed, and competitors with low-cost continuous-strip mills were selling sheets cheaper than this firm could produce them on its hand-style and semiautomatic mills. Its employment already had been reduced by nine hundred because it could not afford new machinery similar to that adopted by other sheet producers. The firm's working capital, in fact, was too low to make even minor, but much-needed, repairs and improvements.

The guiding spirit of the union's research committee, now in charge of SWOC's union-management co-operation programs, reported the following results at the end of the first year.

Dozens of suggestions have been submitted to the Company by our Research Committee. Many of these have been placed in operation and have resulted in reduced costs of production, and at the same time have improved our product. In many cases it has been very difficult to measure the results accurately; but the following cases where the results are tangible and measurable illustrate our success.

The entire Research Committee suggested that pebble lime be substituted for Scioto lime in the furnaces of the Open Hearth. We maintained that pebble lime would bring sulphur down, reduce fuel cost, and increase tonnage. The superintendent vetoed the suggestion. He asserted that Scioto lime was three dollars per ton cheaper, and that the transportation of it was more easily fulfilled since it came a short distance by truck, while pebble lime had to be brought by rail from Indiana. The president overruled him after the suggestion was pressed at subsequent meetings. The results of one week of experimenting showed that fuel consumption was down three gallons per ton; sulphur was down; and production was up. The lime cost remained about the same because less lime of a higher quality was used. On the fuel cost alone, a saving of $6,800 a year was obtained.

After a thorough survey by a firm of combustion engineers, it was agreed that our gas consumption could be reduced in the Soaking Pit Department by installing checker chambers in the pits. A low bid of $33,000 was made by an outside concern, which also guaranteed a 10% saving with an agreement to accept payment in monthly installments according to the amount saved. A member of the Research Committee claimed that he could effect a greater saving with little or no investment. Management treated this claim pretty much as a joke; and those who had succeeded in securing the necessary appropriation for the renovation attempted to ridicule his suggestion. Although we succeeded in reaching the president with our suggestion, he was disinclined to accept it. Notwithstanding all this opposition, we pressed on; and when the chief engineer studied the suggestion he at once insisted that it be tried. It was used on one block of pits and its success was immediate. It worked better than anticipated. It was installed in all the other pits at a total cost of $900, and means a saving of about $18,000 a year, plus $32,100 saved on equipment.

A research committeeman from the Bar Mill suggested the use of solid guides. After much study the idea was carried out. Without evaluating the money saved in increased tonnage and the reduction of man-hours per ton, the Company actually saved in lost time about 18 minutes per turn, or approximately $4,000 per year.

In the Cold Roll Department the Company was experiencing difficulty concerning the rust which was inordinately high. The management requested assistance from the Research Committee. We investigated the problem. After two weeks we reported that one of our members had followed lifts of sheets through to inspection and found that the first eight or ten sheets rolled on each turn were always the ones affected. He concluded that moisture in the rolls at the beginning of each turn was responsible for the rust, and suggested the installation of gas jets to heat the rolls for a few minutes before work began. His ideas were carried out, and the problem was solved. A close estimate based on the price of scrap sheets and a prime product would indicate a yearly saving of $6,200 per year on slow operations.

In the Shear Department the Company was faced with mounting sticker costs, as high as 38 cents per ton, while the industry average in similar plants was about 12 cents. Often the secondary cost in the Inspection Department is higher than the original costs on sticker chopping. The Company tried many remedies, including a charge of a higher "Phos" content in the Open Hearth. At three consecutive meetings of the Research Committee the members tried to persuade the Company to install a cooling conveyor which was to be placed behind the mill. This suggestion was made on the assumption that the sheets were piled too hot and thus were welding. The Company finally agreed to try the idea. First, however, before spending any money on a conveyor, it was decided to experiment with twenty or thirty men who were to scatter the sheets immediately after they left the mill and before they were piled to allow sufficient cooling. This prior testing proved so satisfactory that conveyors were installed at a cost of $6,000. In the last two months we have attained an all-time low in sticker costs which are 4 cents per ton, and there is a resultant improvement in inspection benches. A very conservative estimate on sticker chopping costs, without considering the larger savings at the inspection benches, would be $10,000 annually.

One of the most serious problems of the entire plant was the bad condition prevailing in the hot mills. Scrap percentages in these mills on regular practice black sheets often ran as high as 20% and on enamel iron 22%, most of which was due to stickers, pinchers, floppers, and grease mottle. Our Research Committee learned, after a trip to another plant—at our expense—that our greatest trouble was the lack of water pressure for cooling the rolls. We prevailed upon the Company to install a water line to a small lake on a hill above the mill building. This gave better control of the shape of the iron. We found, however, it was impossible to get square cut sheet bar with the type of bar shearing equipment in the plant. After further study, we suggested an edger-guide. This solved the problem. As a result of these improvements, our material coming from the roughing mills is square, has a very good shape, and is uniform in length. This makes the finish mill operations at least 50% easier.

On the finish mills, in addition to the cooling conveyors, we suggested improvements in the edgers on the rolling tables and on the doubling hammers. These eliminated delays and made the work easier for the men. Our original crew setup for the finish mills was five men on a single iron and seven men on the double iron. We persuaded the Company to maintain a seven-man crew at all times, using the two extra men as utility men. This resulted in increased tonnages and lower scrap percentages, enough, we believe, to offset the wages of the extra men. The results to date are a monthly saving of $8,000, or $96,000 a year.

At the end of the first year the company spent $6,900 for new equipment, but saved $173,100 as a result of suggestions sponsored by the union's research committee—a net gain of $166,200. These savings, in addition to other and, no doubt, more substantial ones resulting from improved morale and other factors that cannot be measured in dollars and cents so easily, carried the company through the 1938 depression and enabled it to restore the old wage scale when World War II upped steel production. The results in this case are remarkable in view of the precarious position of the company at the outset. Its existence still threatened by the continuous-strip mills, this company's life has been prolonged by union-management co-operation. Unlike the McKeesport Tinplate Corporation (three thousand employees), whose problem was the same, yet was permanently abandoned in the fall of 1940, this steel firm is serving the armament program and stands an even chance of survival in the postwar period for several more years.

Having begun with their fingers crossed, the executives of this company, frankly amazed by the results of the first year, are now stanch supporters of union-management co-operation. To officials of other companies who are not sold on co-operation with the union by his company's results, the mill superintendent relates the following costly experience.

In 1935, previous to the advent of our current president, our Company found itself beset by an exasperating problem. There was an epidemic of what we called "alligator hide" on our finished sheets. This imperfection ended in a scrap of 60% of our production. Every resource of the Company was used to solve this distressing condition. Finally a firm of consultant metallurgists was contacted. They sent one of the country's finest metallurgists here. His fee was $500 per day. After a ten day stay and a painstaking survey of all operations, this expert recommended many changes in our practices; but these changes did not reduce the incidence of "alligator hide." In desperation, I urged the president, who at the time was fearful that the Board would order the plant closed, to call upon the union for assistance.

The union responded and immediately appointed a committee composed of members who were experienced and who represented every department. This committee met with us. Each one examined the finished sheets which were afflicted with "alligator hide." Then each member rendered an opinion. One member of the committee, an old experienced hot mill man, stated that he had seen such a rough surface many times. He claimed that it was caused by the pairs soaking too long in the pair furnace. When asked why the pairs soaked too long, he replied that it was because the pickler was working short-handed and couldn't get them back fast enough to keep the furnace going. We scoffed at this explanation until he offered to wager his pay that he could correct the condition if given the opportunity.

We finally agreed to try the plan out. A trial was made, the condition was remedied, and three additional men were placed on the pickling crew. Since the introduction of union-management cooperation perplexing problems such as that are solved in short order and many thousands of dollars saved.

The results for the next two years were equally as impressive. The Federal Steel Company met the ten-cent-an-hour raise of the industry in the spring of 1941 and, in addition, made substantial wage-inequality adjustments. Net profits were earned in 1940, and the next year the firm moved into the class of a good money-maker. But, aside from these economic benefits, union-management co-operation added stature to the individual workers in this mill. Henry Sawyer, who cut fuel costs eighteen thousand dollars a year in the soaking pits and saved the company thirty-two thousand and one hundred dollars in capital expenditures, did not receive a single penny for his contribution. His only economic gain was his share in the gain of the group of workers as a whole. Henry got more personal satisfaction out of his contribution than he could have bought with a year's wages. He is a highly paid heater and always had commanded the respect of his fellow workers. But this contribution increased his social prestige. In the mill the men, almost as one, told Henry, "You sure showed them fancy engineers that a workin' stiff knows more about the steel business than they do."

"They ain't seen nuthin' yet," Henry replied, obviously inspired by this reception. He is working now on a way to cut costs further by creating a more uniform heat on ingots.

The contrast between the social-group approval Henry received and the ostracism suffered by a worker who made a suggestion in a neighboring electrical-manufacturing plant runs to the heart of union-management co-operation. In the latter plant, management also realizes that its employees are filled with practical production ideas that do not find their way into its hands. To tap this knowledge management installed a suggestion-box system that gives cash rewards to employees who contribute usable ideas. At the time the town was buzzing about the co-operative plan in the steel mill, the local paper printed on the front page the picture of a worker from the electrical-manufacturing plant who had received a four-hundred-dollar cash award for making a suggestion that saved the company thousands of dollars. The reaction of the other workers in the department was hostile. They were not organized into any union, but they had their own informal group policies. One of them was that anyone who helped management find a way to eliminate someone else from his job was a "no-good." Six men were eliminated by the suggestion and furloughed temporarily. Although jobs were found for them later in other departments, the group attitude of these unorganized workers remained the same. They congratulated the suggester with the demand that he throw a party for everyone in the department with the money he had won for his idea. He did this reluctantly. Since then management has not received another major suggestion from this department.

The suggester's four hundred dollars could not buy the favor of his fellow workers that Henry naturally received, because the latter participated in cost-saving activities with management as part of a group and with its implicit consent, while the former participated as an individual without the consent of the group of which he was an inseparable part. Management cannot work out with individual unorganized workers effective mechanisms for transmitting their production ideas to the top. The underlying philosophy of such a venture runs counter to the prevailing group attitudes of unorganized workers. These attitudes have grown out of the abuses and planless manner in which management has introduced cost-saving machinery and ideas over the years. When workers organize into a union they carry over these attitudes as part of their union policies, because they associate such activities with the speed-up and other things inimical to their welfare. The first job we have in establishing union-management co-operation is to convince the local union that cost reductions are tied up with its welfare and that of its members. The failure of suggestion boxes to produce anything but "penny-ante" savings is accounted for, in part, by the inability of management to convince its employees that the suggestion system is not inimical to their welfare. Even the suggester who won a four-hundred-dollar award lives under the daily fear that someone else might suggest him out of his job.

That no one shall lose his job as a result of any change is a basic principle of union-management co-operation. It is not difficult to fulfill. A fabricating firm, for example, employing eight hundred workers installed an automatic polishing machine. Thirty-five hand polishers were eliminated. A check of labor turnover showed that seven workers quit, died, or were discharged each month on the average over the previous three years. The union members of the joint research and planning committee consented to the installation on the basis that work would be provided for these thirty-five men at their regular wages until they could be placed on other jobs. Within less than a half year jobs were found for them paying wages comparable to what they had been earning, except for six men. These were given a cash sum and first choice on better-paying jobs when vacancies developed on them. The cost for doing this was added to the original cost of the new equipment and amortized on the same basis.

In a firm that could not afford to absorb such a wage cost, the displacement of seventeen workers was handled in another way. Six months' advance notice was given to the seventeen men at the bottom of the seniority list. They were given an opportunity to acquire experience on other jobs elsewhere in the mill, and as openings developed they received preference. When the technical change was completed, all but four had been placed on other jobs paying comparable wages. The men in the department shared work with these four until a few weeks later, when they also were absorbed on other jobs. In SWOC's union-management co-operation experiences no one has lost his job, nor have suggestions resulting in displacements affected the willingness of union members to continue participating in the program.

Suggestion-box systems fail to get such co-operation, in part, because the savings they produce are not shared equitably between workers and owners. The savings that the electrical-manufacturing firm received from the suggestion that displaced six workers was not shared with its employees as a whole but with one individual worker. Under union-management co-operation the savings are shared with all employees. The difference between these two methods of sharing cost savings is illustrated by one of the most successful suggestion systems in industry.[3] This firm employs eighty-eight thousand and six hundred workers. In 1940 thirteen per cent of them made suggestions that saved the company five hundred and fifteen thousand dollars for the year. Their share in these savings was fifteen per cent, or an annual average of six dollars and seventy-five cents for each employee who made a usable suggestion. The remaining eighty-seven per cent of the employees did not share in the savings at all. The significant fact about this method is not that only thirteen per cent of the employees received a mere fifteen per cent of the proceeds but that they shared for just one year in savings that accrued to the company year after year. From organized labor's viewpoint, to share in only $77,500 of a $515,000 savings is inequitable; from management's viewpoint, to take eighty-five per cent of the savings for the first year and one hundred per cent for all succeeding years is indefensible.

The failure of this firm to share the savings of its suggestion system equitably with its employees shows up in the results. For the year 1940 the savings amounted to less than two-tenths of one per cent, or five hundred and fifteen thousand dollars saved on operating expenses of two hundred and eighty-three million dollars. This is an average saving of not quite six dollars for each of the eighty-eight thousand and six hundred employees. In the first year of union-management co-operation the Federal Steel Company saved one hundred and sixty-six thousand dollars—an average of one hundred and sixty-six dollars for each worker. This is a twenty-seven-times-greater contribution by each worker than under one of the most successful suggestion systems. To be certain, the Federal Steel workers got more than fifteen per cent of the one hundred and sixty-six thousand dollars they helped to save. The failure of suggestion systems, by and large, to produce more than "penny-ante" results does not reflect on the ability of workers to make substantial savings but reveals the unsound foundation upon which these systems operate.

Workers are not a miscellaneous assortment of individuals moved primarily by personal economic incentives, but social beings guided by a combination of social, psychological, and economic motives; as a consequence, their technical knowledge can find expression only through group participation in management. The success of union-management co-operation depends largely upon a small group of imaginative, energetic, and aggressive union leaders and management officials. But this is not unique; it is characteristic of group activities. A union is organized, in the first instance, by a small group of energetic workers, as are industrial concerns which have their birth in the minds of a few men. The success of group activities, of course, varies in direct proportion to which leaders can secure the active participation of all members of the group.

At Federal Steel, for instance, although only a small number of workers contribute usable ideas, they all participate through their union in one way or another. Walk into the open-hearth department and ask any worker, first helper or laborer, how many tons are being produced an hour, what the labor or fuel costs are per ton, how much the company is paying for scrap or pig iron, or any other vital question about running the furnaces, and you will get a precise answer. These workers are cost-conscious. They have an interest in production that they can understand, and that means something important to them as self-reliant individuals, as members of a group fully able to protect their mutual welfare, and as providers for their families. There is nothing incredible about workers mastering the key cost details of their department. They demonstrate such mental ability in their daily lives, though it is usually for nonproductive purposes. Many workers, for example, are rabid baseball fans, and can tell you the batting average of every first-team ball player in the big leagues. That workers generally do not show a like interest in the important facts about their daily work is a reflection upon the character of union-management relations.

Where workers do show such an interest in their daily work the results are revealing. A union-management cooperation program raised the output of a small water-heater firm, employing seventy workers, twenty-seven per cent. The daily production of storage and instantaneous water heaters rose from fifty-one in 1937 to sixty-five in 1940; and the best day's output rose from a high of fifty-five in 1937 to one hundred and twenty-five three years later, a rise of one hundred and twenty-seven per cent. No additional workers were added to the assembly line during this period. At the same time, wastes were reduced. In 1937 an average of four water heaters were returned to the plant daily because of defective parts, faulty assembly, or other defects, but in the entire year of 1940 only one such unit came back. The company's financial position naturally reflected the increased productivity and lowered wastes. Losses in the neighborhood of fifty thousand dollars in 1937 and 1938 were wiped out in the first year of the program, 1939, and the following year net profits reached a new high. The earnings of the men, of course, rose. Between 1937 and 1940 their hourly earnings increased only six and one-half per cent, from sixty-eight to seventy-two and one-half cents per hour, but their annual wages—this is the crux of union-management co-operation—increased thirty per cent, from eight hundred and sixty dollars to eleven hundred and sixty-three dollars. In 1941 the average employee earned thirteen hundred and eighty-five dollars, or twenty per cent more than in the preceding year. The union not only secured the ten-cent-an-hour raise in the spring of 1941 but won additional wage adjustments.

These results were achieved, in the main, by each worker becoming cost-conscious. Nick Rondo, who led the picket line during the strike for recognition in the mid-thirties, is the final inspector. Defective water heaters do not get past him. Four years ago when Nick saw a defective unit on its way out of the plant he said to himself, "Let 'er go. She'll come back." Today he knows a lot about water-heater business that he did not know then. He realizes that only good heaters can sell, that perfect units build and expand a business, and that, in the last analysis, he and his fellow workers pay for defective units in the loss of business and the replacement of returned heaters. This interest in the business has changed Nick's attitude toward his job. "It sure is better around here," he boastfully told us, taking a good deal of the credit for the improvement. "A fellow's time passes fast. It's time to go home before he knows it. Eight hours used to be a helluva long time around here."

George Bryon, the union president, is chairman of the union production committee, which consists of Nick and three other union members. It is jointly responsible with management for productive efficiency, the scheduling of production, and the continuity of work. Tangible results are produced by suggestions that come from workers who formerly kept their ideas to themselves, because they found it useless to try and get them adopted. Box lumber, for example, was scrapped and burned in the yard. One of the men suggested the lumber be salvaged. The ex-vice-president ridiculed the idea, and produced figures to show it would be more costly to save the old than buy new wood. After union-management co-operation got under way the idea was suggested again. Now these boxes, which are full-length lumber, are torn down, nails removed, and used for crating material for which lumber used to be bought at a cost of thirty to thirty-five dollars a thousand feet. This item alone nets a good annual saving.

In recounting other tangible improvements, the present vice-president told us: "Subassembly lines used to be operated on an individual-unit basis which resulted, in many cases, in material being filed and adjusted before fitting. Each man did this differently. One of them suggested that the individual benches be eliminated and the correction in material, if any, be made on the first operation. This resulted in a change being made on one operation and eliminating a duplication of effort at eight or ten different points." Output rose by at least five heaters a day through this change. Had the old management, which operated on a purely authoritarian basis, made such a change, the vice-president added, the men would have made a grievance of it, and might have gone on strike against it as "a vicious form of speed-up." Furthermore, if anyone had made such a suggestion under the old management, he would have been ostracized by his fellow workers, who, the vice-president observed, might even have refused to work with him. In this case the suggester was patted on the back by his fellow workers. He felt that, after all, he was important to the business.

These and other suggestions, together with a harmonious working spirit, contributed toward the substantial increase in production. The men, of course, shared in it. The day of September 16, 1940, is typical—when one hundred and one units were produced. Fourteen men worked on the actual assembly of these heaters. Their hourly wage rates ranged from sixty to eighty cents; the average was sixty-four cents. Their combined earnings for the day were seventy-one dollars and seventy-six cents. In addition, they earned a combined bonus of thirty-one dollars and forty-eight cents, or an average of twenty-eight cents per hour. This brought their total average hourly earnings to ninety-two cents. Prior to union-management co-operation the hourly wage rates were the same, but the men earned less than a ten per cent bonus because production averaged only fifty-one units a day. The doubling of production raised average hourly earnings over forty per cent and cut the company's assembly labor cost per unit thirty-six per cent, from one dollar and forty-four cents to one dollar and two cents. Actually the cut was greater, because fewer men were used in assembly than previously. In addition, the company's overhead per unit was cut in half and both the men and owners realized larger earnings over the year from more business made possible by the increased production.

The boss is the president of the company, although a casual look at the organizational structure of the plant might indicate otherwise. His ability to communicate production ideas to his employees is unhampered by the restrictions inherent in an authoritarian type of management, and the flow of ideas from the men to him is unrestrained. The union production committee is responsible directly to him. The manager of a neighboring firm told us, "The management will soon regret its steps. It has turned the plant over to the union and hamstrung itself."

This water-heater company's president, a short, roly-poly bald man in his mid-forties, laughs at such criticism. "Hamstrung!" He smiles. "Why, this move has released us from the old union restrictions that our critics are still suffering from, and has given us a greater freedom than any of them would dare dream of enjoying."

He continued, "Just look at a few of the things that used to happen around here. We were tied down with departmental seniority. We couldn't transfer a man from a slack to a rush department. Another thing. We always had trouble with foremen doing production work. The union would not tolerate it. That's history here now. The really big thing we have been able to do, however, is bring new work into the plant. We only used to be primarily an assembly plant. The parts were contracted out. The old management did not dare make them here for fear that when it needed vital parts the men might strike key operations to press a grievance or win a sharp bargain. Some parts were made in Cleveland, others in Cincinnati, and when they got here we prayed, often in vain, that they would fit together. This is no longer a problem, and making most of our own parts gives us a better finished product. The water-heater business is seasonal. Our rush period lasts only a few months, and the plant used to be closed down for weeks. This slack is taken up now by the manufacturing of most of our own parts.

"I wonder," he concluded, "how many of these other companies have their union committee come in and show how more work can be done with fewer men, and proceed to do it while also placing the extra men on new jobs. I hear one of my neighbors had an idea on eliminating two men in his shipping crew, but abandoned it after the department and then his whole plant went on strike. I can call on more brains in the production end of our business than any other plant of the same size. That's the heart of our union relations."

Unlike most of the other small companies in the metal-fabricating industries, this one has not been hit by priority unemployment. It foresaw the shortage of materials growing out of the armament program, and was one of the first small firms to get into armament production in the Pittsburgh district. The very nature of their new relations had made management and the union look at their problems from a long-range viewpoint, and since the start of the armament program employment has more than doubled in their plant. The fruits of union-management co-operation in this case go beyond increased earnings for owners and workers. The latter have been protected against priority unemployment, and the former have been saved from the fate of so many other small enterprises that have had to go out of business, or seriously curtail operations, because of the armament program. Furthermore, the nation as a whole has gained. This plant is producing vital parts for one of the most important implements of war, and is keeping ahead of its schedule.

Union-management co-operation has greater possibilities in large profitable firms than in ones that are forced into it by economic adversity. The fact that most of SWOC's experiences have been with the latter type of firms is no reflection on the program, but upon the American character. In all fields of endeavor, in the main, Americans let nature take its own course until the wolf is at the door. This is such a universal trait that it needs no illustration. In firms forced into union-management co-operation by threatened bankruptcy, a bad situation was allowed to become worse over the years. Finally, when all conventional ways of preserving a business enterprise became closed, these firms agreed to a plan of co-operation with their unions. No doubt they felt that they were grabbing at a figurative last straw, but it turned out otherwise. Without an exception union-management co-operation pulled these firms through their dark days, and they all are making net profits at present. In each case the program has been limited by the fact that very little, if any, money has been available to make equipment replacements long overdue. The combined ingenuity of management and workers has had to function within the framework of finding ways to raise output and cut costs without capital expenditures. Where these limitations do not exist the fruits of union-management co-operation naturally are more plentiful.

A large profitable steel firm that has embarked upon a program of union-management co-operation with SWOC is located in Canada. It employs over four thousand workers and is one of the largest steel firms in that country. It may, or may not, be significant that the first profitably managed steel firm to embrace union-management co-operation is located in Canada. Perhaps the national trait of letting nature take its course is as characteristic of Canadians as of Americans. We do not know our northern neighbors well enough to judge. We do know, however, that this firm has accepted SWOC Local Union No. 2251 as a permanent part of the business. The dispute over union security is history in this mill. We also know that the management has not had any fears about what other industrial concerns might say because it adopted full co-operation with the union on vital operating phases of the business. Fear of such criticism in management circles, to date, has blocked the large-scale adoption of the program in the United States. This, of course, merely reflects more fundamental factors in union-management relations in our country, and will not be changed until the leaders of American industry finally make up their minds that collective bargaining with labor unions has become a permanent institution. The most striking impression we got in conferences with the management of this Canadian steel firm is that it appreciated the possibilities of full co-operation with its employees as an organized group, and had the courage to try it out. Its courage has produced tangible results.

The program started in March, 1941. It was launched at a joint banquet attended by more than two hundred management officials and one hundred union representatives from the mill. One of the authors and the head of the firm were the speakers. The very fact of such a gathering tells its own story. Results were forthcoming immediately, and naturally have been more substantial than in firms unable to take advantage of many helpful suggestions because of limited working capital. The program operates through joint union and management committees in each department. Their meetings during the first month are noteworthy of what can happen when the combined brain power of a working force is permitted free expression through organized channels.

The joint committee in the tin mill met. The discussion centered around more efficient maintenance. "The biggest difficulty of maintenance men getting to a job," a union member of the committee observed, "is that the territory we have to cover is so big. It often happens that we lose several minutes before we find out from the whistle whether it's an important job or not that's down."

Another union committee member asked the superintendent if he had any idea of how much a fifteen-minute delay on the hot mills cost. He replied in the negative, but added that it might be a good idea to figure it out. "Maintenance men," he said, "ought to be like firemen—get to the breakdown or where they're needed in a hurry. What ideas do you have to improve the calling of maintenance men?"

Someone suggested a system of lights directing them to the job. Another added that four lights, red, green, white, and blue, ought to go over the clock, where everyone could see them. The red light would mean that the electrician was wanted on the big mill, the green light would indicate that the hot-mill crane was down, etc. The superintendent said the lights would be installed immediately. Maybe the electricians, pipe fitters, millwrights, and other maintenance men that keep the mill going wanted the lights to symbolize their importance. For one thing, the frustrations of answering false alarms were largely eliminated. The alibi for not getting to a job in the quickest possible time was killed. At any rate, lost time in the department declined more than fifty per cent in a few months. It may have been due to the lights, or to the fact, which the men previously had not appreciated, that lost time cost so much money per minute.

The merchant-mill committee's first meeting produced even more tangible results. One of the committeemen, a rougher, pressed a suggestion for increasing production that was also a grievance. "For four years," he complained, "I've been after better guides that would eliminate a lot of turned bars in the roughers. Some time back I took a guide off the other side and cut the heel off it, got the machine shop to narrow the guide, and put it in—and it worked fine. But I haven't been able to get this kind of a guide. It's heavier than needed to stay in and what we get is a light guide that raises every time, and the company loses steel and the men lose time. The guide can be remedied at little expense to make it what it ought to be."

The superintendent said that if the suggestion would reduce "cobbles" and "turndowns" he would be glad to give the roughers what they wanted. Another committeeman wanted to know what a delay meant in dollars. The superintendent figured it was two hundred and forty dollars on the eighteen-inch mill and four hundred dollars on the twelve-inch mill for an hour's delay. These mills had been losing twenty hours a week on the average—a minimum cost of sixty-four hundred dollars a week. Another committeeman said he knew a way to save fifteen minutes every time there was a roll change. "Move the racks behind the welders' shack out to the end of the eighteen-inch walkway. This would also be safer. The welders' shack is right underneath the hoist and if the sling on the roll let go when it was over it there certainly would be an accident."

This, the superintendent assured the committee, would be looked into right away. Another committeeman pointed out other ways of increasing production. "Move the stop blocks on the end of the rails on the down side of the roughing tables back about eight inches, and put in a little wider runway. Then the finishing table could go over and work on the roughing table."

"We'll see what can be done about that," the super replied. He was kept busy until the next month's meeting exploring the possibilities of these suggestions. The twenty-hour-a-week dead time on the mills was cut to twelve hours within a few months. In dollars and cents this amounted to an annual saving in excess of one hundred thousand dollars—more than enough to grant a one-cent-an-hour wage increase to all employees.

The first open-hearth department meeting was no less fruitful. It revolved around running stoppers. This is a shop term that describes the phenomenon of the stopper in the ladle getting stuck while pouring molten steel into molds—which is costly, since steel runs continuously until the ladle is emptied and much of it is lost in moving from one mold to another. The department had been experiencing an epidemic of running stoppers. A long discussion into this problem consumed most of the time of the meeting. Within a few days the problem was licked. It is something that might recur; and if it does, all the technical factors that might cause it will have to be checked until the problem is solved. In such instances now, the knowledge and experience of both management and workers are at work.

The union members of the committee asked all about costs. How much does an hour's delay in the open hearth cost? What are the labor costs per ton? the fuel costs? the scrap costs? Each question was answered promptly. This whole field of information, so vital to their daily work, was opened to the men for the first time. Each figure had been confidential information. Now the men are in "the know," and the results have been apparent in lowered costs on most of the principal cost factors in melting steel.

The joint committees in the rail mill, finishing mill, coke ovens, blooming mill, chipping department, and all other operations in the mill likewise found their first meetings profitable. Not all of them produced usable suggestions, but they all promoted better understanding of one another's problems. Not a single department in later meetings has failed to find one or more profitable cost-reduction ideas. It is too early, at this time, to measure the cumulative effect of union-management co-operation in terms of dollars and cents. However, two important developments since the outset of the program give some indication of what the results of the first year will show. Substantial individual wage adjustments were made at the end of six months. No doubt much of the money for these adjustments came from savings effectuated by the joint department committees and the top union-management committee, because they were not economically possible at the start of the program. The other development took place before a government commission involving another industrial concern in Canada. The head of this steel mill testified about SWOC. He told the commission, "I would not take a million dollars for the union-management co-operation program I have in my mill. I would not think of going back to the days before the union." The commission recommended that the concern in question recognize and sign a collective-bargaining contract with its employees' union—a SWOC local union. But this gain is only incidental.

The important thing is that in a small, isolated town of twenty-five thousand people in a Canadian province a group of workers points the way to greater productive efficiency. Not alone, but in co-operation with their management, these workers point the way to greater results in production for the war effort now and for peacetime purposes later. They point the way for industrial management and labor unions in North America. What they are accomplishing can be repeated in mines, mills, and factories throughout Canada and the United States. The one thing about which there is unanimous agreement is that more production is needed urgently. Organized labor, since the start of the armament program in our country and the war effort in Canada, has been saying to management and to government, "Take us into the inner councils of industry and government. Give us responsibility and authority to match it. And we will see that the maximum effort of which our men and machines are capable is achieved."

The curt reply has been, "No. That's too big a price to pay for maximum production. We can achieve it without bringing you into the administrative councils of government and the managerial councils of industry."

Can they? They did not do it in 1917-18. Nor did they do it in England before Dunkirk. Are they doing it now in Canada and the United States?

These problems are the subject of the last part of this book. Here we are concerned with productive efficiency at the level of the local enterprise. Organized labor said to industrial management long before September, 1939, "Let's get together. Let's co-operate. That's the way to optimum efficiency and maximum output."

Since September, 1939, organized labor has been repeating this more persistently. The answer is well known. It is seen in the refusal of firms that do bargain collectively in good faith to recognize the union for anything except bargaining about wages, hours, and working conditions. It is seen in the practices of union-management relationships that compel the union to be nothing more than an agency to adjust grievances. It is seen in the case of the shipbuilding company that gave up its yard before yielding to the elementary principle of self-preservation, because it applied to a labor union.

As a consequence, the armament program is suffering in most of the mines, mills, and factories. Productive efficiency is greater, to be certain, than in Germany and Italy. Free workers inherently produce more and better goods than slave workers. The advertised efficiency of dictatorship is not at the level of the local enterprise. The man-hour output of German and Italian industries does not begin to approximate that of the United States or even Canada. Their advertised efficiency is at the level of industry-wide and national co-ordination. A dynamic democracy, as we discuss later, can match and excel the efficiency of the dictator countries at these levels, not by imitating them but by giving democracy a chance to work fully at all levels of all types of endeavor. But at the level of the local enterprise in the democracies of North America productive efficiency is not as high as it could be, because the principles of democracy are not allowed to operate fully. This is evident in the case of the Canadian steel firm that has the courage to let the democratic participation of its employees in production realize its natural fruition. It is evident in the marginal firms in the United States that have engaged in union-management co-operation. Evidences of it can be found in other industries—electrical manufacturing, railroads, die casting, textiles, hosiery, printing, coal, millinery, men's and women's clothing, and other fields of production. The results have not been uniform, but they

Part Three

MEANS TO FULL PRODUCTION AND EMPLOYMENT

Chapter X: Industry-wide Collective Bargaining

The natural outgrowth of local-plant and individual-company collective bargaining is bargaining between district or industry-wide organizations of management and unions.

In the industries where union-management relations are of long standing, collective-bargaining contracts have been extended beyond the individual plant or company. Although there are still segments of the men's-clothing and ladies'-garment industries where only individual-company contracts are in force, for instance, a large portion of the members of both the Amalgamated Clothing Workers of America and the International Ladies' Garment Workers' Union are covered by contracts with employers' associations. These contracts cover geographical producing markets with district organizations of management, because of peculiar competitive conditions. The needle-trades industries are not national in scope like steel, coal, or auto; but, significantly, relations have extended beyond the level of the local enterprise. This is likewise the case in the railroad industry. The Association of Railway Labor Executives negotiates the basic terms of a contract with all the carriers represented by the Association of American Railroads, which, in turn, are incorporated into contracts through negotiations with the Eastern, Southern, and Western carriers' associations. In varying degrees, therefore, collective bargaining embraces the entire industry, or geographical sections of it, in those industries which have a long union-management experience, such as pottery, glass bottle, printing, and others. The most notable examples, of course, are in bituminous and anthracite mining.

Industry-wide bargaining in the bituminous-coal industry goes back to 1886, although union organization in some measure had existed for a quarter of a century earlier. In that year the operators and union miners in Ohio, Indiana,

Illinois, and Pennsylvania met in joint conference. The area defined by that conference—the Central Competitive Field—has remained intact with little variation during the intervening years. The tonnage represented in these conferences has varied from forty to seventy per cent of the total national production of bituminous coal. Since the 1933-34 period the United Mine Workers of America (UMW) has greatly extended its organization into coal fields previously unorganized. As a consequence, during the last eight years contract negotiations between the union and operators have become largely all-inclusive and only an insignificant percentage of the approximately four hundred and fifty thousand bituminous miners and sixteen thousand operators are not represented in them. The negotiations between the representatives of the coal-operators associations and the UMW in the Central Competitive Field have a special significance. The wage rates and other basic contractual conditions agreed upon in them determine the level of wage rates and other basic terms of employment in all of the bituminous-coal-producing fields in the nation.

In organizational structure the miners and operators parallel each other. The former are organized into local unions that, as a rule, embrace a single mine. These locals, in turn, are organized into twenty-nine districts. Thus the unit of action and control is one providing for the greatest possible degree of participation by the miners. Upon this base the pyramid of union organization is erected. Each district organization is represented on the Executive Board of the International Union of the United Mine Workers of America. Biennially the International Union holds a convention which is attended by more than fifteen hundred delegates from the affiliated local unions. One of the most important items of business at each convention is the selection of the Policy Committee; it meets prior to the expiration of the UMW's wage contracts in the industry for the purpose of formulating both policies and proposals for contract revisions. This committee is made up of some one hundred and fifty local and international union representatives, and its functions are to serve as the union's general wage-negotiating agency.

On the operators' side the basic unit of organization is a district association comprising the operators within a given geographical area. The Central Competitive Field is divided into Northern and Southern groups. In the Northern group there are more than a score of associations of operators, while the Southern group embraces more than a dozen such associations. Taken together, there is for all practical purposes complete organization, on a workable democratic basis, of all coal operators on the one hand and all coal miners on the other hand. Every two years they negotiate an industry-wide collective-bargaining contract.

The operation of the biennial Appalachian Joint Conference for wage-contract negotiations is an interesting example of industrial democracy at work at the level of an entire industry. On one side of an auditorium sit approximately one hundred and fifty representatives of the operators, while on the opposite side sit an equal number of representatives of the miners. Rules for governing the proceedings of the conference are proposed, debated, and finally agreed upon. They are binding upon both parties. One of these rules is that each party votes as a unit on all questions. A chairman and secretary are elected; alternately one is an operator and the other a miner. A stenographic record of the proceedings is kept. The proposals for contract revision are submitted, and debated within the framework of parliamentary rules formulated and adopted by the participants. Usually the conference is broken down into a small joint subcommittee to which is delegated carefully defined authority. Its work is subject to the review and final action of the larger group. Both parties, of course, have full power to conclude an agreement.

Out of these conferences eventually emerges a written collective-bargaining wage contract. It sets forth the rates of pay, methods of calculating same, schedules of working hours, form of union recognition, vacation rules, procedures for the presentation and adjustment of grievances and complaints, and other terms of union-management relationships that govern the coal operators and the UMW for a two-year period. These industry-wide negotiations are then supplemented with district and local negotiations between the operators and miners that embrace problems peculiar to the respective localities in the bituminous-mining industry. In recent years work stoppages have attended the negotiations of new contracts, although there were no industry-wide stoppages in 1935 and 1937. In the anthracite-mining industry, where industry-wide bargaining has been practiced more universally for a longer period of time, there have been no work stoppages incident to the negotiation of a new agreement for a period of sixteen years up to the brief stoppage in 1941.

The benefits of industry-wide bargaining in bituminous mining have been self-evident. The operators and miners, among other things, have learned how to work together. They have co-operated in securing the passage of federal legislation designed to stabilize their industry, and have presented similar views to Congressional committees on national problems of concern to bituminous mining. They have established joint commissions to study the effects of transportation costs and of technological changes in the production of soft coal, and to study other matters of mutual interest. But, more important, industry-wide bargaining has served to stabilize the soft-coal industry, which suffered disastrously from price cutting and unprofitable operations, in part, because of unfair wage differentials enjoyed by coal operators in certain districts. As early as 1939 a coal operator[1] declared:

> . . . The bituminous coal industry has passed through a period of five years of continuous effort to stabilize wages and prices. The total net result has been a more stable wage scale and lower wage differentials between the northern and southern fields than have been in effect at any period of time in the history of the industry. Prices, on the contrary, remain uncontrolled except in so far as they are stabilized by wages, which represent a large proportion of cost. . . .

Since then, of course, the UMW has eliminated a large portion of the wage differential enjoyed by the Southern districts, and through the Bituminous (Guffey) Coal Act—which, significantly, both the UMW and most coal operators favored—the price structure of the industry has been largely stabilized.

Thus industry-wide bargaining has assisted in the solution of problems beyond the scope of action of local-mine or individual-company relations, and it has paid dividends to both the coal operators and soft-coal miners. Many problems, to be sure, remain unsolved, but these—such as soft-coal competition with other fuels, and the levels of output and employment in relation to the rate of national business and industrial activity—are beyond the scope of effective action by a single industry. They require, as we discuss in the concluding chapter, national action of management, organized labor, and government.

Industry-wide bargaining is virtually nonexistent in such industries as steel, auto, rubber, aluminum, electrical manufacturing, and textiles, which have only recently embraced collective bargaining at the level of the local plant and individual company. We have previously noted some of the deficiencies of union-management relations growing out of the absence of effectively organized industry-wide associations of management designed to bargain collectively with labor unions that are already organized along parallel lines. Before examining these deficiencies, however, let us look briefly at the extent of industry-wide bargaining in other democratic countries.

In Great Britain and Sweden collective bargaining not only has assumed industry-wide proportions but in many respects, has become national in scope.[2] "The expression 'collective agreement' does not mean an agreement between a single employer and his workers, or even an agreement between a single employer and a union. It means an agreement negotiated collectively by representatives of a group or association of employers (commonly an industry-wide association) and representatives of a union or a group or association of unions," President Roosevelt's Commission on Industrial Relations in Great Britain reported in 1938. Many of the agreements thus negotiated "are national in scope, regulating the terms of employment" of all workers in the categories covered by them; and when agreements are negotiated with individual employers they "generally conform to the national agreements." Collective-bargaining agreements in Sweden likewise are mostly industry-wide, many being national in scope; and the local or district agreements that are negotiated also "generally follow the standards set for that particular industry by the national agreements." Gerard Swope, Chairman of the President's Commission on Industrial Relations in Sweden, reported that in December, 1938, "the Federation of Swedish Employers and the Confederation of Swedish Trade Unions, both nation-wide Swedish associations of employers' and workers' organizations" voluntarily negotiated a national agreement, designed to promote industrial peace and eliminate as many stoppages of work as humanly possible. It covers virtually every union and company practicing collective bargaining in the country.

Experiences in other democratic countries and in our own industries with long union-management practices indicate, it seems clear, that the tendency of labor organizations to extend their collective-bargaining contracts beyond the individual plant or company naturally follows the almost complete unionization of any given industry. Already the flat-glass industry, which embarked upon collective bargaining in the last decade, engages in partial industry-wide negotiations with the Federation of Flat Glass Workers. As collective bargaining grows and matures in the newly organized industries it will assume, from year to year, a broader industrial scope. This is so because of the natural limitations on union-management relations at the level of the local plant and individual firm. Let us look at a few of the problems typified by the steel industry that cannot be solved effectively at this level.

Industry-wide bargaining is necessary to correct the indefensible differentials existing between maintenance- and production-workers' wage rates in steel. These inequities in the wage structure have grown over the years. The methods of computing costs arbitrarily divided labor costs into direct wages and "overhead." Each penny spent for a millwright, a rigger, an electrician, and other maintenance man-hours was considered a drag on profits. As a result, this group of workers received inadequate consideration from management when it was free—unhampered by collective bargaining—to distribute wages as it saw fit. Complaints from maintenance workers for more money usually brought the rejoinder, "If you want to make more money, then you should take a production job where you can earn it." Evidence of this attitude is found in the promotional sequence. As noted in the discussion of seniority, a motor inspector, for example, has precedence for the soaking-pit-crane job over cranemen working on other cranes in a particular mill. Logically this job should go to experienced cranemen on lower-rated cranes, but for more than thirty years the line of promotion has been from motor-inspector helper to motor inspector to soaking-pit craneman. By converting highly trained tradesmen into production workers, which is quite typical, steel management has temporized with the problem of the wage differential between maintenance and production workers. And the problem is still with the industry.

Advancing technology has radically changed the status of the maintenance worker in recent decades. The electrician, for instance, tending the huge electrical motors driving the rolls of a modern continuous-strip mill, in many ways, is as important as the roller or his assistant who directs the flow of electric power with buttons and levers. The ratio of maintenance to production workers has been rising in the last two decades due to the replacement of muscular energy by electricity as the primary source of productive power. In fact, one argument advanced by management to counteract the view that continuous-strip mills have created technological unemployment has been that, although the number of workers on primary production is reduced, more maintenance workers are required to tend these huge mills than were needed for the old hand mills. Yet this increased importance of the maintenance worker has not been recognized in the distribution of wages. An electrician, who has spent several years learning his trade, in most continuous-strip mills receives about half as much in wages per hour as an assistant roller or speed operator—both of whom have learned their jobs in a considerably shorter period of time. As a consequence, maintenance workers have begun to stir; their objective is to see that the compensation for their work is raised in direct proportion to which advancing technology has been raising their importance.

Evidence of this unrest, particularly during the armament boom, has been interpreted as a reversion to craft consciousness. The several groups of skilled tradesmen in the steel industry—machinists here, pipe fitters there, and other groups of maintenance workers—since the increased demands for such trained workers under the armament program became evident, have been pressing SWOC and management for higher wages. But this is hardly the result of a sudden consciousness of craft skills, because similar wage problems have risen simultaneously in blast furnaces and coke plants in the industry—where wage rates are disproportionate in relation to the other departments of an integrated steel works. Like the maintenance workers' wage-inequality complaint, that of blast-furnace and coke workers can receive only partial treatment within the framework of collective-bargaining contracts with individual companies that substantially freeze wages for a definite period of time.

We have noted this in the discussion of wage inequalities in the case of four hundred and eighty-three maintenance workers in a steel mill employing over five thousand workers; they demanded that their wages be equalized with (1) wage rates for similar work elsewhere in the steel industry, (2) wage rates of production workers in their own mill. Management adjusted their wages as compared with those paid by competitors, but was helpless—as was SWOC—to do anything about the dissatisfaction over the differential between their earnings and those of production workers.

Obviously one company could not grant a general increase to its maintenance workers without putting its costs out of line with the rest of the industry. Such a large-cost problem requires simultaneous consideration and action throughout the whole of an industry. This problem is so fundamental that even industry-wide collective bargaining would probably have to evolve a long-range policy to eliminate it. We believe that if and when the first industry-wide steel conferences are convened the negotiators should say to the maintenance workers, for example, "We recognize the justness of your grievance. However, it cannot be solved in one step. We have agreed, therefore, that maintenance workers shall receive a five-cent-an-hour higher increase than production workers as a result of these conferences. We have also agreed upon the establishment of a joint commission to make an evaluation of the several maintenance jobs with a view toward placing the wage rates for these jobs in proper relation to those paid production workers. The commission will report back to the next conference, and further steps, at that time, will be taken to adjust your grievance."

A long-range program of this kind involves granting some workers a larger increase than others. Hence it is again obvious that the union-shop form of recognition is essential. In this connection SWOC's success has been due, in part, to the fact that its basic wage policy has been to secure the same amount of wage increase for all its members—so many cents per hour. Any other type of general wage increase may have proved fatal to SWOC with membership in the union purely voluntary. "Equal treatment to all" has been SWOC's policy. This is an integral part of its program and, in turn, is a long-range approach to a more serious wage-differential problem in the steel industry's wage structure than that of maintenance and production workers.

The steel industry, in more ways than one, is a "feast or famine" undertaking. When SWOC entered the industry in 1936, laborers were starving for forty-seven cents an hour alongside of rollers making three dollars and fifty cents an hour. The last time steel management was free to decide by itself how to raise wages, November, 1936, it granted a ten per cent wage raise; the laborer at the bottom of the ladder got five and one-half cents an hour (slightly more than ten per cent), while the highest-paid roller got thirty-five cents an hour. The indefensible spread was increased. SWOC halted this unhealthy trend, and for the first time in the industry's history introduced the principle of flat hourly raises. The two ten-cent raises, one in 1937 and the other in 1941, have brought the laborer up to seventy-two and one-half cents an hour, or thirty-eight per cent. The roller has gone from three dollars and eighty-five cents to four dollars and five cents an hour, or only five per cent. In four years SWOC reduced the spread of the top man from seven and one-half times as much as the laborer to five and one-half times. The administration of this policy has not been easy. We have had five-hundred-dollar-a-month workers in the furnace department of a tool-steel firm, for example, strike because the ten-cent raise was an insult to them. But this kind of difficulty has been rare in comparison with the furor that percentage wage raises would have created in 1937 and 1941. Narrowing the spread between high and low rates in the steel industry is essential to the development of a wage structure that will be most conducive to industrial peace.

But the eventual solution to this problem requires industry-wide action, because advancing technology—the power age attaining maturity—is making the entire concept of the basis for wage payments obsolete. Industry's wage system has been predicated upon the muscular contribution of workers in the several classifications of work, while increasingly during the last two decades this source of productive power has been losing its dominant role in the conversion of America's raw materials into finished goods. The continuous-strip steel mill is a typical example of the shift from muscular effort to electrical energy as the primary source of productive power. The old hand mills are dirty, noisy, hot places; that is, the few that are still remaining. Here scores of men, using hand tongs, grab the steel out of a hot furnace, push it through power-driven rolls, catch it on the other side of the rolls, push it back and forth, throw it to a doubler who folds it up, and then put it back into the furnace and through the rolls for some more "passes" until the steel is reduced to the desired thickness. The muscular energy and skill of these hot-mill workers in this steel-making process is more important than the steam or electrical power that drives the rolls. Each man on the hot-mill crew is paid a specific tonnage rate according to his particular degree of "skill, responsibility, and so forth." The more muscular energy the hot-mill workers put into their work, the more money they earn.

Contrast this with a modern strip mill. The huge building is clean, neither noisy nor hot like the hand mills, and the usual hordes of men are conspicuous by their absence. In their place is a new kind of skilled worker. He does not have a pair of tongs in his hands, since human hands never touch the steel going through the strip mill. Instead, one of these skilled workers pushes a button—and a slab of steel looking like a double-sized mattress and weighing two or more tons slides out of a reheating furnace. Another worker throws a lever, and the slab starts through the first breakdown stand of rolls; from there on, a succession of buttons and levers operated by the crew of the strip mill carry the slab along a conveyor until it is rolled—at the rate of more than a half mile a minute—into a thousand-foot coil, like a reel of motion-picture film. From here the coil moves along an automatic conveyor for further treatment by automatic machinery. Electricity is the source of power that enables a crew of two score workers to produce a thousand tons in eight hours—twenty-five times more steel than the same number of workers can produce on the old sheet hand mills. Yet these forty strip-mill workers, whose chief function is to direct the flow of electrical energy with buttons and levers, are paid a specific tonnage rate according to their "respective degrees of skill, responsibility, and so forth." Although the shift to electrical power has been complete, they are paid on the basis of the identical wage structure that prevails in the few old hand mills that are still operating.

Consequently, the wage structure of the strip mills is an anomaly. The roller, for example, is paid a guaranteed hourly rate plus so much per ton or per hundred tons over a certain predetermined standard of output. This is the same method by which the old hand-mill roller was paid, except that he usually received tonnage rates without any hourly guarantee. These tonnage rates were set years ago and changed very little, if at all, except at times when the industry's wage levels moved upward or downward. The harder the roller and his crew worked, the more they produced and the more they earned. Management was glad to get the extra tonnage and let them have the extra earnings. The primary factors that contributed to higher output were the skill, physical effort, and responsibility of the roller and his crew. On the strip mills these factors are of secondary importance in production, and thus every time output rises for any one of a score of reasons—most of which have their roots in the fact that electricity is the primary source of productive power—the wage structure is thrown out of line.

The Ohio River Steel Corporation, for example, installed a strip mill in 1934. It set tonnage wage rates on the basis of an expected average hourly output of fifty tons. By 1937 the mill, with no change in the size of the crew, was producing an average of one hundred tons an hour. Management asked SWOC to raise the basis of the tonnage wage system from fifty to seventy-five tons an hour—a twenty per cent cut in average hourly earnings for the crew, as its tonnage earnings would not start until after the seventy-five-ton-per-hour level would be exceeded. The twenty per cent cut in the crew's earnings was requested on the grounds that the increased output over the four-year period was due to nine hundred and thirty-three thousand dollars' worth of improvements, and not to any increased physical effort, or skill, of the men operating the mill. The soaking pits had been enlarged; this meant that more ingots could be fed to the blooming mill and, in turn, it could produce more slabs for the strip mill to roll. A new bottleneck then developed, and management eliminated it at a substantial cost. The reheating furnaces could not handle all the slabs coming from the blooming mill, and so they were enlarged. Thus still more slabs were available for the strip mill to roll. Other improvements were also made. They were all directed at supplying the strip mill with more steel to roll, but its appetite seemed insatiable. The more steel fed, the more rolled.

Management contended that the only factors to be considered in determining the extent to which earnings should rise in relation to increased output were "skill, efficiency, and physical requirements and hazards." These factors, of course, did not entitle the men to much of an increase in earnings, because the chief factor in the rising output was electricity and not physical effort. They did not have to break their backs handling the steel with hand tongs, as in the hand mills; all the increased output required of them was a keener perception and greater degree of alertness in throwing the levers and pushing the buttons directing the electric power that turns the rolls and moves the conveyors. A time study by management revealed that the increase in bonus earnings from eleven per cent in 1934 to sixty-one per cent in 1937 was unjustified on the basis of increased physical work, and recommended that the crew's earnings be cut twenty per cent. From the viewpoint of wages paid workers in other parts of this huge integrated steel works—some of which had not yet felt the full impact of the shift from muscular to electric power—the strip-mill crew's wages were out of line and, after some bickering, SWOC consented to part of the requested cut. But the cut was economically unsound and would not have been requested, let alone made, if the basis for wage payments had not been obsolete.

These simple facts reveal the extent to which advancing technology is making the entire concept of the basis for wage payments obsolete. In measuring wage earners' share of the benefits of increased output, it is plain, other factors besides "skill, ability, and physical requirements" should be given consideration—because, if these factors were all-determining, wages would be frozen at their present levels and wage earners would automatically be denied a fair distribution of the benefits of increased output. The basis of wage payments, therefore, should be an equitable distribution of the proceeds of production to wage earners, as well as the factors of physical requirements now given exclusive consideration. Hence a new concept of the basis of wage payments is imperative. Collective bargaining at the level of the local plant or individual company not only has been unable to evolve such a concept but has been unable even to give official recognition to the need for it. Through industry-wide bargaining a formula could be devised whereby the proceeds of a particular technological change affecting a small number of workers could be distributed to all workers in a given mine, mill, or factory. In this way the earnings of those workers immediately affected would not be put out of line with the rest of the plant, and at the same time an equitable share of the proceeds of increased output going to workers would be distributed to them. This, in turn, is related to another wage problem that advancing technology is creating, which may strain union-management relations to a breaking point unless solved through the processes of industry-wide bargaining.

Not only is the power age rendering entire mills and processes of production obsolete; it is making obsolete the complicated wage-incentive systems that have grown up over the years, with their accompanying time and motion studies and job evaluations. In their place, it seems to us, will evolve a simple wage structure recognizing that the prevailing source of productive energy is no longer muscular power, and therefore workers should no longer be compensated on this basis alone. The management of one steel works in America has already gained a full appreciation of the devastating effects of the power age on the traditional wage system of American industry. Unlike the steel industry generally —whose wage structure is complicated and embraces more than one hundred thousand different wage rates—the system of wage payment in this single steel works is the essence of simplicity.

There are only twenty-one wage rates in this steel works—all hourly rates. Not a single incentive rate exists in the entire works, from coke ovens to cold finishing mills. The lowest rate is one dollar an hour, the highest rate is two dollars an hour, and the remaining nineteen rates are at five-cent-an-hour gradations. Workers know what their earnings will be each pay before they draw their envelopes; management wastes no time or energy figuring out earnings through an antiquated wage system. But what about efficiency, production, and profits? The answer is simple. No steel company in the United States matches this steel works as a successful, efficient, and profitable business enterprise. Though organized labor in coming years may be the champion of a wage system consisting exclusively of flat hourly wage rates with measured production, fundamentally the power age will be responsible for consigning American industry's traditional wage system to the scrap heap.

Obviously collective bargaining between unions and individual companies is not broad enough in scope to handle adequately the basic economic and wage-payment problems that are already with us or in the making by advancing technology. Maintenance workers will hardly receive twenty- to seventy-five-cent-an-hour wage raises to bring their earnings in proper relation to those of production workers. The spread between the lowest- and highest-paid workers in industry, as typified by steel, is not likely to be reduced to proper proportions. Neither are the proceeds of increased production likely to be distributed equitably to workers as long as their basis of compensation is outmoded. Nor will the entire basic concept of American industry's wage system be revamped while the status of unions is still in doubt and the natural growth of geographical district or industry-wide bargaining is impeded. The limitations on union-management relations at the level of the local plant and individual firm are a constant, irresistible pressure on unions and management alike to extend their relations. In no small measure the industrial strife of the last few years is attributable to the absence of industry-wide associations of management designed especially to work out many of these problems with national unions.

A narrow-visioned leadership, on either the union or the management side, that conceives of collective bargaining as a device whereby organized wage earners acquire power to wrest from their individual firm all that they can possibly secure, in higher wages, shorter hours, and other conditions of work, fails to understand the processes of democracy and the social and economic forces at work. Society as a whole is dynamic—not static. As a consequence, the position of organized labor does not remain stationary. Once wage earners successfully establish organization and collective bargaining at their point of actual employment, their new relationship with management undergoes a transition from one of conflict in varying degrees to that of co-operation in some degree. The extent of co-operation may vary from mere mutual agreement on wages and other terms of employment to union participation in raising productive efficiency. Instead of this leading to collective bargaining on a permanent status in a single plant or firm, it serves to open up a larger area of common interests and objectives. This is so because the level of wages and other economic conditions in any given industry is influenced, in large measure, by the prevailing conditions in the nonunion segments. Also local unions are tied together through their affiliation with a national or international (the latter is one that embraces both the United States and Canada) union, which gives their members a sense of being part of something larger than the productive unit in which they are directly employed. They develop out of their union experiences an industry consciousness, and an awareness of participation in a movement that transcends a whole industry and encompasses the organized employees of a great variety of industries.

Two weeks after SWOC signed its first contract with the largest steel firm in the spring of 1937, its officers presented several admittedly meritorious grievances involving big cost items. Management said, "We have signed a contract with your union. But most of our major competitors have not. We have taken on costs through our contract which these competitors have not yet assumed. We're hard-pressed enough. Why don't you bring these other companies into line? Then we'll see what can be done about these grievances you are pressing that would only raise our costs at present." The union recognized these reasons to be sound, it accepted the fact that the extent to which it could advance the economic interests of its members was limited until every major producer in the industry was organized and operating under a like collective-bargaining contract. Several weeks later SWOC unsuccessfully tried to extend its contractual relations to all of the principal steel firms. Four years later it succeeded. Meanwhile these grievances involving substantial additions to the cost of production went unsettled in the industry.

Now that almost the entire industry is under contract with SWOC, the next step is industry-wide bargaining. That such a step is eminently practical is demonstrated by the fact that traditionally the steel industry has for all practical purposes acted on an industry-wide basis in the formulation of wage and price policies. Though the "Little Steel" firms refused to follow a majority of the companies in the industry in recognizing SWOC in 1937, they followed the actions of the majority on wages and prices that were taken simultaneously. The history of the steel industry's formulation of price and wage policies is well known. For decades it has enacted its own economic legislation without the participation of workers, consumers, or the government. The effect of this legislation has been so far-reaching that in the nineteen-twenties the federal government took action designed to stop the industry from passing such economic legislation arbitrarily. The success of the federal government's intervention is not our present concern; we cite it merely to illustrate the effectiveness achieved by the industry in acting informally as a unit. This was industrial dictatorship, since the larger numerical groups in the industry were denied participation in formulating and administering this economic legislation. On behalf of one of the groups—workers—SWOC has already achieved some degree of effective participation.

In 1941 the steel industry adopted an economic policy that permitted wages to be raised only two and one-half cents an hour. For a year earlier the auto, aluminum, glass, and other basic industries had operated under a similar law—passed arbitrarily by the financial and industrial leaders of these industries. Evidence of this is found in the inability of the auto workers, glass workers, or aluminum workers to secure wage raises in excess of two to three cents an hour. In 1941 Philip Murray, on behalf of the organized steel workers, told the steel industry, "SWOC moves that the wage-raise law you passed without consulting it be amended to provide for a ten-cent-an-hour increase instead of a two-and-one-half-cent one." The largest steel firm immediately consulted with many of the other large firms in the industry. The reply in effect was, "We will accept a five-cent amendment." SWOC argued the merits of its original motion. It was finally accepted. The steel industry as a whole simultaneously followed suit.

At the same time, the steel industry passed an economic law raising prices several dollars a ton and proceeded to publicly announce it. Whereupon the federal government—now more representative of the consuming public than in the nineteen twenties and more powerful—told the industry, "We wish to amend the price law you passed without consulting the consumers of steel products as follows: steel prices shall not be raised under present circumstances." The industry argued. But the same facts that SWOC used to argue its case were used with equal effectiveness by the federal government. The increased rate of steel operations more than enabled the industry to make a fair return on its investment after granting the ten-cent raise and without raising prices. At this point the industry, which had originally ignored SWOC in formulating its own 1941 price and wage laws, asked it to participate in passing the price law it had arbitrarily drafted. SWOC refused this invitation. For all practical purposes this threw its weight behind the federal government, and no general increase in steel prices was made in 1941.

Thus in steel the patterns of industrial democracy on an industry-wide basis that prevail in the coal industries are becoming visible. That they will eventually develop into formal conferences between two coequal industry-wide organizations, fully empowered to negotiate the basic terms of employment for the industry, seems to us to be both a natural and a necessary development. It is not our purpose in this discussion to offer detailed solutions for specific problems that will face such a conference when it is convened. Our present purpose is merely to point out some of them and to explore the possibilities for creating practical machinery, democratically conceived and operated, through which these difficult economic, social, and political problems can be reconciled.

One of these problems in steel, and in most of the other basic industries, is the marginal producer. Although the larger steel firms were able to absorb the 1941 wage raise without a general price increase and maintain their earnings positions, this has not been the case with the marginal firms. For years they have been following the lead of the "big fellows," and were helpless to do otherwise in this instance. Their problems are peculiar to them and are not shared by the larger companies. The smaller firms are nonintegrated or semi-integrated, poorly located in a single area or operating obsolete equipment. By themselves they are helpless. One of these firms tried to organize this group of companies into an independent association. It was immediately given rough treatment by the large company that supplies it with semifinished steel. Its material began to decline in quality, and it was unable to get any of the other big companies to sell it steel bars. This small firm soon dropped the idea of an independent association, whereupon its steel bars started to arrive in good condition.

No longer do the "big fellows" protect the interests of the "little ones." For example, the latter are being gradually strangled to death. A nonintegrated firm that buys semifinished steel for conversion into finished steel has seen the spread between semifinished and hot-rolled strip drop from twelve dollars a ton in 1927 to eight in 1940, going as low as three dollars in 1938 and one dollar in 1939. In order to make any profits this nonintegrated firm's labor, sales, and other costs have to be less than the spread. Obviously in 1938 and 1939 it lost heavily. Unless steps are taken to arrest the present course of events, the pressures of economic concentration and expensive technological advances will leave only the "big fellows" producing steel in a relatively short period of time. Maybe the more than half-billion-dollar investment in these companies and the more than fifty thousand workers they employ should be sacrificed for the national welfare. We think not. But, in any event, whether or not steps should be taken to enable them to live and thrive should not be left to the arbitrary decision of the large steel producers. Organized labor, the smaller firms, and other interested groups should have a voice in making such an important decision. Industry-wide bargaining, in part, provides the democratic machinery through which these groups can participate in deciding the fate of the "smaller fellows."

Of course, the largest single problem that makes industry-wide bargaining procedures in the basic and mass-producing industries almost inevitable is that of equitably distributing the proceeds of production. Previously in this discussion we have noted how most of the major wage raises won by organized labor in the last five years have been either eaten up by technological changes or burned up by rising prices. This process creates a vicious circle of rising hourly wage rates and increasing prices and lower production costs that tends to prevent a net rise in the plane of living of workers and their families. Such conditions, it seems evident, are inevitable as long as union-management relations are confined to the level of the individual plant and competitive company. Hence organized labor seeks industry-wide bargaining as a means of raising the real earnings of its members on a relatively permanent basis. In the quest of a higher plane of living, organized workers have begun to sense a certain frustration because their hourly increases in wages afford them only temporary gains. Consequently, the major problems facing industry-wide collective-bargaining conferences when they are inaugurated in the newly unionized industries will be to determine:

1. What share of the industry's income should go to wage earners? to owners? to consumers?
2. How shall the respective shares be distributed so that they will stay so distributed?

These problems, in turn, raise the question of industrial price policies. The problem of the marginal firms is also tied into this question, since the survival of many of these firms depends, in large measure, upon the price level. Should the formulation of industrial price policies be left in the hands of organized industry and organized labor? If so, to what extent? If not, then in what manner should the federal government, on behalf of the ultimate consumers of industrial products, participate? Clearly these problems will have to be worked out simultaneously with the creation of industry-wide bargaining procedures in the newly unionized industries. It is not the purpose of this discussion to deal with them. Our concern is with the significance of organized labor's persistent drive for geographical-district or industry-wide bargaining, depending upon the economics of the respective industries. Ordway Tead in his *New Adventures in Democracy*[3] points this out.

> . . . As they [labor unions] gain inclusive membership, maturity and able, continuing leadership, they are associations profoundly concerned to advance the total effectiveness of the specific calling or industry in the total economy. The well-established union is, and has to be, as much concerned as the associated employers of an industry with the development of conditions which foster that industry's prosperity. There is a real sense in which the affiliated workers of an industry have more at stake in helping an industry to thrive than the salaried managers or the scattering of absentee stockholders.

In demanding and securing participation in making the almost two thousand shops in the New York dress market more efficient, the International Ladies' Garment Workers' Union has given real meaning to Ordway Tead's words with its slogan "There can be no security in an insecure industry."

Chapter XI: National Democratic Planning

The future of industrial democracy depends upon the attainment of full production and employment on a sustained basis during and after the war.

Industrial democracy is dynamic—an ever-changing, ever-growing way of life. Like its political counterpart it cannot become static, except at its peril. Inexorably it seeks to embrace everything that vitally affects the workingman in his work, community, and home. Personal happiness, family security, community integration, and a constantly rising plane of living are the fundamental objectives of industrial democracy. Their fulfillment depends upon full production and employment on a sustained basis. By the same token, the failure to solve the twin problems of mass unemployment and scarcity production threatens the extension of democratic methods in industry that, step by step, we have traced in the preceding pages. Likewise it is certainly open to doubt whether America's free institutions can again endure a breakdown in industrial output and jobs, such as the nineteen thirties witnessed. Finally, the widespread fear in our country that after the armament boom America is bound to return to the chaos, the mass unemployment, the restricted production, the economic and social poverty, and the political confusion of the last decade is, at once, a threat to the speedy prosecution of the war effort and the survival of democracy in the postwar era.

The dynamics of industrial democracy require that full production and employment be achieved on a sustained basis. The future holds little promise for collective bargaining between individual unions and firms if the unions' members and the firms' machines are not kept continuously busy. The application of democratic methods in the settlement of grievances, adjustment of wage rates, negotiation of general wage raises, development of seniority rules, joint determination of other working conditions, and establishment of the union-shop form of recognition, as we have discussed earlier, is a vital component of industrial democracy but, in itself, will not provide workers with that plane of living and measure of security needed to satisfy these basic human needs.

There is little future for union-management co-operation unless the resulting increased productive efficiency is converted into higher sales, lower prices, increased annual earnings, and sustained employment the year around. Obviously the solution to these problems is beyond the scope of the individual unions and firms practicing union-management co-operation. Thus the extension of democratic methods to actual production in the local plant will avail those workers affected very little in permanent gains unless their increased annual output is absorbed by the economy as a whole. Similarly the extension of industrial democracy to an entire industry will be seriously impeded. The future security of all the gains that the United Mine Workers of America has brought its members in the soft-coal fields, for example, is threatened by the failure of American industry as a whole to operate at a sustained level that in time will provide miners with year-round employment and adequate annual incomes. The persistent union demand for a minimum of two hundred days of work annually that is made at each biennial contract conference in the bituminous-coal industry is a recognition of this fact. "There can be no security in an insecure industry." Consequently the ultimate success of industrial democracy—in fact, the ultimate survival of political democracy—depends upon full production and full employment, because anything short of this cannot satisfy the basic motives that originally impelled workers to organize their unions and implement political democracy by the extension of its methods to their economic life.

Of course the future of political and industrial democracy —which the march of economic and technological events, nationally and internationally, has made mutually dependent

—is tied up with a decisive defeat of the Nazi regime in Germany and the war regime in Japan. Personally we have no doubt about such a military victory over the antidemocratic forces that Hitler has let loose in the world. We believe with Ernest Bevin, Minister of Labor in England, that this war is not one between democracy with its back against the wall and tyranny on a victorious march. This war is between democracy on the march and tyranny that once again, in a last effort for centuries, has reared its head out of the Middle Ages to challenge the worth and virility of the democratic way. It is our conviction that democracy will prevail over the Nazis and war lords of Japan, and in so doing will prepare the way for democratic methods and rights in the larger part of the world for generations to come.

Such a victory, however, consists of more than a military one, since the armies of democracy can be victorious on the battlefields and the cause of democracy may still be lost. The victory of the forces of democracy in the postwar era depends as much upon the effective solution of the problems of unemployment and scarcity production, though, to be certain, one battle cannot be won without the other. But more. The length of time it will take the forces of democracy to win their decisive military victory may be prolonged, in terms not only of months or years but of human lives, toil, and money, unless democratic planning is applied to our national economy in the execution of the armament-production program. In this final chapter we attempt, in broad outline, to indicate those methods that may reasonably be expected to accomplish such planning. Our concern in this discussion is not with the entire field of economic endeavor —such as credit, taxation, farm surpluses, foreign trade, and so forth—but is confined to the problem of achieving and maintaining full industrial production and employment for both the war period and the postwar era.

The weakness of free America is the lack of adequate national democratic planning. American industry has outdistanced every other country in productive efficiency at the level of the local enterprise—though even here efficiency, as we have seen, can be raised still higher through the further extension of democratic methods to industry. But this is where American industry excels. Never in its history, however, has it achieved a comparable degree of efficiency at the level of an entire industry or combination of vital industries. In mid-1940 there were no co-ordinated industries, integrated into a national whole, to which the federal government could turn for effective armament output. The only vital industries—aluminum and nickel—that functioned as a unit pursued restricted production policies and, it soon became evident, were incapable of supplying military needs alone to say nothing of essential domestic requirements. Here is where the dictator countries have free America whipped—so far. They operate their separate industries as co-ordinated units and these, in turn, are managed as integral parts of the economy as a whole. This is the basis for the prevalent impression that dictatorship is more efficient than democracy, but this is not necessarily inherent in the two systems. American industry can achieve a higher level of national efficiency than the dictator-regimented German industry, not by imitation but by co-operating with government and organized labor in a national democratic-planning effort. Herein, we believe, lies the means toward full production and employment during and after the war.

Before examining national democratic planning, let us briefly look at our national inefficiency. This is illustrated by both the 1917-18 armament-production failure of American industry and the equally inadequate output of implements of war during the first fifteen months of the current armament program, as well as by the dismal nineteen thirties.

The Commander in Chief of the American Expeditionary Forces, General John J. Pershing, testifies[1] that if his army had not been armed by England and France in all probability it would have lost the last battle. Of twenty thousand heavy field guns ordered from American industry only thirty were fired in battle. No American-built fighting plane ever flew at the front; nor were any American-manufactured tanks available for the First Army when the actual concentration of its troops and material was begun in the St. Mihiel region, and its thirty-one hundred artillery guns of all calibers were entirely supplied by the Allies. America even failed to deliver raw materials to French factories with whom Pershing had contracted for tanks, airplanes, and engines for the planes. He reported in *My Experiences in the World War:*

> . . . after nearly eighteen months of war it would be reasonable to expect that the organization at home would have been more nearly able to provide adequate equipment and supplies, and to handle shipments more systematically. It was fortunate indeed that we were not operating alone, for, in that case, the failure to meet our demands would have caused us serious trouble, if not irreparable disaster.

The War Department developed what was publicized during the generation after the Armistice as an Industrial Mobilization Plan, popularly termed M-Day, which was to insure against a repetition of the 1917-18 failure. But amidst the inadequacies and outright failures of the armament program at the end of 1941 the M-Day Plan was almost completely forgotten, and it was obvious that American industry could not achieve effective armament production without national planning. The outbreak of war in the Pacific in December revealed the inadequacy of aircraft, tank, ordnance, shell, powder, and naval-fighting-craft output; this is all in the public record.[2] Thus in more than a year—aided by several additional advance months of preparation in armament production for France and Great Britain—American industry again demonstrated its inability to produce armaments on time and in needed quantities. That its performance could have been larger and speedier was indicated by the extent to which England—slightly more than one-third the size of the United States—was outproducing American industry in November, 1941, in its aircraft factories, munition plants, tank arsenals, and shipyards. And doing so despite severe bombings since Dunkirk, and the failure of the Conservatives to mobilize its industries fully before that fateful retreat.

But the inadequacies of the armament program extended beyond actual output and effective administration. Sixty large corporations received more than three-fourths of the contracts and failed to let out "bits and parts" to smaller producers. As a consequence the largest single result of the armament program at the end of the year 1941 was "priority unemployment," not just a scattering of displaced workers but mass displacements—two to three million workers began to be added to the four to five million idle workers not yet absorbed in armament output. They symbolized America's national inefficiency. Auto workers were being laid off by the thousands, steel workers were being reduced to part-time work by the hundreds, and workers in scores of industries were beginning to suffer from the hazards of "priority unemployment" for the same basic causes that American industry had failed in 1917-18, and was failing in 1941, to produce implements of war on time and in needed quantities. There was nothing new about such national inefficiency; it had especially characterized the nineteen thirties.

During this dismal decade coal miners were lucky to get one hundred and seventy days of work in a year. Steel workers were being displaced by technological changes by the thousands. Auto workers were compelled, year in and year out, to suffer prolonged periods of seasonal unemployment. The industrial section of America was overrun with millions of unemployed workers, and there were evidences of the development of a permanent group—numbering in the millions—of American workers who never again would secure sustained private employment. Simultaneously during this decade, as we have noted previously, productive efficiency at the level of the local enterprise continued to rise—man-hour output, in fact, showed signs of rising faster and to a greater extent than in the previous decade of relative prosperity. But—and here was demonstrated the need for national democratic planning—this record of industrial efficiency was not being translated into full production and employment.

In the fall of 1939, for example, industrial output returned to the levels of 1929 without providing jobs for at least ten million workers. The steel industry had used technology to make fifty per cent of capacity operations profitable. Invention and research had been used by private industry to make scarcity production profitable rather than to increase total employment and raise the plane of living. This chronically depressed economic situation made many American workers, if not most of them, despair of any effective solution to their problems within the framework of our free democratic government and private economy. Then America started to wipe out unemployment with a huge armament program. In so doing, however, the federal government not only failed to take steps to assure effective armament output and to inspire hope of continued jobs and prosperity in the postwar era but, by virtually turning the government administration of the program over to the industrial leaders who had been identified with the economic failures of the nineteen thirties, created the prevailing impression that the postwar era portends a return to the dismal thirties.

The significance of this was immediately sensed by Philip Murray. A few weeks after he assumed the presidency of the CIO he proposed to President Roosevelt, in December, 1940, that each defense and basic industry be organized into a single production unit to achieve total armament production, to maintain simultaneously as high a level of essential domestic output as possible, to expand facilities where needed, and to plan for the continuation of full production and employment in the postwar era by converting production from war materials to peacetime goods. In each such industry, he proposed, an Industry Council[2] should be created, consisting of an equal number of representatives of management and of organized labor with a government chairman; and that these Councils should function under the direction of a National Board, similarly constituted,

[2] A fuller elaboration is contained in Appendix I.

whose duties it would be to integrate their work, plan for the date and place of delivery of the government's armament needs, formulate policies to meet these needs, and execute them through the several Councils. Though this proposal for national democratic planning was advanced to speed up the armament program, it had originated in Philip Murray's mind before the outbreak of war in the fall of 1939—it took form during the dismal decade of the thirties—and is no less concerned with achieving full production and employment in the postwar era.

At the outset the armament program was characterized by the absence of national planning and an administrative agency organized along industry-wide lines. Originally the National Defense Advisory Commission and later the Office of Production Management (OPM) were organized exclusively on a functional basis. A separate division was created for each major function—production, labor, materials, prices, transportation, and so forth. No administrative machinery was created to put policies into effect in the several industries; this was left to the relatively autonomous and unco-ordinated firms within each industry, and thus this obvious gap in American industry's national inefficiency was not bridged. Nor were effective national plans made to match existing productive facilities in the vital defense and basic industries against the military and domestic demands that would increasingly be made upon them.

By the end of 1941 the tragic consequences of this utter lack of national planning was evidenced by the huge backlogs of five-dozen large firms that had not been converted into implements of war, by the idle and unused facilities of smaller firms throughout the country, and by the failure of key-material industries to inaugurate and execute expansion programs.[3] Six months earlier the ineffectualness of the OPM setup could no longer be denied, and it was reorganized along industry-wide lines. The need for national planning was also recognized, and the Supply Priorities and Allocations Board (SPAB) was created in the fall of 1941. Thus, step by step, the administrative mechanism of the armament program began to evolve toward the Industry Council idea, though a month after Pearl Harbor, unfortunately, it was far from the kind of national planning necessary to achieve the production levels outlined by President Roosevelt in his message to Congress, January 6, 1942. A few days afterward the War Production Board was created—replacing OPM and SPAB—the success of which, in our judgment, will be largely determined by the extent to which it bridges the gap between the OPM-SPAB failure and the Industry Council idea.

The nature of this idea is illustrated in a survey of the steel industry, *How to Speed Up Steel Production*, submitted by Philip Murray to President Roosevelt on January 24, 1941. The Industry Council Proposal—Philip Murray explained—

> is founded on the fact that the entire Iron, Steel and Tin producing industry should be organized into one great production unit in order to assure this country of an adequate supply of iron and steel for civilian and military needs. This plan proposes to obtain this steel in two ways: first, through the most efficient co-ordination and use of present steel producing facilities; and second, through a well-reasoned, responsible program to expand steel melting and finishing capacities where necessary. . . . The disorganized state of the industry, growing out of the inefficient, individual order, and cross purpose state of affairs existing among separate companies, prevents the full use of the existing steel facilities as well as the execution of an effective expansion program. Unless the industry is organized into a single production unit, serious shortages of steel will follow. . . . The plan has its foundation in the creation of a "Top Scheduling Clerk" for the entire steel industry. Each mill and each company has a scheduling clerk to achieve the highest possible productive efficiency. This method of co-ordinating steel needs with steel facilities is precisely what is required for the entire industry, and what is lacking at present. It is as practical to achieve this type of industry-wide co-ordination as it is to achieve mill-wide and company-wide co-ordination of steel orders with production facilities.

The survey, at the time, showed almost six million tons of idle steel capacity. It pointed out, for instance, that:

> The industry is reported operating at ninety-nine per cent of ingot capacity, yet the actual production of both steel ingots and finished steel is substantially below the level of which present melting and finishing facilities are capable. Large steel firms are overloaded with orders, backlogs are running from two to four months, while smaller steel firms are operating their open hearth departments as little as forty-five per cent of capacity.

The veracity of this statement was flatly challenged by one of the industry's trade journals. But it soon discovered, upon SWOC's advice, small firms operating below fifty per cent of capacity, and apologized. In so doing, however, the journal went on to argue that Phil Murray's proposal was technically impractical, because one of the firms lacked the converting mills with which to reduce its ingots into usable semifinished products for rolling in other mills. This argument fell of its own weight a few months later when the Ford Motor Company purchased some of the ingots of this small firm and, lacking the capacity in its steel mill to reduce the ingots into slabs for rolling on its hot strip mill, farmed out this job to a neighboring steel firm which had the necessary converting facilities.

This is the kind of industry-wide co-ordination that is possible, but which the industry was not achieving to any substantial degree even by the end of 1941. In fact, the inability of the industry, functioning as a score or more of individual and separate firms, to achieve maximum efficiency was illustrated at the end of 1941 by plate production: the industry as a whole was producing plates at only three-fourths of capacity, while at the same time there were serious delays in the production of ships, freight cars, and so forth, for lack of steel plates. The OPM Iron and Steel Branch early in January, 1942, recommended a program of partially pooling plate orders and estimated that plate output, as a result, could be raised twelve per cent in January and another ten per cent in February on existing facilities. But the success of this effort could hardly result in full plate production, because the steel industry was still hobbling along as a score or more of individual firms.

Let us look at an illustration. At the beginning of 1942 Company A was operating one of its strip mills—annual capacity seven hundred and twenty thousand gross tons—two to three days a week. It had been built in the mid-nineteen thirties exclusively for the purpose of supplying light sheets to the auto industry and other essentially domestic industries. This mill has an auxiliary fifty-four-inch blooming mill which is capable of producing large-size slabs for conversion on the strip mill into from three-eighth-inch to probably as thick as three-quarter-inch plate. Yet, a year and one-half after the armament program started, it had not been converted for this purpose. Instead, the parent firm, which had received more armament contracts (in money value) than any other firm in the country, was hanging onto as much of its domestic business as possible through this mill. Had Philip Murray's proposal been adopted in January, 1941, the auxiliary equipment, such as runout tables and shears, needed for the production of plates could have been installed by year's end. But it had been ignored, and as a consequence this mill, among others, was kept out of the production of the type of steel plates in which the armament program was suffering a shortage.

In the meantime Company B, a smaller producer with only one integrated steel works, was compelled to divide the production on its strip mill—which was working seven days a week—between heavy flat-rolled products (plates) and lighter products (sheets). As a result, its total output of finished flat-rolled steel products was less than it would have been if it had been operating entirely upon lighter products. Thus the maximum output of which this mill was capable was not being achieved. More plates for the armament program and more sheets for essential domestic goods could have been achieved through the co-ordination of these two strip mills; that is, by placing the strip mill of the large firm exclusively on plates for ships, tanks, and so forth, and that of the smaller firm exclusively on sheets for essential domestic goods. The steel industry is replete with such cases, as evidenced by the fact that its 1941 output fell more than two million tons below capacity, and estimates of 1942 output, by both the OPM and the industry itself, indicate that only eighty million of the industry's eighty-nine million tons of capacity will be used. The 1942 output estimates were based, among other things, upon an alleged shortage of iron and steel scrap, which could be corrected, as proposed by SWOC, through industry-wide co-ordination of both the iron- and steel-scrap and the basic steel-producing industries.

That an entire industry is the unit of maximum efficiency is demonstrated even more forcibly by the automotive industry. Two days before Christmas, 1940, young, able Walter P. Reuther of the United Automobile Workers of America submitted to President Roosevelt, through Philip Murray as president of CIO, a proposal "to transform the entire unused capacity of the automotive industry into one huge plane production unit." This proposal was accompanied by a survey which showed that "the automobile industry as a whole is not using more than fifty per cent of its maximum potential capacity if that capacity were properly coordinated and operated to the fullest degree." Within six months, Walter Reuther concluded, the automobile industry could be expected to turn out "500 of the most modern fighting planes a day, if the idle machines and the idle men of the automotive industry were fully mobilized and private interests temporarily subordinated to the needs of the emergency."

It is not necessary to illustrate the merit of Reuther's proposal, since the course of events has clearly proved its validity. Raymond Clapper, noted reporter of national affairs, said on the last day of 1941, "The Reuther plan to put the auto plants to work on war contracts was brushed aside as a CIO crackpot idea just a year ago. Today OPM is driven by force of circumstances to put the Reuther plan into effect."[4] About OPM's failure to act favorably on this proposal of organized labor Walter Lippmann wrote, "That piece of Philistinism cost us not merely an unconscionable delay in using the resources of the motor industry but it cost us the enthusiastic participation of labor in national defense."[5] Reuther's proposal was twofold: that the automotive industry convert its facilities for armament production and, secondly, pool each firm's facilities into one great production unit. A month after Pearl Harbor management agreed to conversion—it had no alternative since SPAB had cut off raw materials for further domestic output—but refused to pool facilities. Each firm insisted upon continuing to operate as a separate unit. Before total armament production is achieved, it seems clear, management in the automotive and other basic and vital armament industries will have to accept the second part of Reuther's proposal.

The Industry Council program, of which Reuther's proposal is a part, is predicated upon two additional fundamentals, designed respectively to achieve planning on a national basis and within the framework of democratic methods. The co-ordination of the several firms in each of the key industries into industry-wide production units requires the creation of a national planning board. This is outlined in Appendix I. Such a board would act as a general staff, preparing the production programs to be executed and securing the co-operation of all the industries required to participate in each such program to the point of maximum efficiency, and so forth. The plans of the board, in turn, would be carried out by the respective industries acting as co-ordinated units. Obviously, national planning requires two major mechanisms: a top board to determine appropriate national needs and to prepare plans, with efficient industry-wide organizations to execute them. One without the other cannot succeed. Both without the effective participation of organized labor would soon become undemocratic. Let us, briefly, examine the reasons for this.

The philosophy underlying Philip Murray's Industry Council program is intrinsically democratic. It is the philosophy expounded throughout this book; namely, that the principal groups in our free society should get together to solve their mutually dependent problems instead of either neglecting them or leaving them to a centrally constituted governmental bureaucracy to try and solve. During the nineteen thirties we became disillusioned by the opposite philosophy. It is basically impractical, since it is predicated upon the idea of referring unsolved economic and social problems to someone else. Instead of organized labor and management, in co-operation with government, getting together to solve their mutual problems they turn them over to Congress, then let Congress pass legislation and thereby turn them over to an administrative agency. The weakness of this procedure is that the problems do not get solved in anything like a fundamental manner, and it is not conducive to the development of democratic methods. This comes close to being a one-sentence history of the "running-to-the-government" trend of the last decade.

The formula for democratic control of a national planning effort should include the participation of organized labor as a coequal with management, with the government acting as the arbiter between these two relatively independent groups in a free society. Of the two groups labor is the only one that proposes such planning. To exclude labor from participating in the work of a planning agency after it has been accepted by management would almost insure its failure, since the former is the only group that has an uncompromising interest in full employment. Every time management has undertaken by itself to control the destinies of an industry or group of industries the result has been monopolistic and essentially undemocratic, because its primary preoccupation has been with profits and competitive positions. This is demonstrated by the history of the National Industrial Recovery Act in 1933–35.

Certainly it was obvious eighteen months after the industrialists had been invited to Washington in June, 1940, that by themselves they were incapable of achieving full production of armaments and, in turn, full employment. But they did not have to come to Washington to demonstrate this, since they had done it so dramatically in the production of domestic goods throughout the dark days of the nineteen thirties. In fact, before the vital armament and basic industries meet the full requirements of war production—through both the industry-wide co-ordination of each industry's facilities and a top planning board—the full participation of organized labor will be necessary. In all its spheres of activity, as we have seen, industrial democracy is characterized by the participation of labor, and this is no less true in the extension of democratic methods to our industrial economy as a whole.

Organized labor is the one force that has the will and the independence to make its knowledge effective, which is so essential to national democratic planning. Furthermore, its basic interests are inseparably tied up with the establishment and maintenance of equitable price levels; this is at once a protection to consumers and a guarantee that labor will not combine with industry in unwarranted price changes. It is on this point that government's participation in a planning effort is most vital, not only in preventing industry from raising its prices so high that its output cannot be consumed but in protecting the real wages of workers and the interests of consumers. There is a price level for all commodities that is most likely to result in full production and employment on a sustained basis, and it can be achieved democratically only through the participation of organized labor and government with industrial management in making the all-important decisions on production levels, wages, and prices. Only in this way also can the benefits of technological changes be passed on to the great bulk of the American people through higher real wages and lower prices.

The relation of organized labor's participation and the preservation and extension of democratic methods in industry and government alike is demonstrated, in our judgment, by the story of England since Dunkirk. When organized labor entered the national councils of Britain in that fateful summer, the Nazis were expected momentarily to land and conquer the British Isles. Eighteen months later they still stood unconquered, and seemingly unconquerable. In England, in America, and throughout the democratic world there is almost unanimous agreement among diverse groups and individuals that British labor—the workingman, the small man—has been the most important force that saved Britain's free existence through the year 1941, and promised to do so indefinitely. The men and women in England's mills, mines, and factories converted a halfhearted war-production program into an all-out successful effort. The participation of these humble people in the vital affairs of their country created a national morale that the most severe air bombings have failed to destroy or weaken. The significance of this remarkable record of achievement is that the organized-labor movement—acting for the working people of England—is the one power that continues to give the government the dynamic force needed for effective resistance and a successful victory program.

In a word, Great Britain has had a rebirth of democracy. Democratic methods have been increasingly extended not only to the councils of government but to industry; and before the war is won, they will be extended still more. The full participation of the working people of England in the vital phases of the war effort has let loose a dynamic force that cannot be equaled by the constituents of a dictator—political or industrial. The dynamics of British democracy, to be certain, are altering the social and economic structure in many essential ways, and apparently the conservative groups are willing to pay this price for a victory over the pagan forces and ideas that the Nazis have temporarily revived. To the working people, of course, this is only one objective of the war. The other, and to them more important, one is the promise of full production and employment in the postwar era. One of the prices of complete victory for England's conservative groups, it seems, is a stronger, more virile, more significant labor movement together with changed social and economic conditions in the postwar era. Apparently they are willing to pay this price.

Herein lies the answer, in large measure, to the heroic strength and tremendous energy of the British people since Dunkirk. Herein, also, lies the answer, in part, to the failure of the armament program in our country to produce the vital implements of war on time or in needed quantities.

In all democratic countries resisting aggression, it seems evident from the example of England, the only power that can give the war effort the dynamic character needed for complete success is the organized-labor movement. This is clear from the statement of John Curtin, Labor party leader, when he became Prime Minister of Australia in October, 1941: "The war involves the interests of labor more than those of any other class." The persistent demand of the American labor movement for the substance as well as the appearance of democratic participation in the war effort is evidence in our country that the working people believe that this is truly their war. The American labor movement has no political arm, such as the British Labor party, through which its members can secure a sense of, and actual, participation in the armament-production program. The creative force that is bottled up inside America's working people—that alone can give the war effort the dynamic character it needs for complete success—therefore has to be brought into play in a different way than in England. The form of participation, at least initially, for America's organized-labor movement has to be along industrial lines, since it lacks a political party through which it can secure real participation in the armament-production effort.

One of the authors advanced the proposal for such industrial participation by labor through Industry Councils, under the direction of a National Board, at a *Fortune* Round Table[6] in September, 1941. The proposal and its underlying philosophy stimulated considerable discussion by the industrialists, government officials, economists, agriculturalists, and practical scientists who participated in the Round Table as well as by the labor representatives present. Except for the latter "most members of the Round Table," it reported, ". . . fear that the tendency of any such national councils would be restrictive and that, judging by experiences abroad, government would soon dominate both the capital and labor involved." The report of the Round Table, in addition, quoted one participant, an ex-chairman of the French aluminum trust, to the effect that Industry Councils would lead to fascism and the corporate state that prevails in Italy. This was the only fundamental objection advanced to the participation of labor in industrial production. It reveals a lack of appreciation of the causes of fascism. Democracy has not been supplanted by fascism where it has been strong, where it solved its major economic and social problems. Fascism has arisen out of chaotic and weak democracies that failed to solve these problems adequately. In his penetrating study "The March of Fascism,"[7] Stephen Raushenbush cites a story he uncovered in Germany that illustrates the causes of fascism. We quote:

> A young man . . . who escaped from a certain German concentration camp, recounts a little game the guards at that camp had developed to occupy their leisure time. After the day's work was over for the prisoners and they had finished their thin supper, the guards separated them out: Here the Social-Democrats, there the Catholics, here the Jews, there the Communists, here the Freemasons, there the objecting Protestants. Then all had to get down on all fours and, in groups, advance barking on each other, the one group against the other, encouraged by kicks in the buttocks. As they growled and barked at each other, under orders and force, dignified older men, doctors, professors, pastors, businessmen, teachers, the guards laughed themselves hoarse. It was a child's history of the fourteen years of democracy in Germany reenacted before their own eyes, and reexplained assuringly to the Nazi guards why they had had such an easy conquest and could count on a future of easy conquests in other democracies.

The future of free America might well hinge on the extent to which industry will go in co-operation with organized labor, and government will go in encouraging it. The alternative, we are fearful, may be a re-enactment of the concentration-camp scene—only with the nationality of the actors changed from German to American. Imagine a fascist guard in an American concentration camp making leaders of industry, labor, and government get down on "all fours and, in groups, advance barking on each other, the one group against the other, encouraged by kicks in the buttocks." . . .

"Strikes, work stoppages, irresponsible, greedy labor leaders are holding back the war-production program!"

"Selfish, profit-seeking, antidemocratic rulers of industry and finance are using the nation's peril to make money, thwart the legitimate aspirations of labor, prevent the needed expansion of industrial capacities, and make the production of the implements of war a failure by insisting upon 'business-as-usual' policies!"

"The New Dealers are trying to use the nation's peril to further their socialistic schemes upon free enterprise!"

"Dollar-a-year men in Washington are trying to wreck all the social gains of the New Deal and take away from the poor all the gains for which the war is worth prosecuting!"

If such a scene is ever enacted in our own country the participants will deserve all the kicks in the buttocks inflicted upon them by the fascist guards. Yet this is the fate awaiting the financial and industrial leaders of American industry (who will also pull labor down with them) unless they reconcile themselves to a postwar era in which the role of organized labor is far different from that of any previous time. Likewise they will have to cease their opposition to the extension of industrial democracy to the national economy as a whole, and accept the growth of democracy in the local mines, mills, and factories through the adoption of the union-shop form of recognition—the relation of which to industrial democracy we have discussed earlier. And the leaders of the federal government have to conceive it as their function to bring labor and management together in a co-operative effort, extending from the top to the bottom of industry, and vest them jointly with the responsibility for a successful armament program. But even after Pearl Harbor they, like the leaders of industry and finance, had not yet realized that to win a decisive military victory over the Nazi regime and Japanese war lords a permanent, strong, virile, dynamic, all-embracing labor movement is essential. They seemed to think that such a victory could be achieved without the full extension of democratic methods to industry and the American economy as a whole.

Instead they appealed to labor "to keep democracy from dying." This phrase, and the concept of democracy that it implies, rankled in the minds of America's workers. And it will continue to do so until democracy is conceived of as a program of action rather than something static, like a skyscraper or power plant, to be defended. Labor's conception of democracy is similar to that held by the pioneers on the American frontier which enabled them to conquer a wilderness and create the richest nation in the world.

They were driven ever onward, to be sure, by the quest for riches; but they were constantly inspired by a dream of a free way of life, of a new world. They had little vision of just how their dream might work out in detail, and probably cared less. The idea of a political democracy where the rights of man would reign supreme was their major source of inspiration. And it carried them through difficult times and even disaster. A dream made them strong and, in the end, victorious. The lack of an equally inspiring dream made free America weak—militarily as well as spiritually—by the time it had formally entered World War II.

The American people should be able, through a national democratic planning program, to visualize the next armistice as the beginning of a new era of industrial prosperity and national well-being, rather than a return to the dismal nineteen thirties. To this latter view, shared by most Americans, can be traced in large measure America's lagging armament output. Millions of our citizens have been making the same fatal assumption since the present world conflict developed into actual warfare in 1939. In all walks of life—industry and finance, labor and farm, the professions, and government—it has been assumed that "there must come a day of reckoning," that free America and private enterprise are incapable of full production and employment on a sustained basis. Various groups give expression to this assumption in different ways. The financier warns of the danger of inflation—he sees the value of his bonds and other assets being wiped out by worthless paper money. The industrialist argues against expanding his capacity to meet war needs, because in the postwar era it might result in ruinous competition. The farmer demands one hundred and ten per cent of parity and more for his products. The typical industrial worker says, "I have to suffer the depressions, so I might as well enjoy prosperity." The vice-president of a large corporation told us, "What's the hurry in completing our backlogs? What is there for us after the war's over? We've never had such regular work before, and probably never will have again!"

This same despair, fatalism, and lack of vision is shared by industrial workers. They express themselves in different ways. Perhaps the most typical is intensive concern with the present, reluctance to talk about the future, and universal fear of what lies ahead. It is the rare one who can put this feeling into words. "Roosevelt's right. We gotta lick Hitler, and save Johnny Bull," a machinist in a shell plant told us. "But what's goin' to be in the armistice for me this time? They won't be needin' these shells any more. Fact is, the whole plant'll go down. And the whole damned country will go to hell again. They're huntin' for machinists like me now. Then us machinists will be huntin' for jobs. Oh, well, what's the use of thinkin' about it? We'll all be in the same stew. I won't be alone."

This machinist fought in the first World War. He returned to see his fellow workers' efforts to unionize smashed in one of the most brutal assaults upon organized labor, the 1919 steel strike. He saw the "open-shop campaign" of industry —encouraged by the federal government after the war—reduce the labor movement to its lowest ebb in half a century. Industry's opposition to the union shop in this war looks to this machinist as a preparatory effort by industry to destroy unionism when this war is over. Hence the armistice in World War II appears to him as the beginning of another life-and-death struggle between his union and the steel industry. But, more important, he cannot see regular employment for himself and others when the armistice does come. A national planning program to execute the armament program could turn this machinist's despair about the future into hope, perhaps even an inspiring vision of a better life.

The shell plant in which he works is alongside a huge steel mill. The men in this and neighboring steel mills do not see any difference in the methods of management. Daily they talk about the many things, of the nature we have previously pointed out, that could be done, but are not being done, to raise output. An Industry Council directing the industry as a co-ordinated unit would take advantage of these opportunities to raise production. Likewise workers would feel a greater sense of being a part of the war effort by their participation in the Council through their union officers. The Council would encourage the creation of joint union-management production committees in each mill along the lines described in Part Two of this discussion. In this way each worker could acquire a recognized status in the war effort, as a soldier in the army of production. But, more important, a postwar division would be established within the Council, and its activities would be publicized. To the nation's steel workers it would say:

"We are preparing for a better day when the war is won.

"This war has shown how we can produce at capacity for almost an indefinite time. True, it is for purposes of destruction. But we are making plans to continue capacity output and steady jobs for peacetime purposes.

"Normally the railroad industry consumes twelve per cent of the annual steel production. Its facilities are in great need of modernization, which will be even more imperative when the war is won. Plans are being made to transfer a portion of the steel industry's output now going into armaments for steel rails, new locomotives, new passenger and freight cars, new bridges, and the other equipment and facilities that the railroads will need when the war is won.

Thus, when we finish producing steel to win the war, we shall be prepared to produce steel for a bigger and better railroad system in America.

"More than fifteen per cent of yearly production of steel goes into automobiles and trucks. Plans are in preparation to continue the production of at least this portion of steel for the automotive industry. We are producing large quantities of steel for tanks, guns, shells, airplanes, and the other armaments being manufactured in the auto plants. When these implements of war have destroyed Hitler and Japan's military forces, the auto plants will return to car and truck production. Plans will be ready to continue you at your jobs producing steel for these auto plants that, after the war is won, will again produce the things that we are having to go without during the war.

"Another fifteen per cent of the steel industry's output usually goes to the building and construction industries. The steel normally consumed by these industries is going to win the war now. When this job is done, we shall be prepared to continue you at work producing steel for the many buildings, new bridges, and other public works our country will badly need.

"Three to five per cent of the steel normally goes to the nation's farms. When the war is won, we will keep you at your jobs producing the steel America's farms will badly need in farm implements, fences, wire, and other steel products.

"Before the war, exports took around five per cent of our annual steel output. After the war is won, America will have to help rebuild large sections of the world. From ten to twenty-five per cent of our steel production may go for exports after we win the war. We do not know the exact amount, but whatever it turns out to be we will be prepared to keep you at work producing it."

And so plans could also be prepared, and publicized, to continue capacity steel output to supply the other steel consumers after the war. Similarly plans could be prepared for the other basic and vital armament industries. Auto workers, for instance, would be inspired to learn that they will not have to suffer the prolonged period of idleness from the transition to domestic goods from military output that they had to suffer during the change-over from domestic to military output in 1941-42. These brief examples give some indication of the manner in which the fear of what lies ahead in the postwar era may be converted into a hope—in fact, a dream—through national democratic planning.

The American people require a vision of a better future. They need to see the war effort as a great opportunity, as an effort that has begun to fully utilize the country's industrial and man power. The postwar era should become a hopeful prospect, one in which this tremendous power of men and machines will continue to be used for the production of peacetime goods. Here is something people can dream about: full production and employment on a sustained basis, almost unlimited production of those nonmilitary goods which mean more of the necessities of life and some of the finer things; no fear of mass unemployment, low farm prices, poverty, insecurity, misery, and inadequate industrial earnings for workers and owners alike.

No such vision has been held out for the American people. Instead they have been called upon to make sacrifices, to fight for the purpose of beating Hitler. This is essentially a negative appeal. Nor is the additional appeal to defend democracy, freedom, and liberty positive enough to free the tremendous energy and dynamic forces that are bottled up within the American people. With all these appeals we fervently agree. But more is needed to inspire a people and galvanize them into united, self-sacrificing, wholehearted action. They need to hear more about "freedom from want." This inspiring appeal of President Roosevelt has to be translated into positive action and carried to its logical conclusion.

It is on this score that the challenge of Hitler is most dangerous. For his people he holds out the hope of economic prosperity after the war. The Nazi regime is waging more than a military war; it is waging a social, economic, and political revolution. It promises full production and employment. This is one of its sources of strength. By the same token it is a challenge to free America that cannot be ignored, lest our people be tempted to barter their freedom for the promise of security. As *Fortune*[8] puts it:

> The only modern statesman who has so far succeeded in giving his people a vision of the future is Adolf Hitler. The German future is for us a thing of horror: nevertheless, it satisfies and even inspires the Germans. And as a result Germany . . . has become a nation with an integrated purpose. . . . Mr. Roosevelt and Mr. Churchill made an attempt in this direction in formulating . . . the Atlantic Charter. But . . . it was just more fine words. . . .
>
> The one thing that Mr. Roosevelt must do, without which further progress in the defense of freedom is unlikely, is to open up, or begin to open up, a new future. This he cannot do with just a ringing speech. . . . He must, rather, set about achieving some kind of basic agreement in the multiplying issues that have been tearing the American people apart and depriving them of hope. . . . [This can only be done] with and not against labor and agriculture and management and capital; the retailer and the manufacturer; the educator and the theorist—honest and intelligent representatives of the many basic interests of the U. S. that are now in conflict and in the process of self-destruction.

Men live by dreams as much as by bread, if not more so. They fight for ideals more than they fight to keep material things. Industrial democracy is still largely a dream—an objective toward which the workingman strives, an inspiration that drives him and his chosen leaders onward. It is still a vision of the future, because without the solid base of full production and employment industrial democracy cannot endure and grow; nor, for that matter, can political democracy in the face of the constant challenge of totalitarian philosophies to provide, at least, regular work and sustained incomes. The forces of democracy are fighting more than the military machine of the Nazis; they are fighting their kind of promise for abundance and security.

The war against the Nazis and Japanese war lords must

be fought with more than bullets, shells, and bombs. It has to be waged with ideas, with hopes, with dreams of a better life. These natural aspirations of any people—the rich and abundant life—cannot be ignored during the conduct of a modern war. They, in a real sense, are more vital instruments with which to wage and win the war than planes, and tanks, and ships. In the hands of a free people, led by courageous and imaginative leaders, these aspirations can become unconquerable weapons of war. This requires a dynamic conception of democracy of the sort possessed and treasured by the pioneer Americans. Such a concept is a prerequisite to conquering the totalitarian philosophy and the nations that preach it, and to creating in America a full-fledged democracy—an ever-growing, creative, and developing form of society.

America was founded and developed by a people who were moved by the greatest dream in human history. In leaving the Old World for the New, the millions who settled and cultivated the great expanse of the North American continent were inspired by a dream of a new life, a free life, an independent and happy existence. They built the greatest democracy in the history of civilization. Our great industries, our rich cities, and the other monuments of a mature industrial society are the results of democracy, and not democracy itself. Fighting for democracy is not fighting for the defense of these material belongings, no matter how dear we hold them. Fighting for democracy is fighting for a way of life that made these things possible. Democracy is a program of action. Put to work in American industry—and we have tried to indicate throughout this discussion how it might be translated into practical democratic mechanisms for human co-operation—democracy can win the war and, more important, win the peace that follows.

Whatever the practical mechanisms, though, to be successful they must be coupled to a dream—a dream of a free, prosperous, secure, happy life. Only by the dream of great things have a free people been able to accomplish great things.

Appendix I: Industry Council Program

By PHILIP MURRAY

President, Congress of Industrial Organizations

The following program is an excerpt from President Murray's report to the Fourth Constitutional Convention of the Congress of Industrial Organizations, Detroit, Michigan, November 17, 1941.

INTRODUCTION

With the initiation of our national defense program over a year and a half ago, certain tasks were created for this nation. From a peacetime economy we were to be directed into an economy of producing primary materials for the defense of those nations struggling against the fascist aggressors. Obviously the first task, and the one of greatest importance, was to produce the necessary quantity of materials within the shortest period of time.

To accomplish this goal it was essential that our existing plant facilities be utilized to the full with adequate provision for any increase in productive facilities that may be necessary, together with a maximum utilization of the available labor supply of the nation. At the same time, it was also necessary that wherever possible production of civilian goods for our domestic needs be maintained as fully as possible. The effectuation of the national defense program would necessarily involve severe sacrifices on the part of the American people. However, it is essential that no one segment or group within our nation be unduly burdened.

To achieve this end it is necessary that our economy be as well ordered as possible, in the effort to avoid inflation which would bring in its wake such dire distress for those with fixed incomes, particularly the labor group. Price control therefore becomes an essential part of our national defense program.

The problem of production to meet our national defense and civilian needs demands extremely careful planning measures on a national scale. Of equal importance is the obvious need of making preparation for the emergency situation which will develop following the termination of the world hostilities.

The effectiveness of our existing national defense agencies as compared to the program submitted by the CIO to effectuate our national defense program must be evaluated in light of the following factors:

(a) the need of producing within the shortest period of time a maximum of tanks, guns, airplanes, and other materials required by the nations abroad as well as our own Army and Navy, together with our own domestic civilian demands;

(b) the need of planning on a national basis in order to utilize our full available labor supply together with all of our production facilities and raw materials and to provide for any necessary expansion; and

(c) the need of preparing adequate and comprehensive plans for maintaining a well ordered economy for our nation to meet the economic problems that will arise following the cessation of hostilities abroad.

INDUSTRY COUNCIL PROGRAM

In December, 1940, your President submitted to the President of the United States a program which in our judgment met the basic needs of the national defense program. The plan received the unanimous endorsement of the CIO Executive Board. This plan has been offered as a constructive proposal to assure the effective execution of our national defense program.

The Congress of the United States has appropriated specific sums of money for the national defense program. These appropriations call for the production and supply of definite required materials. The War and Navy Departments of the United States, in cooperation with those nations which we seek to aid, have estimated the amounts of specified goods which are required both for those nations as well as for the United States.

The problem which now confronts this nation is basically the problem of production—how to produce the required quantities of materials within the shortest period of time. It is the judgment of your President and of the Executive Board that this problem can be met and solved through the Industry Council Plan that has been presented to the federal administration. In essence the Industry Council Plan has as its theme that:

(1) Through adequate and centralized planning each basic defense industry could be advised as to the materials that must be produced by such industry and the general price level that should be maintained for such industry; and

(2) The persons directly involved in each such industry, as management and labor, are the ones best equipped and trained to attain the goal set for the industry. The Industry Council Plan contemplates a direct and active participation within each industry on the part of management and labor. For labor we are demanding such representation not merely to protect labor's interests, but of equal importance, to obtain the full benefit of the resourcefulness and tech-

nical skill of labor's representatives who are fully acquainted with the problems and needs of the industry.

For the national defense program to be effectuated, it is necessary to unleash the energies and resourcefulness of all our people and not merely of any one segment. There is no monopoly of brains on the part of any one group. Our national defense program demands the full participation of all the people.

The administrative machinery contemplated under the Industry Council Plan is simple:

(1) It is suggested that the President of the United States shall establish for each basic defense industry an Industry Council. Each such Council would be composed of equal representation for management and the labor unions in the industry, together with one government representative, the latter to serve as chairman.

(a) Each Council will be advised of the domestic and armament requirements of its industry, and the general price level that should prevail for the industry. It will be the duty of each Council to coordinate the production facilities of that industry to meet these requirements with the maximum degree of speed and, where necessary, to expand the production facilities to meet the requirements. It will also be the duty of each Council to maintain the price level within the industry as has been established under the general planning program.

(b) To accomplish this goal it will be the obligation of the Industry Council to allocate available raw materials within the industry, allocate the outstanding contracts and also any new contracts among the available plant facilities in any industry, to adjust the labor supply to the plant facilities without compelling any forced labor, arrange for necessary and appropriate facilities for housing, and make arrangements for necessary training to meet the labor requirements.

In this manner the abuse which is now prevalent wherein certain concerns in an industry have contracts which they cannot fulfill within the next 3 or 5 years will be eliminated. All firms within the industry having available plant facilities will not only be entitled to but will be obligated to participate in the production program to effectuate national defense requirements. Further, this program will be carried out by those who are best equipped with knowledge and training, namely, those who are actively participating within the industry—management and labor. In this manner we will not have the spectacle of plants which are idle, people unemployed in a particular industry, with the accompanying hue and cry that production is lagging.

(c) Each Council will have to constantly engage in active planning in order to make certain that it is achieving the greatest possible output within the industry for domestic and armament requirements as well as planning for the maximum utilization of its facilities and labor supply in terms of post-war needs.

(d) In effect, the Industry Councils must be implemented with full executive and administrative authority to carry out the program for each industry. All legal and executive authority must be delegated to the Councils for the purpose of carrying out the task for which the Councils will have the responsibility for fulfillment. Within the discretion of the Councils there may be organized within each industry regional and local machinery which would obtain the full participation of local management, labor, and others in the communities. The highest degree of morale on the part of the American people can be established with the maximum assurance of fulfillment of our national defense program through such participation.

(2) The President of the United States shall establish a National Defense Board consisting of an equal number of representatives for industry and labor unions, over which the President or his designee shall be the Chairman. The National Defense Board shall establish rules and regulations for the operation of the Industry Councils. The general policies of the national defense program shall be promulgated by the National Defense Board. The basic planning in order to determine the domestic and armament requirements for each industry will have to be determined by this National Defense Board. The National Defense Board will operate as a general staff. The Industry Councils will act as the generals in charge of their respective armies to carry through the national defense program for their respective spheres of activity.

The Board will act as an appeals agency for the Industry Councils, and coordinate the work of the Councils by serving as a clearing house for inter-industry matters.

(3) The Industry Councils will furnish an excellent basis for promoting industrial peace through the perfection and extension of sound collective bargaining relations between management and organized labor. However, it must be clear that the established relations between unions and management through collective bargaining will continue. Collective bargaining procedure is not to be superseded by the Industry Council program. Negotiations through collective bargaining between recognized unions and management regarding wages, hours and working conditions, must continue in order to assure the continued existence of our democratic procedures. In addition, the Industry Councils will not supersede but rather will secure the compliance, within their respective spheres, with all laws affecting the rights and welfare of labor, such as the Social Security Law, the Wages and Hours Act, the National Labor Relations Act, the Walsh-Healey Act, and others.

(4) Former Attorney-General Robert Jackson and present Attorney-

General Francis Biddle have issued opinion letters in which they have indicated that, in the interest of National Defense, manufacturing concerns will be permitted, under the supervision of the Federal government, to collaborate in the pooling of facilities, allocation of contracts and subcontracts, and in the procurement and use of raw materials. The Industry Council program is intended to accomplish this very end.

CONCLUSION

The Congress of Industrial Organizations, with its millions of members, is determined to protect and safeguard America and its democratic institutions. It is for this basic reason that we are wholeheartedly and completely in support of the national defense program. We are determined that the program must be effectuated and fulfilled with all possible speed. We are convinced that our national policy and program for increasing production can be fulfilled only through the full and active participation of all our people.

In this endeavor the Congress of Industrial Organizations, through your President and the Executive Board, has submitted its Industry Council Plan. We do not submit that this Plan is the only blueprint that can serve our national defense effort. In our judgement it meets the basic needs of the situation. We merely ask the opportunity for discussing this Plan with the responsible officials of the United States government in order that it be given full consideration. We are deeply appreciative of the defects of the present administrative machinery which seeks the accomplishment of the national defense effort. The CIO does not wish it to be understood that it will refrain from participation in the national defense program unless its own Industry Council Plan is adopted.

To the contrary, the CIO, as an American institution with loyal Americans as its members, will do all in its power to assist in the national defense program. At all times we shall attempt to point out what we may consider to be the shortcomings of the program or its administrative machinery from the point of view of ever pressing for a stronger and more effective national defense effort.

The CIO is firmly convinced that this nation must participate in the defeat of Nazi Germany. Toward this end we have offered our analysis of the national defense program and have submitted our recommendations for a more vigorous and more militant and comprehensive plan to effectuate the goal desired by all Americans.

Acknowledgments

Thanks are due to the editors of *Reader's Digest*, *Harvard Business Review*, and *Advanced Management* for permission to use material that first appeared in their pages. We are particularly indebted to the Committee on Work in Industry of the National Research Council for permission to use material that one of the authors, as a member of the committee, contributed to its report *Fatigue of Workers—Its Relation to Industrial Production*, Reinhold Publishing Corporation, New York City, 1941.

We are indebted to many co-workers and friends for their counsel and assistance at various stages in the execution of the manuscript. Among those who have been especially helpful are Joseph Scanlon, Stephen Levitsky, and Meyer Bernstein of the staff of the Steel Workers Organizing Committee; Dr. Bernhard Ostrolenk, Economics Department, College of the City of New York; P. Alston Waring, Solebury, Pennsylvania; Marjorie S. Gavin, Pittsburgh, Pennsylvania; and finally our wives and helpmates, Dora O. Golden and Katherine M. Ruttenberg, who helped with the typing and research work, and without whose co-operation and inspiration this book could never have been written.

We are grateful to Benjamin C. Sigal, Attorney at Law, Pittsburgh, Pennsylvania, with whom we discussed and argued many sections of this book; his is the kind of help most difficult to acknowledge but most deserving of acknowledgment.

The debt we owe the members and leaders of organized labor, past and present, who are responsible for bringing a measure of democracy to industry, and the management officials who have co-operated in the establishment and growth of collective bargaining, cannot be acknowledged in words; it can merely be noted.

All responsibility for the shortcomings of the book, of course, belongs to us.

THE AUTHORS

Notes and References

CHAPTER I

[1] *Handbook of Labor Statistics,* 1929 edition, Number 491 Bulletin of the United States Bureau of Labor Statistics, page 686; "Factory-Labor Turn-Over, 1931 to 1939," Serial Number R.1175, United States Department of Labor, Bureau of Labor Statistics, from the *Monthly Labor Review,* September, 1940; and the National War Labor Board report printed in the *New York Times,* August 5, 1918, page 9, column 5.

[2] *Time,* March 17, 1941, page 19, column 1.

CHAPTER II

[1] "Six Years of the National Labor Relations Act," by H. A. Millis, *Labor Information Bulletin,* United States Department of Labor, Bureau of Labor Statistics, Washington, D. C., August, 1941, page 1.

[2] "In an American Factory," by Stoyan Pribichevich, *Harpers,* September, 1938, pages 362-373.

CHAPTER III

[1] "Industrial Peace," by Andrew Carnegie, Address at the Annual Dinner of the National Civic Federation, New York City, December 15, 1904.

CHAPTER V

[1] *Business Week,* July 12, 1941, pages 61 and 62.

CHAPTER VI

[1] *Hearings before the Temporary National Economic Committee, Congress of the United States,* Part 30, "Technology and Concentration of Economic Power," April 12, 1940, pages 16,491 through 16,508.

[2] *New York Times,* July 3, 1941, page 25.

[3] The most extensive elaboration of the Western Electric Researches is contained in *Management and the Worker,* by F. J. Roethlisberger and William J. Dickson, Harvard University Press, Cambridge, Massachusetts, 1939. They are evaluated in *Fatigue of Workers—Its Relation to Industrial Production,* a report by the Committee on Work in Industry of the National Research Council, Reinhold Publishing Corporation, New York City, 1941.

[4] *Iron Age,* February 6, 1941, page 96-D.

CHAPTER VII

[1] *The Open Shop,* by Clarence S. Darrow, Charles H. Kerr and Company, Chicago, an undated pamphlet.

[2] *American Metal Market,* 111 John Street, New York City, August 8, 1941, page 1.

[3] *New York Times,* August 14, 1941, page 12.

[4] *New York Times,* August 14, 1941, page 12.

[5] *New York Times,* August 17, 1941, page 1, section 1.

[6] *Pittsburgh Press,* February 28, 1941, page 2.

[7] *The Open Shop,* by Clarence S. Darrow.

[8] *American Metal Market,* August 22, 1941, a quotation from the *New York Times.*

[9] *American Metal Market,* August 26, 1941, page 7.

CHAPTER VIII

[1] *Pittsburgh Sun-Telegraph,* June 11, 1941, page 1.

[2] *Amalgamated Journal,* 500 South Main Street, Pittsburgh, Pennsylvania, February 20, 1941, page 7.

[3] *Management and Defense,* Proceedings of the National Defense Management Conference, Washington, D. C., November 15, 1940, auspices of the Society for the Advancement of Management, Washington Chapter, page 41.

[4] *Waste in Industry,* by the Committee on Elimination of Waste in Industry of the Federated American Engineering Societies, Foreword by Herbert Hoover, McGraw-Hill Book Company, Inc., New York City, 1921.

[5] *Reader's Digest,* Pleasantville, N. Y., October, 1938, page 16.

[6] "Public Policy and Labor's Role in Industry," by Morris L. Cooke, Address delivered before the Institute of Public Affairs, University of Virginia, at Charlottesville, Virginia, June 27, 1941.

CHAPTER IX

[1] Division of Industrial Economics of the National Industrial Conference Board, as reported in the *American Metal Market,* September 23, 1941, page 5.

[2] *Modern Industry,* 347 Madison Avenue, New York City, May 15, 1941, pages 16 and 17.

[3] *American Metal Market,* February 8, 1941.

[4] *Advanced Management,* the Society for the Advancement of Management, 29 West Thirty-ninth Street, New York City, April-June, 1941, pages 49 and 80.

CHAPTER X

[1] "Stabilization of the Bituminous Coal Industry," by Frank G. Smith, Assistant General Superintendent, the Sunday Creek Coal Company, *Harvard Business Review,* Winter, 1939.

[2] *Report of the Commission on Industrial Relations in Great Britain Appointed by President Roosevelt,* and *Report of the Commission on Industrial Relations in Sweden Appointed by President Roosevelt,* United States Printing Office, Washington, D. C., 1938; and a letter of Mr. Gerard Swope, Chairman of the President's Commission on Industrial Relations in Sweden, *New York Times,* May 21, 1939.

[3] *New Adventures in Democracy,* by Ordway Tead, Whittlesey House, McGraw-Hill Book Company, Inc., New York City, 1939, page 92.

CHAPTER XI

[1] *My Experiences in the World War,* by John J. Pershing, Frederick A. Stokes Company, New York City, 1931, Volume I, pages 27, 107, 131,

144, 160, 161, 222, 232, 320, 325, 326, 334; Volume II, pages 260, 261, 310.

[2] The performance of American industry in armament output for the first fifteen months (July, 1940, to October, 1941) of the armament program, and the first half year of the British-aid program is recorded in *Congressional Record,* Volume 87, No. 179, October 9, 1941, pages 7978 to 7985; *Life,* September 29, 1941, pages 27 to 31; "Where Do We Stand in Production?" Office of Production Management, November 2, 1941, press release, PM 1411; "Our 'Arsenal of Democracy' Begins to Function," by Hanson W. Baldwin, *New York Times,* November 2, 1941, Section 4, page 3; *Wall Street Journal,* October 21, 1941, page 1, and October 25, 1941, page 1; "The Failure of Our National Defense Program," by U. S. Senator Harry F. Byrd, *Reader's Digest,* November, 1941, page 16; "The Crisis in Production," by Michael Straight, *New Republic,* November 3, 1941, page 577; "Little Industry—'What Now?'" by R. L. Duffus, *New York Times Magazine,* October 5, 1941, page 3.

[3] *Recommendations on Full Utilization of America's Industrial Capacity and Labor Supply in the War Effort,* Second Interim Report of the Select Committee Investigating National Defense Migration, House of Representatives, December 19, 1941, United States Government Printing Office, Washington, D. C., 1941.

[4] *Pittsburgh Press,* December 31, 1941, page 13.

[5] Quoted in *Time,* January 5, 1942, page 58.

[6] The tenth *Fortune* Round Table, "On Demobilizing the War Economy," supplement to *Fortune,* November, 1941.

[7] *The March of Fascism,* by Stephen Raushenbush, Yale University Press, New Haven, 1939, pages 106 and 107.

[8] "The American Struggle," *Fortune,* January, 1942, page 35.

Index